MASONIC SONGS,

OLD AND NEW:

INCLUDING THOSE PUBLISHED IN "THE FREE-MASONS' MELODY," 1818: TOGETHER WITH

AN APPENDIX,

CONTAINING MANY ORIGINAL MASONIC SONGS AND POEMS, WRITTEN EXPRESSLY FOR THIS WORK.

STONE GUILD PUBLISHING
PLANO, TEXAS
HTTP://WWW.STONEGUILDPUBLISHING.COM/

2009

Originally Published By:
W. S. BARLOW
1885

This Edition Copyright © 2009
Stone Guild Publishing, Inc.
Plano, Texas
http://www.stoneguildpublishing.com/

First Paperback Edition 2009

ISBN-13 978-1-60532-047-2
ISBN-10 1-60532-047-1

10 9 8 7 6 5 4 3 2

PREFACE.

THE first part of the present volume consists of a reprint of "The Free-Masons' Melody" published by BRO. J. R. HELLAWELL, of Bury, under the direction of the Officers and Members of Prince Edwin Lodge, Bury, in the year 1818, and which had become very scarce. It contained the greater part of those old and favourite songs known to the brotherhood prior to, and about the time of, its publication, and many of which have now become "familiar in our mouths as household words." The antient orthography has been retained, although the instances are not very numerous where variations of any importance occur in the spelling.

The Appendix contains about eighty additional Songs, Chorales, Hymns, Cantatas, &c., mostly original, and not a few of them written expressly for the present work. Besides these there will be found a few Songs of early date, which have not hitherto, so far as is known, been published in any modern collection of Masonic Songs. Whilst thus, for a time at least, preserving the songs, it is much to be regretted that the names of their authors could not, in every case, be rescued from oblivion.

The Publisher desires to thank most cordially the Brethren who have directly assisted him by composing songs specially for the work, and also those who have in other ways aided in its compilation. The names of these Brethren will be found at the head of their respective contributions.

In the Prospectus it was stated that the volume would contain 250 pages; it has, however, extended to 456 pages. This has very considerably increased the cost of printing, &c., therefore, Subscribers' Copies only will be issued at the prices originally advertised.

It is hoped that the Craft generally will approve of the work—both the old and new portions—and that it may assist in promoting not only good-fellowship, but good Masonry also, and add a pleasant and wholesome zest to the social intercourse of the Brethren.

W. S. BARLOW.

Bury,
   July, 1885.

MASONIC SONGS, &c.

I.

THE FAREWELL.

To the Brethren of St. James's Lodge, Tarbolton.

BY ROBERT BURNS.

(Tune, *"Good Night, and joy be wi' you a'."*)

A DIEU! a heart-warm fond adieu!
    Dear brothers of the mystic tie!
Ye favour'd, ye enlighten'd few,
    Companions of my social joy!
Tho' I to foreign lands must hie,
    Pursuing fortune's slidd'ry ba',
With melting heart and brimful eye,
    I'll mind you still, tho' far awa'.

Oft have I met your social band,
    And spent the cheerful festive night;
Oft, honour'd with supreme command,
    Presided o'er the sons of light:
And by that hieroglyphic bright
    Which none but craftsmen ever saw!
Strong mem'ry on my heart shall write
    Those happy scenes when far awa'.

May freedom, harmony, and love,
    Unite you in the grand design,
Beneath the omniscient eye above,
    The glorious Architect divine!
That you may keep the unerring line,
    Still rising by the plummet's law,
Till order bright completely shine,
    Shall be my prayer when far awa'.
And you, farewell! whose merits claim
    Justly that highest badge to wear!
Heaven bless your honour'd, noble name,
    To masonry and Scotia dear!
A last request permit me here,
    When yearly ye assemble a',
One round, I ask it with a tear,
    To him, the bard that's far awa'.

II.

WRITTEN BY BROTHER J. WILLIAMSON,

(Tune, *"Dear Tom, this brown jug."*)

ADVANCE, each true brother, my song now attend,
And assist in full chorus a brother and friend,
With good humour he calls you, then socially join,
That the ceiling may ring with a theme that's divine.
  Cho.—Then join, brother masons, aloft raise the song,
    All the virtues in life to true masons belong.

The wisest of men was a mason, we know,
From him our chief honours and dignities flow;
He founded the temple, the pillars he rais'd,
And Solomon still in our songs shall be prais'd.
  Cho.—Then join, &c.

With square and with compass, with level and line,
We constantly work to complete our design;
By prudence we steer, and the passions subdue,
What we learn in our youth in our age we renew.
  Cho.—Then join, &c.

On freedom and friendship our order began,
To deal squarely with all is the chief of our plan;
The sneer then of fools we esteem as a feather,
Since virtue's cement 'tis that joins us together.
  Cho.—Then join, &c.

Till the ocean be dry, and hard rocks melt away,
Till the globe shall dissolve, and no sun cheer the day,
So long shall the masons their order maintain,
And the arrows of slander be shot forth in vain.
  Cho.—Then join, &c.

III.

A HEALTH to our sisters let's drink;
 For why should not they
  Be remember'd, I pray,
When of us they so often do think.
'Tis they give the chiefest delight;
 Tho' wine cheers the mind,
  And masonry's kind,
These keep us in transport all night.

IV.

By Brother JOHN RICHARDSON, *of the Royal Brunswick Lodge, Sheffield.*

ALONE from arts and science flow
 Whate'er instructs or charms the eye,
Whate'er can fill the mind with awe,
 Beneath yon arched azure sky.

With heav'nly, true mechanic skill,
Our great Almighty Master wrought;
And in six days did he fulfil
What far surpasses human thought.

Firm in the centre fixëd he
The sun, to guide the rolling spheres;
The moon, by night a light to be,
And mark us out the months and years.

What tho' no powerful lever's seen?
Nor axle, wheel, or pulley there?
Yet they have ever constant been,
As time and truth to us declare.

Just so our true Masonic fame
On lofty, lasting columns stands:
Grac'd with a royal Brunswick's name,
And rear'd beneath his ruling hands.

V.

A MASON one time
   Was cast for a crime,
Which malice had put a bad face on;
  And then, without thought,
  To a gibbet was brought
The free and the accepted mason.
Chos.—And then without thought, &c.

  And when he came there,
  He put up his pray'r
For heaven to pity his case on!
  His king he espy'd,
  Who in progress did ride,
Was a free and an accepted mason.
  His king he espy'd, &c.

Then out a sign flew,
Which the grand master knew,
Who rode up to know the occasion;
Ask'd who had condemn'd
So worthy a friend
As a free and an accepted mason.
Ask'd who had condemn'd, &c.

He then tried the cause,
And found out the flaws,
According to justice and reason:
He tuck'd up the judge,
And all that bore grudge
To the free and the accepted mason.
He tuck'd up the judge, &c.

Though ignorant pride
Our secrets deride,
Or foolish conjectures occasion,
They ne'er shall divine
The word or the sign
Of a free and an accepted mason.
They ne'er shall divine, &c.

VI.

(Tune, *"Young Damon."*)

A MASON'S daughter, fair and young,
The pride of all the virgin throng,
Thus to her lover said:
Though, Damon, I your flame approve,
Your actions praise, your person love,
Yet still I'll live a maid.

None shall untie my virgin-zone,
But one to whom the secret's known
    Of famed Freemasonry;
In which the great and good combine
To raise, with generous design,
    Man to felicity.

The lodge excludes the fop and fool,
The plodding knave, and party-tool,
    That liberty would sell;
The noble, faithful, and the brave,
No golden charms can e'er deceive,
    In slavery to dwell.

Thus said: he bow'd and went away;
Apply'd: was made: without delay
    Return'd to her again;
The fair complied with his request,
Connubial joys the couple blest;
    And long may they remain.

VII.

By J. BISSET, *Steward of St. Alban's Lodge, and Provincial G.S. for the County of Warwick.*

(Tune, *"A Sailor's life's a life of woe."*)

A MASON'S life's the life for me:
    With joy we meet each other,
We pass our time with mirth and glee,
    And hail each friendly brother;
In lodge no party feuds are seen,
But careful we in this agree,
    To banish care or spleen.

The Master's call we one and all
   With pleasure soon obey;
With heart and hand we ready stand,
   Our duty still to pay.
     But when the glass goes round,
     Then mirth and glee abound,
       We're happy ev'ry soul;
   We laugh a little, we drink a little,
   We work a little, we play a little.

Cho.—We laugh a little, we drink a little,
     We sing a little, are merry a little,
       And quaff the flowing bowl.
       And quaff, &c.

   See in the east the Master stands,
     The wardens south and west, sir,
   Both ready to obey command,
     Find work, or give us rest, sir.
The signal given, we all prepare,
With one accord obey the word,
   To work by rule or square:
Or, if they please, the ladder raise,
   Or plumb the level line;
Thus we employ our time with joy,
   Attending every sign.
     But when the glass goes round,
     Then mirth and glee abound,
       We're happy ev'ry soul;
   We laugh a little, and drink a little,
   We work a little, and play a little.

Cho.—We laugh a little, we drink a little,
     We sing a little, are merry a little,
       And quaff the flowing bowl.
       And quaff, &c.

Th' Almighty said, "Let there be light;"
    Effulgent rays appearing
Dispell'd the gloom, the glory bright
    To this new world was cheering:
But unto Masonry alone,
Another light, so clear and bright,
    In mystic rays then shone;
From east to west it spread so fast,
    That, faith and hope unfurl'd,
We hail with joy sweet charity,
    The darling of the world.
        Then while the toast goes round,
        Let mirth and glee abound,
            Let's be happy every soul;
        We'll laugh a little, and drink a little,
        We'll work a little, and play a little.

Cho.—We'll laugh a little, and drink a little,
        We'll sing a little, be merry a little,
            And quaff the flowing bowl.
            And quaff, &c.

VIII.

(Tune, *"Attic Fire."*)

ARISE, and blow thy trumpet, Fame!
    Freemasonry aloud proclaim
To realms and worlds unknown:
Tell them it was by David's son,
The wise, the matchless Solomon,
    Priz'd far above his throne.

The solemn temple's cloudcapt towers,
Th' aspiring domes are works of ours,
    By us those piles were rais'd:

Then bid mankind with songs advance,
And through th' ethereal vast expanse
 Let Masonry be prais'd!

We help the poor in time of need,
The naked clothe, the hungry feed,
 'Tis our foundation stone;
We build upon the noblest plan,
For friendship rivets man to man, } *Chorus three times.*
 And makes us all as one.

Still louder, Fame! thy trumpet blow;
Let all the distant regions know
 Freemasonry is this:
Almighty wisdom gave it birth,
And heaven has fix'd it here on earth,
 A type of future bliss!

IX.

(Tune, *"Dear Tom, this brown jug."*)

ARISE, gentle muse, and the wisdom impart
 To each bosom that glows with the love of our art;
 For the bliss that from thy inspiration accrues,
Is what all should admire, and each mason pursues.

Cho.—Hence harmony springs, the cement 'tis of love,
 Fair freedom on earth, and bright union above.

Tho' malice our joy should attempt to control,
Tho' discord around like an ocean should roll;
To the one we'll be deaf, to the other be blind,
For wisdom alone is the strength of the mind.

 Cho.—Hence harmony, &c.

The bright charms of beauty for ever will shine,
Our art to adorn with a lustre divine,
Till time, circling round, shall unfold the great truth,
Which thus has united the sage and the youth.
      Cho.—Hence harmony, &c.

X.

AS I at Wheeler's lodge one night,
    Kept Bacchus company;
(For Bacchus is a mason bright,
    And of all lodges free:)

Said I, "great Bacchus is a-dry,
    Pray give the god some wine;"
Jove in a fury did reply,
    "October's as divine."

It makes us masons more complete,
    Adds to our fancy wings;
Makes us as happy and as great
    As mighty lords and kings.

XI.

AS long as our coast does with whiteness appear,
    Still masons stand foremost in verse;
Whilst harmony, friendship, and joys are held dear,
    New bands shall our praises rehearse.

CHORUS.

Though lodges, less favour'd, less happy, decay,
    Destroy'd by Old Time as he runs;
Tho' Albions, Gregorians, and Bucks fade away,
    Still masons shall live in their sons!

If envy attempts our success to impede,
   United we'll trample her down;
If faction should threaten, we'll show we're agreed,
   And discord shall own we are one.
      Cho.—Though lodges, &c.

Whilst with ardour we glow this our Order to raise,
   Promoting its welfare and peace;
Old masons return, our endeavours to praise,
   And new ones confirm the increase.
      Cho.—Though lodges, &c.

Go on, cry our parents, for Time is your friend,
   His flight shall increase your renown;
May Mirth be your guest, smiling Bacchus attend,
   With joy all your meetings to crown.
      Cho.—Though lodges, &c.

XII.

BY BROTHER LAURENCE DERMOTT.
(Tune, *"Mutual love."*)

AS Masons once on Shinar's plain,
   (Met to revive their arts again),
     Did mutually agree;
So now we're met in Britain's isle,
And make the royal craft to smile,
     In ancient Masonry.

The masons in this happy land,
Have now reviv'd the ancient grand,
     And the strong Tuscan laid;
Each faithful brother, by a sign,
Like Salem's sons each other join,
     And soon each order made.

Thrice happy, blest fraternity,
Whose basis is sweet unity;
   And makes us all agree;
Kings, dukes, and lords to us are kind,
As we to strangers, when we find
   Them skill'd in Masonry.

How happy are the ancient brave,
Whom never cowan can deceive;
   And may they so remain;
No modern craftsman e'er did know
What signs our masters to us show,
   Though long they strove in vain.

My brethren, all take glass in hand,
And toast our Noble Master Grand,
   And in full chorus sing
A health to Ancient Masons free,
Throughout the globe, where'er they be,
   And so, God Save the King.

XIII.

AN ALLEGORY ON CHARITY.

(Tune, *"How happy a state does the Miller possess."*)

AS Poverty late in a fit of despair
   Was beating her bosom and tearing her hair,
Smiling Hope came to ask, what her countenance told.
That she there lay expiring with hunger and cold.

Come, rise! said the sweet rose herald of joy,
And the torments you suffer I'll quickly destroy?
Take me by the hand, all your griefs I'll dispel,
And I'll lead you for succour to Charity's cell.

On Poverty hobbl'd, Hope soften'd her pain,
But long did they search for the goddess in vain;
Towns, cities, and countries, they travers'd around;
For Charity's lately grown hard to be found.

At length at the door of a lodge they arriv'd,
Where, their spirits exhausted, the tyler reviv'd,
Who when ask'd (as 'twas late) if the dame had gone home,
Said, "no; Charity's always the last in the room."
The door being open'd, in Poverty came,
Was cherish'd, reliev'd, and caress'd by the dame;
Each votary, likewise, the object to save,
Obey'd his own feelings, and cheerfully gave.

Then shame on the man who the science derides,
Where this soft-beaming virtue for ever presides.
In this scriptural maxim let's ever accord—
"What we give to the poor we but lend to the Lord."

XIV.

ST. JOHN. (Tune, *"The Huntsman."*)

ASSEMBL'D and tyl'd, let us social agree,
 With the monarch that sits on the throne,
For he charges a glass, and round let it pass,
 To celebrate ancient St. John.

Though babblers may prattle in showing their spleen,
 Their spite we compare to the drone,
For in sweet harmony, in love we'll agree,
 To celebrate ancient St. John.

The world is in pain our secrets to gain,
 In ignorance let them think on,
For in sweet harmony, in love we'll agree,
 To celebrate ancient St. John.

With toast after toast let us drink to the king,
    Remem'bring the great Solomon,
For his actions were rare, by the compass and square:—
    Thus celebrate ancient St. John.

Then join hand in hand, in a body firm stand,
    Our cares and our troubles begone,
Let us love, laugh, and sing; love the ladies and king:
    Thus celebrate ancient St. John.

XV.

Written by the EDITOR, *and intended to have been sung at the Grand Feast, May 11th, 1796,**

(Tune, *"Hearts of Oak."*)

A SYSTEM more pure ne'er was modell'd by man,
    Than that which we boast as the Freemason's plan;
It unites all the world by the strongest of ties,
And adds to men's bliss, while it makes them more wise.
    From the prince to the boor,
    Be he rich, be he poor,
    A mason's a brother,
    And each will help t'other,
So grateful the tie is of Freemasonry.

That hence flow the purest enjoyments of life,
That banish'd from hence are dissension and strife,
That the lessons are good which we practice and teach,
Are truths that our foes vainly try to impeach.
    From the prince, &c.

---

*The 4th, 5th, 6th, 7th, and 8th verses may be omitted on ordinary occasions, for the purpose of shortening the song, The first three verses with the last verse make a song which most hearers, perhaps, will think long enough.

The greatest of monarchs, the wisest and best,
Have masons become, and been true to the test;
And still with that sanction our rites are pursu'd,
Admir'd by the wise, and approv'd by the good.
    From the prince, &c.

"The King and the Craft" having claim'd our applause,
The guardian the one, t'other firm to the laws,
In union, my brethren, assist me to sing,
"Ever true be the Craft to a patriot King!"
    From the prince, &c.

To George, Prince of Wales, our affections we owe,
To his health let libations with due honours flow;
With zeal let "Our Royal Grand Master" be giv'n,
And the blessings be sanctioned and granted by heaven.
    From the prince, &c.

His consort may health and enjoyment attend,
The Craft are assur'd that she's firmly their friend:
For her offspring we crave but this boon from above,
"Be the meed of her virtues a whole nation's love!"
    From the prince, &c.

Of York and of Clarence (while o'er land and sea
The toils of the brave serve to keep Britain free)
May the deeds furnish subjects for many a lay,
And their mem'ry ne'er die till all nature decay!
    From the prince, &c.

Yet let not the "man of our hearts" be unsung,
Nor forget the effects of his well-pleading tongue;*

   Alluding to a collection of upwards of £550 being made for the Cumberland School, after a Speech of the Earl of Moira's in its behalf, at a public dinner, April 11th, 1796, at Freemasons' Hall.

May the pray'rs of our orphans to heaven ascend,
And secure its best blessings for Moira, their friend!
    From the prince, &c.

The task were too tedious the deeds to record
Of the great and the good that our annals afford;
In a word, let us utter this truth to mankind,
There's no temple more pure than the true mason's
    From the prince, &c.   [mind.

XVI.

By Brother JOHN CARTWRIGHT, *of Cheadle, in Lancashire.*

(Tune, *"Smile, Britannia."*)

ATTEND, attend the strain,
  Ye masons free, whilst I,
To celebrate your fame,
  Your virtues sound on high;
Accepted masons, free and bold,
Will never live the dupes of gold.

  Great Solomon, the king,
    Great Architect of fame,
  Of whom all coasts did ring,
    Rever'd the mason's name.
Like him accepted, free, and bold;
True wisdom we prefer to gold.

  Since him, the great and wise
    Of every age and clime,
  With fame that never dies,
    Pursued the art sublime,
Inspir'd by heav'n; just and free,
Have honour'd much our mystery.

> The glorious paths of those
> With heav'n-born wisdom crown'd
> We every day disclose,
> And tread on sacred ground;
> A mason righteous, just, and free,
> Or else not worthy Masonry.

XVII.

(Tune, *"Derry down."*)

ATTEND, loving brethren, and to me give ear,
Our work being ended, let's lay aside care;
Let mirth and good humour our senses regale,
And mind that our secrets we never reveal.
> Derry down, down, down, derry down.

With leave of his worship who there fills the chair,
Who governs our actions with compass and square;
We'll sing a few verses in Masonry s praise;
Not fond of ambition, we look for no bays.
> Derry down, &c.

Our Ancient Grand Master, inspir'd by the Lord,
On holy Moriah, as scriptures record,
Began the magnificent structure to frame
In the month called Zif, the fourth year of his reign.
> Derry down, &c.

With level and square the foundation begun,
In length sixty cubits, breadth nineteen and one;
Here Masonry shone above all other arts,
So sublime's the great secret the artist imparts.
> Derry down, &c.

Old Hiram of Tyre, King David's great friend,
Did fir, pine, and cedar from Lebanon send,
To build the sanctorum by Masonry's skill,
In obedience unto the great Architect's will.
      Derry down, &c.

One hundred and fifty three thousand six hundred,
Employed for the temple, we find they were number'd;
With Crafts many thousands, and bearers of loads,
And Masters six hundred, as scripture records.
      Derry down, &c.

These form'd themselves all into lodges, they say,
Some east and some west, some north and south way;
In love and truth still they go happily on,
In all well-governed countries under the sun.
      Derry down, &c.

Now let the brisk bumper go merrily round;
May our Worshipful Master in honour abound;
May his precepts instructive to harmony move,
And we live like true brethren in friendship and love.
      Derry down, &c.

All health to our brethren of ev'ry degree,
Dispers'd round the globe, or by land or by sea;
Preserve them, ye pow'rs, their virtues improve:
When we part from this world may we all meet above.
      Derry down, &c.

XVIII.

A SONG FOR THE KNIGHTS TEMPLAR.

Written by T. DUNCKERLY, ESQ., *late Grand Master.*

(Tune, *"At the bright Temple's massy dome."*)

AT the bright temple's awful dome,
    Where Christian knights in arms are drest;
To that most sacred place we come,
    With cross and star upon the breast;
Pilgrims inspir'd with zealous flame,
    Through rugged ways and dangers past;
Our sandals torn, our feet were lame,
    But faith and hope o'ercame at last.

Remember, knights, the noble cause,
    Let Simon's fate prevent your fall;
Be firm and true, obey the laws,
    Nor let the cock unheeded call.
Let none the sacred word profane,
    Nor e'er, like Peter, Christ deny;
Your conduct still preserve from blame,
    Nor let the urn be plac'd on high.

Unite your hearts, unite each hand,
    In friendship, harmony, and love;
Connected thus Knights Templar stand,
    Our love and charity to prove.
Until that awful final day
    When fire shall melt this earthly ball,
Your courage and your faith display;
    Attend to freedom's sacred call.

True to our God, our Laws, and King,
    Devout, obedient, loyal, free.
The praise of royal Edward sing,
    The patron of our mystery.
In uniform each knight is drest,
    Distinguish'd all by *black, red, blue,*
The cross and star upon the breast,
    Adorn the heart that's just and true.

XIX.

BEGIN, O ye muses, a Freemason's strain;
    Let the numbers be gentle, and easy, and plain;
Though sometimes in concert sublimely we sing,
Whilst each brother mason joins hands with a king,
And princes disdain not companions to be
With the man that is own'd for a mason and free.

Why seek our best nobles our mystery to know,
And rather sing here than sip tea with a beau?
The sweet notes of knowledge more powerfully call,
Than a fav'rite at court, or a toast at a ball:
For truth's sake, a lord is of equal degree
With the man that is own'd for a mason and free.

'Twas heav'n first lighted the glorious flame
Of science, that sages Freemasonry name.
From Adam it flow'd to the patriarch of old;
The wise king preferr'd it to coffers of gold;
And Hiram of Tyre join'd with him to be
Of the number of those that we e masons and free.

The grigs, antigallics, and others, they say,
Have set up their lodges, and mimic our way;
But frogs claim a curse when they croak from the fen.
And monkeys a kick when they imitate men.
In vain, shallow mortals, ye rivals would be
To the man that is own'd for a mason and free.

The wisdom of Greece and old Rome we explore,
Nay pass to the learn'd of the Memphian shore,
What secrets Euphrates and Tigris have known,
And Palestine gather'd, are made all our own.
Well may the world wonder what strange things we see,
With the man that is own'd for a mason and free.

Though the fair from our rites are for ever debar'd,
Ah, ladies! repine not, nor censure too hard:
You have no rivals here, not ev'n in glass,
Where fribbles so dote on the shade of an ass.
Your own dearest pictures, our hearts could you see,
Would be found in the man that's a mason and free.

The brightest of graces with virtue here join,
No such angel looks in the drawing room shine,
Bless'd concord, and eagle-ey'd truth hover round,
And face to face, friendship says, see the bowl crown'd:
Here's a health, let it pass with the number of three,
To the man that is own'd for a mason and free.

XX.

By Dr. William Perfect.

Sung by Brother Sylvester Harding, *at the Grand Provincial Anniversary Meeting at the Ship Tavern, Feversham.* (Tune, *"Mulberry Tree."*)

BEHOLD, a cloud breaks, and Urania descends,
    The sky-mantled nymph our convention attends!
It is for the Craft that she sweeps the loud strings,
And science attunes her sweet notes as she sings.
Cho.—All the arts inform'd by me,
    Bow to thee, blest Masonry;
    Creation spreads her charms to thee,
    And thou immortal e'er shalt be.

Elated, all own that thy source is divine,
The bible thy standard, thy square, and thy line;
That truth is thy handmaid, and reason thy soul,
And justice thy guide to the farthermost pole.
    Cho.—All the arts, &c.

As wide and extensive as Sol's boundless ray,
All cheering as spring, and as bright as her May,
The system Masonic, of mystical rite,
Spreads an ocean of rapture and infinite light.
    Cho.—All the arts, &c.

Sense, truth, and good humour, and harmony join,
By Masonry warm'd, they unite and combine;
To the bower of friendship she leads them along,
To taste of her banquets and chorus her song.
    Cho.—Then the arts, &c.

Behold the Freemason, how glorious his plan!
It enlarges the mind, and ennobles the man;
It teaches the hand and the heart how to bless,
And melts e'en the miser to soften distress.
    Cho.—Then the arts, &c.

To time's latest period the Craft so divine
As the rays of their art shall diffusedly shine;
Their laws, rules, and orders all others excel,
And Kent here stands foremost their virtues to tell.
    Cho.—While the art, &c.

XXI.

By Brother LAURIE, *of the Lodge of Alloa, 1758.*

(Tune, *Derry down.*)

BEHOLD in a lodge we dear brethren are met,
    And in proper order together are set;
Our secrets to none but ourselves shall be known,
Our actions to none but Freemasons be shown.
    Derry down, down, down, derry down.

Let brotherly love be among us reviv'd;
Let's stand by our laws, that are wisely contriv'd,
And then all the glorious creation shall see
That none are so loving, so friendly as we.
    Derry down, &c.

The temple, and many a magnificent pile,
E'en buildings now standing within our own isle,
With wisdom contriv'd, with beauty refin'd,
With strength to support, and the building to bind—
    Derry down, &c.

These noble, grand structures will always proclaim
What honour is due to a Freemason's name;
E'en ages to come, when our work they shall see,
Will strive with each other like us to be free.
    Derry down, &c.

What though some of late by their spleen plainly show
They fain would deride what they gladly would know;
Let ev'ry true brother these vermin despise,
And the ancient grand secret keep back from their eyes.
    Derry down, &c.

Then, brethren, let each put his hand to his heart,
And resolve from true Masonry ne'er to depart;
And when the last trumpet on earth shall descend,
Our lodge will be clos'd, and our secrets shall end.
    Derry down, &c.

XXII.

BY GAVIN WILSON.

(Tune, "The Banks of Invermay.")

COME, all ye gentle springs, that move
    And animate the human mind,
And by your energy improve
    The social bond by which we're joined.
The social lodge, of care devoid,
    And haggard malice always free,
Shall by your aid be still employ'd
    In social love and harmony.

How must the heart with rapture glow
    When every nerve's with virtue strung,
When from the kindly bosom flow
    Unfeigned expressions of the tongue!
The social virtues thus practis'd,
    Express'd by symbols of our art,
Engage us to be exercis'd
    In studies that improve the heart.

XXIII.

(Tune, "Entered Apprentice's Song.")

COME, are you prepar'd?
    Your scaffolds well rear'd?
Bring mortar, and temper it purely;
    'Tis all safe, I hope,
    Well brac'd with each rope,
Your ledgers and putlogs securely:

Then next your bricks bring,
It is time to begin,
For the sun with its ray is adorning;
The day's fair and clear,
No rain you need fear:
'Tis a charming and lovely fine morning.

Pray, where are your tools?
Your line and plumb-rules?
Each man to his work let him stand, boys,
Work solid and sure,
Upright and secure;
And your building, be sure, will be strong, boys.

Pray, make no mistake,
But true your joints break,
And take care you follow your leaders;
Work, rake, beck and tueth,
And make your work smooth,
And be sure that you fill up your headers.

XXIV.

COME, boys, let us more liquor get,
 Since jovially we are all met,
Since jovially, &c.
 Here none will disagree;
Let's drink and sing, and all combine,
In songs to praise that art divine,
In songs, &c.
 That's called Freemasonry.

True knowledge seated in the head,
Instructs us masons how to tread,
Instructs us, &c.
 The paths we ought to go;

By which we ever friends create,
Drown care and strife and all debate,
Drown care, &c.
    Count none but fools our foes.

Here sorrow knows not how to weep,
And watchful grief is lull'd asleep.
And watchful, &c.
    In our lodge we know no care;
Join hand in hand before we part,
Each brother takes his glass with art,
Each brother, &c.
    And toasts some charming fair.

Hear me, ye gods, and whilst I live,
Good masons and good liquor give,
Good masons, &c.
    Then always happy me;
Likewise a gentle she I crave,
Until I'm summoned to my grave;
But when I'm summon'd to my grave,
    Adieu my lodge and she.

XXV.

By Brother W. UTLEY, *of the Lodge of Prince George, No. 574, Bottoms in Stansfield.*

(Tune, *"True Courage."*)

COME, brother Freemasons, in clothing most shining.
    For your work be prepared, no longer delay;
Truth, friendship, and love, in your emblems
    entwining,
Bespeak you are ready, and cheerful, and gay.

Then on with your labour, pursue the great lecture
By Hiram invented, and to true masons giv'n;
Of working the science of fam'd architecture,
Sent down for Freemasons as a blessing from heav'n.

Then on, my dear brethren, improve the grand blessing,
Let faith, hope, and charity, be guides on the way;
Whilst with brotherly love and true friendship caressing,
We've support in each other, dispelling dismay:
Join'd firm in a body, we've fellowship's strength, sirs,
Our works in fair beauty, none shall them outdo:
For planned in wisdom, in truth they are rear'd, sirs,
So as we've begun them, we'll carry them through.

See th' Apprentices ready, and Craftsmen attending,
And the Master directing the whole, you may see;
The pile being rais'd, and completed the building,
Then all are refresh'd, and from labour set free;
Then jovial and merry, their toil being ended,
They most freely and friendly each other do greet;
And in acts of fair charity, with sympathy blended,
The ancients and moderns their union complete.

Then blest be the union, thus happily binding
Each brother to aid, and support, and befriend:
Whilst working, his tools his duty reminding,
Square, level, and upright, his actions should end:
So then within compass let your actions be bounded,
As the pencil a plan of your life may record;
From a line of the skirret, strict and true founded,
And held, and recorded by those who've the word.

Thus gauged our time, our work fairly measur'd,
The rudeness of nature by the gavel remov'd,
And smooth'd with the chisel, in lodge it is treasur'd
As a polish'd, pure ashlar, by labour improv'd:

So blest be the art, let each brother revere it,
Go on most sincerely, on its maxims improve;
Let a Freemason's toast, whilst loudly he cheers it,
Be concord, and union, and brotherly love.

XXVI.
COME, BROTHERS, SING.

In general use at the Lodges in Germany, extracted from Render's Tour through that empire.

COME, brothers, sing with me,
    Join brethren all;
Wisdom our Goddess be,
    List to her call.

Laugh at the foolish throng,
    Heedless and vain;
Wisdom inspires our song,
    Blest be her reign.

Masons we all are bound,
    Heart, voice, and hand;
Her laws to spread around
    O'er ev'ry land.

Nature directs us still,
    Mortals to aid;
This we with joy fulfil,
    Well we're repaid.

We need no borrow'd beams,
    Brethren, behold!
From the bright east still gleams
    Radiant gold:

Which on our joyful way,
    Is to us given;
Till an eternal day,
    Greets us in heaven.

XXVII.

COME, come, my dear brethren,
    Great news I proclaim:
Our King's a Freemason,
    A mason of fame:
And tho' he's a king,
    He's a brother to me:
No mortals but masons
    So great then can be.
Cho.—So great then can be,
        So great then can be;
        No mortals but masons
        So great then can be.

Who would not be proud, say,
    Of such a great name?
He that's a Freemason
    Is a true son of fame;
Since kings, dukes, and princes,
    Men of high degree,
Throw by their distinctions,
    With us to be free.
Cho.—With us to be free, &c.

We're sons of antiquity,
    But not of pride;
The fathers of old, they
    Were all on our side.
Being struck with surprise
    The grand temple to see,
They all were ambitious
    Freemasons to be.
Cho.—Freemasons to be.

We're true and we're trusty,
    We're just and sincere;
We're bless'd by the poor,
    And ador'd by the fair.
Kings are our companions,
    So noble are we;
Then who would not wish
    A Freemason to be?
Cho.—A Freemason to be, &c.

Why, then, should we mind
    The reflections of fools,
Who know not the value
    Nor use of our tools?
We keep within compass;
    Square conduct have we;
To plumb, line, and level
    Our actions agree.
Cho.—Our actions, &c.

With innocent mirth,
    And with social soul,
Let's taste the pure nectar
    That flows in the bowl.
Then fill up a bumper—
    My toast it shall be,
A health to our masters,
    Our wardens, and we.
Cho.—Our wardens, and we, &c.

XXVIII.

COME, come, my brethren dear,
　　Now we're assembled here,
　Exalt your voices clear,
　　　With harmony;
Here none shall be admitted in,
Were he a lord, a duke, or king!
He's counted but an empty thing,
　　　Except he's free.
Cho.—Let ev'ry man take glass in hand,
　Drink bumpers to our Master Grand,
　As long as he can sit or stand
　　　With decency.

　By our grand arts we prove
　Emblems of truth and love,
　Types given from above,
　　　To those that are free;
There's ne'er a king that fills a throne
Will ever be asham'd to own
Those secrets to the world unknown,
　　　But such as we.
Cho.—Let ev'ry man, &c.

　Now, ladies, try your arts,
　To gain us men of parts,
　Who best can charm your hearts,
　　　Because we're free;
Take us, try us, and you'll find,
We're true, we're loving, just, and kind,
And taught to please a lady's mind,
　　　By Masonry.
Cho.—Let ev'ry man, &c.

Grand Chorus.

God bless King George! long may he reign,
To curb the pride of foes who're vain,
And with the conq'ring sword maintain
    Freemasonry!

XXIX.

COME, fill up a bumper, and let it go round,
    Let mirth and good fellowship always abound;
        And let the world see,
        That Freemasonry
Doth teach honest hearts to be jovial and free.

Our lodge, now compos'd of honest free hearts,
Our Master most freely his secret imparts;
        And so we improve
        In knowledge and love,
By help from our mighty Grand Master above.

Let honour and friendship eternally reign,
Let each brother mason the truth so maintain;
        While all may agree,
        That Freemasonry
Doth teach honest hearts to be honest and free.

In mirth and good fellowship we will agree,
For none are more blest, or more happy than we;
        And thus we'll endure,
        While our actions are pure.
Kind heaven those blessings to us doth insure.

XXX.

(Tune, *"Fairy Elves."*)

COME, follow, follow me,
　　Ye jovial masons free;
　Come, follow all the rules,
By Solomon, that mason king,
Who honour to the Craft did bring.

　　He's justly call'd the wise,
　　His fame doth reach the skies;
　　He stood upon the square,
　　And did the temple rear;
With true level, plumb, and gauge,
He prov'd the wonder of the age.

　　The mighty, mason lords,
　　Stood firmly to their words;
　　They had it in esteem,
　　For which they're wise men deem'd;
Why should not their example prove,
Our present Craft to live in love.

　　The royal art and word,
　　Are kept upon record
　　In upright hearts and pure,
　　While sun and moon endure;
Not written, but indented on
The heart of every Arch-mason.

　　And as for Hiram's art,
　　We need not to impart;
　　The scripture plainly shows
　　From whence his knowledge flows;
His genius was so much refin'd,
His peer he has not left behind.

Then let not any one
Forget the widow's son;
But toast his memory
In glasses charg'd full high;
And when our proper time is come
Like brethren part, and so go home.

XXXI.

The ENTERED APPRENTICE'S SONG.

COME, let us prepare,
    We brothers that are
Assembled on merry occasion,
    To drink, laugh, and sing;
    Be he beggar or king,
Here's a health to an accepted mason.

    The world is in pain
    Our secrets to gain,
And still let them wonder and gaze on;
    They ne'er can divine
    The word, or the sign,
Of a free and an accepted mason.

    'Tis this, and 'tis that,
    They cannot tell what,
Nor why the great men of the nation
    Should aprons put on,
    And make themselves one
With a free and an accepted mason.

Great dukes, kings, and lords,
Have laid by their swords,
Our myst'ry to put a good grace on;
And ne'er been asham'd
To hear themselves nam'd
With a free and an accepted mason.

Antiquity's pride
We have on our side,
To keep up our old reputation;
There's naught but what's good
To be understood
By a free and an accepted mason.

We're true and sincere,
And just to the fair,
Who will trust us on any occasion;
No mortal can more
The ladies adore,
Than a free and an accepted mason.

Then join hand in hand,   (STANDING).
By each brother firm stand,
Let's be merry and put a bright face on;
What mortal can boast   } *Chorus*
So noble a toast   } *three times.*
As a free and an accepted mason? }

XXXII.

(Tune, *Of noble race was Shenkin*).

COME, now, lov'd loving brothers,
　　Since serious work is ended,
　　　Let wine give birth
　　　To social mirth,
With tuneful songs attended.

　　Charge then with liquid powder,
Each his sound-bottom'd bumper;
　　　For as to the king
　　　And the craft we sing,
It should be with a thumper.

　　Off with it; clap; huzza boys!
As do our rites require;
　　　Thrice three make nine;
　　　Mind discipline,
And all as one give fire.

　　Again replenish high lads,
To the grand lodges' grand master,
　　　And his wardens two,
　　　Our next toast's due;
Heav'n shield them from disaster!

　　Next, to all worthy masons,
Howe'er by fortune batter'd,
　　　And poor as Job,
　　　Where, o'er the globe,
Them providence hath scatter'd.

　　And, as the fair sex ever
By masons are ador'd,
　　　Health to their charms
　　　Who in masons' arms
Lig, in true love assur'd.

SONGS. 37

XXXIII.

The FELLOW-CRAFT'S *song, as sung at the Lodge in Carmarthen, South Wales.*

COME all ye (1) elves that be,
   Come follow, follow me,
All ye that guards have been
Without, or serve within:
Come, sing for joy, thro' us, tis found
That all this Lodge is sacred ground.

* Guides too, (2) that fairies are
   Come, five by five prepare;
   Come, buy fresh oil with speed,
   The dying lamps to feed;
All trimm'd anew in glitt'ring light,
For welcome garments must be white.

* Come, (3) seraphs too, that be
   Bright rulers, three by three,
   Attend on me, your queen,
   Two handmaids led between;
And all around the healths I name
Make you the hallow'd stones proclaim.

* While (4) sylphs and sylvan loves
   Of mountains and of groves,
   With gnomes and sprightly dames
   Of fountains and of flames,

---

1. The five external senses and ideas of the soul.
2. The five internal senses, or faculties of the soul, viz.: perception, reflection, imagination, attention and invention.
3. The three superior graces, or faculties of the mind, wisdom, knowledge and skill.
4. The seven influences, both natural and divine, of the heart, or gradual successions and acquirements.

The joyful noise with hands and feet
Shall echo, and the noise repeat.

All we who sing and love,
Who live in springs above,
Descend, descend do we,
With masons to be free;
Where (5) springs of wine revive each face,
And streams of milk spill all the place.

Where (6) cherubs guard the door
With flaming sword before,
We thro' the keyhole creep,
And there we deeply peep;
O'er all their jewels skip and leap,
Or trip it tip-toe step by step.

Or, as upon the green
We fairies turn unseen,
So here we make (7) a ring,
And dance while masons sing:
Around their crowns we whirl apace,
Nor yet one single hair misplace.

Or when from thence we jump
All down with (8) silent thump,

---

†Here might be drank the following health, viz.:
    All hail the crafty sisters three!
    The dame that blows the fire, and she
    That weaves the fine embroidery;
    But chief of all, hail masonry!
  5. The liberal arts and sciences of masons.
  6. The two keys of scripture and nature which belong to the logos, or word of rational judgment, whereby we distinguish truth from falsehood, and evidence from darkness, &c.
  7. Alluding to the revolutions of our thoughts, or rumination, &c.   (8) Alluding to the secrecies of our thoughts, and obedience of our wills, &c.

None hear our feet rebound
Round, round the table, round,
Nor see us while we nimbly pass
Thrice round the rim of ev'ry glass.

Hence, (9) satyrs, hence, begone,
Foul vesture ye have on;
No naked nymphs here be,
Each five and sacred three,
With virgins and with graces join
In sacred songs the feast divine.

Two (10) stones of crystal clear
Our squared cloth shall bear;
Five loaves of oaken mast
Shall be our firm repast;
Five acorn cups of pearly dew
Shall serve to pledge each health anew.*

If any (11) crumbs withal
Do from their table fall,
With greedy mirth we eat,
No honey is so sweet;
And when they drop it from the thumb,
We catch each *supernaculum*.

---

9. Such ideas as are impurely dressed, or too open and familiar, &c.

10. Alluding to the foundations whereon this sacred order is laid, &c.

  * N.B.—Here might be drank this health, viz:—
    To all true housewives and their bearns,
    To every damsel that has charms,
    But chiefly those in masons' arms.

11. The lessons, &c. given in this lodge.

* The (12) tongues of nightingale,
   The (13) eyes of unctuous snails,
   The (14) serpent's brain with blood
   Of (15) doves, is charming food;
But (16) brains of worm, and marrow of mice,
Are foolish and of filthy price.

* Whilst we enchant all ears
   With (17) music of the spheres,
   No (18) grasshopper nor fly
   Serves for our minstrelsy;
Such locusts leave, and all such flies
To Beelzebub, the (19) prince of lies.

* Grace said, while all awhile
   In songs the time beguile;
   Or pleasant healths, or at
   The table sit and chat;
Then, (20) female-like, on teas we feast,
As we first (21) taught it in the east.

   Of (22) grass the tender (23) tops
   Infus'd in (24) dewy drops,

---

  12. The oratory of teachers.   13. The curiosity of enquirers.
  14. The understanding of the crafty.
  15. The spirit of the innocent.
  16. The blind and covetous.
  17. The harmony of the several degrees of life, soul, and mind, & c.   18. No busy-bodies nor ramblers, &c.
  19. The author of maggots, chimeras, &c.
  20. The learning of lectures, and explanation of secrets, &c.
  21. Alluding to the natural light of the Chinese;
  22. Or rather the first restorer of masonry, who fed on the tops of wild herbs, wild honey, &c.
  23. The newer terms of art and science derived from nature, &c.
  24. The older terms of scripture, &c.

SONGS. 41

 With (25) crystal bags of bees,
 Make us delicious teas;
So sweet and fragrant of the (26) flow'r,
None taste the bitter or the sour.

 Meanwhile, the (27) house new swept,
 And from uncleanness kept;
 If all things shine with grace,
 And nothing's out of place,
Then do we praise the (28) household maid,
And (29) four fold surely she's repaid.

 But if the house be foul,
 With (30) hammer, axe, or tool;
 If wardens fall asleep,
 Or fellows drink too deep;
If (31) smoke perchance or (32) flames arise,
Or if the lodge (33) untiled lies;

 Then in the (34) dead of night,
 With (35) goblins we affright;
 Or lead some into (36) pools,
 Or (37) steal away the tools;

---

25. The sweet collections and digestions of us the labourers in masonry, &c.
26. Beautiful moral of it, such that neither its religion nor law displeases any.
27. Implying that the whole economy being reformed and purified, ought to be kept in decency and order.
28. The memory, &c.
29. For every idea points out four several ways, viz:—To things celestial and angelical, terrestrial and human, &c.
30. Low, vulgar, and litigious notions, &c.
31. Discoveries, &c.   32. Disputations, &c.
33. Unveiled, &c.   34. The times of ignorance, &c.
35. Enthusiasms or superstitions, &c.
36. Libertinisms or abominations; the consequences of mystery and darkness, &c.
37. Deprive the mind, &c. of its proper testimonies, emblems, &c.

Or else (38) we pinch both arms and thighs,
Till some one hears, or us espies.
   Thus of true masonry,
   Tho' (39) females we are free;
   Made free by us all are,
   Tho' none us see nor hear.
When in (40) the morning signs are seen
Where we (41) the eve before have been.
   Yet what we hear and see
   In lodges where we be,
   Not (42) forc'd nor offer'd gold
   Can masons' truths unfold;
Besides, the craft we love, not gain,
And secrets why should we profane?
   † We taught masons' school,
   To walk by square (43) and (44) rule,
   On level (45) just to act,
   And work all (46) upright fact;

---

38. Alluding to the arts whereby masons awake men's minds.
39. As external forms begetting our ideas, may be metaphorically styled males; so the faculties inter-conceiving them, may be elegantly styled females, &c.
40. The age of reformation, &c.
41. The age of accomplishments, &c.
42. Implying that sublime truths are not obtained any otherwise than by a right study, and an endeavour to find out the real sense, which being always veiled, are therefore holy and sacred, such as are all general truths, &c.
   † Here likewise may be drank this health:
   May therefore bounty, faith and love,
   The lodge's lasting cement prove,
   While dark confusion shame them all
   Who dare her freedom to enthral.
43. The justice of our actions, &c.   44. The rule of law, &c.
45. With regard to our equals, &c.
46. With regard to our superiors, &c.

To live in (47) compass by our due,
And keep our hearts for ever (48) true.

That when the world's at (49) rest,
And snoring in her nest;
When (50) sun has long been set,
And (51) stars no rays beget;
When (52) moon her horned glory hides,
Their (53) lighted tapers are our guides.

CHORUS.

* Then fairies hand in hand,
   Thrice at the word's command,
   And seraphs make a ring,
   While merry masons sing,
That as their lodge, so always they
Stay'd always, and shall always stay.

* And rise up ev'ry elf,
   Come join the sacred twelve;
   Sing also whilst they sing
   Their ancient, glorious King,
That as he is, so ever we
Were ever, and shall ever be.

---

47. Within our proper stations, &c. 48. To every master, &c.
49. Returned to a state of illiterature, and inactivity.
50. The light of the gospel, i.e., of reason and of judgment.
51. Both priests and philosophers, &c.
52. Scripture, which, according to the learning of the times, increases or diminishes alternately in the glory of her writers.
53. The perfect patterns, &c. of free-masons.

N.B.—The verses marked with an Asterisk may be omitted when it is requisite to shorten the song.

XXXIV.

Sung at Provincial Grand Lodge, Truro, on the Festival of St. John the Baptist, June 24th, 1799.

(Tune, *Come, thou rosy, dimpled boy.*)

COME, ye masons, hither bring
The tuneful pipe and pleasing string,
Exalt each voice,
Aloud rejoice,
And make the spacious concave ring:
Let your hearts be blithe and gay,
Joy and mirth let all display,
No dull care
Shall enter here,
For this is masons' holiday.
Cho.—Let your hearts, &c.

Friendship here has fix'd her seat,
And virtue finds a calm retreat;
Go, tell the fool
'Tis wisdom's school,
Where love and honour always meet.
Cho.—Let your hearts, &c.

Social pleasures here invite
To fill the soul with sweet delight,
While hand in hand,
Our friendly band
In love and harmony unite.
Cho.—Let your hearts, &c.

May we oft assemble here,
And long the badge of honour wear;
May joy abound,
And we be found
For ever faithful and sincere.
Cho.—Let your hearts, &c.

Take the flowing glass in hand,
And drink to your provincial grand;
   Long may he reign,
   The cause maintain,
And lodges flourish through the land.
  Cho.—Let your hearts, &c.

XXXV.

A ROYAL ARCH SONG.

Communicated to W. Utley by Bro. J. Sutcliffe of Burnley.

C OMPANIONS all agree,
   For masonry to be
  A something that's divine;
Tradition hath us told,
Beneath the hallow'd ground,
'Till happily it was found,
  With lustre it did shine.

Long time it lay conceal'd
Before it was reveal'd,
  And did in darkness lay;
But God, who's just and true,
Did with the work pursue,
The grand art bring to view,
  Then led us the right way.

Jehovah being our guide
Our footsteps ne'er can slide,
  He'll make our paths secure,
Though dangers may abound
When trav'ling under ground;
Yet our anchor, hope, is found,
  Our helper still is sure.

My wandering feet at last
On solid ground was cast
   Although in shades of night;
But darkness being withdrawn,
Behold the lovely morn
With light did it adorn,
   Conspicuously bright.
Secrets which long I'd sought
By light divine were brought,
   That made all things accord.
I blest the happy day
That pointed out the way,
No longer to delay
   To find the long lost word.
Resplendent works arise
That're dazzling to the eyes,
   No beauty e'er excell'd.
In golden lines I did see
The grandest mystery,
In amazing ecstacy
   That e'er my eyes beheld.
Such glorious things I found
Within the sacred ground,
   As cannot be express'd.
Industrious masons may
By travelling the same way,
As sure as light makes day,
   Receive the solemn test.
Then let us bless the Lord,
Who gave the solemn word,
   And did the cause maintain.
As sure as He did send,
He ever will defend,
Until the world shall end,
   His great and glorious name.

XXXVI.

DIVINE Urania, virgin pure!
    Enthroned in the Olympian bow'r,
  I here invoke thy lays!
Celestial muse, awake the lyre,
With heav'n-born, sweet, seraphic fire,
  Freemasonry to praise.

The stately structures that arise,
And brush the concave of the skies,
  Still ornament thy shrine;
Th' aspiring domes, those works of ours,
"The solemn temples—cloud-capt towers,"
  Confess the art divine.

With prudence all our actions are,
By Bible, compass, and by square,
  In love and truth combin'd;
While justice and benevolence,
With fortitude and temperance,
  Adorn and grace the mind.

Let masonry's profound grand art,
Be rooted in each brother's heart,
  Immortal to remain;
Hence for ever mayst thou be
Beyond compare, of masonry,
  Unrivall'd in thy reign!

XXXVII.

ERE genius, fire, or science fair, illum'd my infant mind,
Ere books had knowledge taught me the manners of mankind,
E'er virtue had instructed me to curb my passions weel,
My sire would oft impress my mind with fears of the deil.

The circling years pass'd round me, this matur'd me into age,
Then did the various ways of life, my varying life engage;
To know the great masonic art, its sacred joys to feel,
Yet something oft would whisper me, that masons rais'd the deil.

I had a friend and one sincere, I strait to him did hie,
Who long had been a brother true, of masons' mystic tie;
Says he, if thou wilt with me go, I'll soon convince thee weel
That masons have no contract nor dealings with the deil.

Admittance being granted me I join'd the social few,
The master took me by the hand, and taught me what to do;
His hand the sacred volume bore, by which I ken'd full weel,
That masons have no contract nor dealings with the deil.

He told me that my duty was to improve life's passing hour,
To aid a brother all I could to th'utmost of my power:

Father to the orphan be, the widow's sorrow heal,
And when I left this earthly lodge, I need not fear the deil.
To trace a part I now had learn'd, I straight began to try,
A magic wand was given me, joy sparkled in each eye;
A brother dash'd the hand aside, for which I thank'd him weel;
Th' impression ne'er will be effac'd, not even by the deil.
Beneath the mystic order there three heav'nly sisters rise,
Faith leads the way with looks benign, Hope points towards the skies;
Next Charity, O pleasing thought! that taught me how to feel,
And kindly whisper'd, happy few, you need not fear the deil.
Blithe tem'prance bids us all depart, when from the lodge we come,
My wife, while pleasure beams her cheek, cries ever welcome home:
My little ones around me press, and smiling say as weel,
My daddy's a freemason and we need not fear the deil.
When love and truth and social joy reign in each breast or heart,
When death a faithful brother gives each warning to depart;
Approving conscience whispers then, thou hast done thy duty weel,
Go, join the bless'd celestial lodge, and never fear the deil.

XXXVIII.
THE PAST MASTER'S SONG.
(Tune, *Rule, Britannia*).

ERE God the universe began,
  In one rude heap all matter lay,
Which wild disorder over-ran,
  Nor knew of light one glimmering ray;
While in darkness o'er the whole,
Confusion reigned without control.

Then God arose, his thunders hurl'd,
  And bade the elements arise;
In air He hung the pendant world,
  And o'er it spread the azure skies;
Stars in circles caus'd to run,
And in the centre fix'd the sun.

Then man He call'd forth out of dust,
  And form'd him with a living soul;
All things committed to his trust,
  And made him lord of all the whole;
But ungrateful unto heav'n
He proved, and was from Eden driv'n.

From thence proceeded all our woes,
  Nor could mankind one comfort share;
Until free-masons greatly rose,
  And form'd another Eden here;
Where true pleasure ever reigns,
And native innocence remains.

Here crystal fountains bubbling flow,
  Here naught that's vile can enter in;
The tree of knowledge here doth grow,
  Whose fruit we taste, yet free from sin;
Whilst here sweet friendship does abound,
And guardian angels hover round.

XXXIX.

E'ER since the temple first was rear'd
    Has masonry extended,
The widow's son, so much rever'd,
    The sacred art amended;
He wrought by compass and by square,
    By level and by plumb, sir,
For neither axe nor hammer there,
    Was heard within the dome, sir.

CHORUS.

Then O! support with hand and heart,
    Be mindful of its glory,
Free-masonry, that sacred art,
    So long renown'd in story.

Full oft has persecution strove
    To crush our sacred order,
By those who either curious prov'd,
    Or those who lov'd disorder;
But all such efforts are in vain,
    Whilst faith and truth we nourish;
Again we'll show them, and again,
    That masonry shall flourish.
    Cho.—Then O! support &c.

E'en kings, by evil men advis'd,
    Free-masonry suspected,
But for a moment tho' despis'd,
    When known 'twill be respected,
E'en good Queen Bess her courtiers sent,
    Resolv'd on our dismission;
They came, return'd, the queen content,
    Said, "let them have permission."
    Cho.—Then O! support &c.

And, now, while some of every band,
 'Tis feared are disaffected,;
Free-masonry most firm does stand,
 By king and law protected;
Then let us fill a bumper glass,
 And drink it whilst we stand, sirs,
With proper honours let it pass,
 The rulers of our craft, sirs.
  Cho.—Then O! support &c.

XL.

EXCUSE my weak, untutor'd muse, who thus presumes to climb;
For who to sing could e'er refuse, of masonry sublime;
Sure errors gross or dangers flow could never taint a brother,
Free to the solemn old new laws of loving one another.
  Lol de rol, &c.

Such God-like reason still at hand, no clouds o'er us are seen;
By moral rectitude we stand, we work, we act like men;
How oft by our august retreat are bounteous succours given!
O this is mercy's darling seat, the attributes of heaven.
  Lol de rol, &c.

Astræa, as the poets feign, on earth can never rest;
They lie, for o'er our lodge she reigns, and in each mason's breast;
Where truth and peace sits on each face, and friendship smiles around;
No biting envye'er takes place, but social joys abound.
  Lol de rol, &c.

So let our union e'er subsist, and never know decay;
For since the creation it did exist, and will till its final
    day:
We'll fill the sparkling, flowing bowl, and toast his
    memory,
Who lived with a firm unshaken soul, and died for
    masonry.

XLI.
A ROYAL ARCH SONG.
By Brother LOWE, *of Stockport.*

FATHER Adam created, beheld the light shine,
    God made him a mason and gave him a sign,
Our royal grand secret to him did impart,
And in paradise often he talk'd of our art.

Then Noah found favour and grace in his sight,
He built up an ark by the help of our light;
In clouds, God His rainbow then set, to insure
That his mercies and cov'nants should ever endure.

Abram, Isaac, and Jacob, partook of the same,
And Moses, that excellent mason of fame,
Whom God had appointed His chosen to bring
From bondage, and humble proud Egypt's great king.

Bezaleel and Aholiab were likewise inspir'd,
By the spirit of wisdom, and for it admir'd,
Well skilled in all workmanship, curious and true,
Of scarlet and purple, fine linen and blue.

In the wilderness, taught by our great architect,
A grand tabernacle they then did erect,
And vessels they made of gold that was good,
Wrought silver, brass, stones, and fine shittim-wood.

Then Joshua was chosen to have the command,
Who led them all safe into the holy land;
And to show that the Lord would His mercies fulfil,
Sun and moon at the order of Joshua stood still.

Next David and Jonathan a cov'nant made,
By the son of great Saul he ne'er was betray'd,
And, tho' strange, yet 'tis scriptural truth that I tell,
That the love of Saul's son did all women's excel.

David's heart sore did ache this kind love to return,
When for Saul's seven sons the Lord'sanger did burn;
Then the sons of great Saul king David did take,
But spared Mephibosheth for his oath's sake.

Our noble grand masters appear next in view,
Who built up the temple so just and so true;
The pattern which David from God had receiv'd,
Who, not suffer'd to build in his heart was sore griev'd.

Our secret divine which lay long concealed
By a light from above unto me was revealed;
Surpris'd at the radiance with which it did shine,
I felt and confess'd it was something divine.

Then having pass'd three, and both offer'd and burnt,
I soon gained admittance on that holy ground,
And revealed unto me were the myst'ries sought,
Tho' the light was by darkness comprehended not.

Being thus consecrated I soon did accord
To acknowledge Jehovah for God and for Lord,
Believ'd Him the source of the light that did shine,
And confess'd Him to be our Grand Master divine.

Then join hands and hearts your voices to raise,
With the whole of creation unite and sing praise;
To the power divine all glory be given,
By men upon earth, and by angels in heaven.

XLII.

(Tune, *Tantararara, &c.*)

FATHER Adam when first he beheld the light shine,
God made him a mason, and gave him a sign,
He freely unto us the same did impart,
And oft'times in paradise talk'd of our art.
   Cho.—Sing tantararara, truth all, &c,

The apostles were masons I'll tell you straightways,
Christ order'd a temple to be rais'd in three days,
They knew what he meant while the ignorant gaz'd,
Then these masons clapp'd hands and their master pleas'd.
   Cho.—Sing tantararara, clap all, &c.

We're bid by the scriptures no longer be blind,
But to knock at the door and the truth we shall find;
And the scripture advises us free-masons further,
To join hand in hand and to love one another.
   Cho.—Sing tantararara, love all, &c.

The ladies say masonry's a dangerous trade,
And are surely afraid when their husbands are made;
But take their own words, and deny it who can,
They ne'er knew a mason but what was a man.
   Cho.—Sing tantararara, men all, &c.

We live by a rule that is just and upright,
Free-masons are known to be children of light;
With conscience clear white like the aprons they wear,
Here's a health to free-masons wherever they are.
   Cho.—Sing tantararara, drink all, &c.

XLIII.
(Tune, *Derry down*).

FIDELITY once had a fancy to rove,
And therefore she quitted the mansions above;
On earth she arrived, but so long was her tour,
Jove thought she intended returning no more.
    Derry down, down, down, derry down.

Then Mercury was hasten'd in quest of the dame,
And soon to this world of confusion he came;
At Paris he stopped, and enquired by chance,
But heard that Fidelity ne'er was in France.
    Derry down, down, down, derry down.

The God then to Portugal next took his route,
In hopes that at Lisbon he might find her out;
But there he was told she had mock'd superstition,
And left it for fear of the grand inquisition.
    Derry down, down, down, derry down.

Being thus disappointed to Holland he flew,
And strictly enquired of an eminent Jew;
When Mordecai readily told him thus much,
Fidelity never was lik'd by the Dutch.
    Derry down, down, down, derry down.

Arriving at London, he hastened to court,
Where numbers of great little men do resort,
Who all stood amaz'd when he asked for the dame,
And swore they had scarce ever heard of the name.
    Derry down, down, down, derry down.

To Westminster Hall did the God next repair,
In hopes with dame Justice she might be found there;
For both he enquir'd; when the court answer'd thus,
"The persons you mention, sir, ne'er trouble us."
    Derry down, down, down, derry down.

Then bending his course to the Cyprian grove,
He civilly asked of the young God of Love;
The urchin replied, "could you think here to find her,
"When I and my mother, you know, never mind her?
  Derry down, down, down, derry down.

"In one only place you can find her on earth,
"The seat of true frieneship, love, freedom and mirth;
"To a lodge of free-masons then quickly repair,
"And you need not to doubt but you'll meet with her
 there."
  Derry down, down, down, derry down.

XLIV.

FROM henceforth ever sing,
 The craftsman and the king,
With poetry and music sweet,
Resound their harmony complete;
And with geometry in skilful hand,
 Due homage pay,
 Without delay,
To the king and to our master grand;
 He rules the free-born sons of art,
 By love and friendship, hand and heart.
  CHORUS.
 Who can rehearse the praise,
  In soft poetic lays,
 Or solid prose of masons true,
 Whose art transcends the common view;
Their secrets ne'er to strangers yet expos'd,
 Reserved shall be,
 By masons free,
And only to the ancient lodge disclos'd;
 Because they're kept in masons' heart,
 By brethren of the royal art.

XLV.

FROM the depths let us raise
    Our voices, and praise
The works of the glorious creation;
    And extol the great fame
    Of our Maker's great name,
And his love to an accepted mason.

    In primitive times,
    When men, by high crimes,
Occasion'd a great devastation,
    The flood did abound
    And all men were drown'd,
Save a free and an accepted mason.

    In an ark that was good,
    Made of gopher wood,
It was built by divine ordination;
    And first in his time,
    That planted a vine,
Was a free and an accepted mason.

    Then Pharaoh, the king
    Of Egypt, did bring
Into bondage our whole generation:
    But that king got a fall,
    And his magicians all,
By a princely and great learned mason.

    Four hundred and thirty years
    By scripture appears,
Was their bondage in th' Egyptian nation,
    But by providence great,
    They made their escape,
Unto the Egyptians vexation.

> Then through the red sea
> Heaven guided their way,
> By two pillars of divine ordination;
> But Pharaoh's great train
> The sea did restrain
> From pursuing an army of masons.
>
> On the plains they did rear
> A pavilion fair,
> It was built by divine inspiration;
> Each part in it square,
> None could it prepare
> But a free and an accepted mason.
>
> Thro' Jordan they go,
> To face their proud foe,
> I mean the great Canaanite nations;
> But their gigantic train
> Could not sustain
> The force of that army of masons.
>
> Next Amalek's king
> Great forces did bring;
> Likewise the great Midianite nations;
> But their kings got a fall,
> And their great nobles all,
> And their wealth fell a prey to our masons.
>
> King Solomon, he
> Was known to be free,
> Built a lodge for the use of the masons;
> Each beautiful part
> Was due to the art
> Of that princely and great learned mason.
>
> Let each mason that's free
> Toast his memory;

Join hands without dissimulation;
    Let cowans think on,
    For they are all wrong,
  Drink a health to an accepted mason.

XLVI.

(Tune, *Goddess of ease*).

GENIUS of masonry, descend,
    And with thee bring thy spotless train;
Constant our sacred rites attend,
    While we adore thy peaceful reign;
Bring with thee virtue, brightest maid,
    Bring love, bring truth, bring friendship here;
While social mirth shall lend her aid,
    To smooth the wrinkled brow of care.

Come, charity with goodness crown'd,
    Encircled in thy heavenly robe,
Diffuse thy blessings all around,
    To every corner of the globe.
See where she comes, with power to bless,
    With open hand, and tender heart,
Which wounded feels at man's distress,
    And bleeds at every human smart.

Envy may every ill devise,
    And falsehood be thy deadliest foe,
Thou, Friendship, still shalt towering rise,
    And sink thine adversaries low:
Thy well built pile shall long endure,
    Through rolling years preserve its prime,
Upon a rock it stands secure,
    And braves the rude assaults of time.

Ye happy few, who here extend
    In perfect lines, from east to west,
With fervent zeal the lodge defend,
    And lock its secrets in each breast:
Since ye are met upon the square,
    Bid love and friendship jointly reign,
Be peace and harmony your care,
    Nor break the admittance chain.

Behold the planets how they move,
    Yet keep due order as they run;
Then imitate the stars above,
    And shine resplendent as the sun:
That future masons, when they meet,
    May all our glorious deeds rehearse,
And say, their fathers were so great,
    That they adorn'd the universe.

XLVII.

GLORIOUS craft, which fires the mind
    With sweet harmony and love;
Surely thou wert first design'd.
    A foretaste of the joys above.

Pleasures always on thee await;
    Thou reformest Adam's race;
Strength and Beauty in thee meet;
    Wisdom's radiant in thy face.

Arts and virtues now combine,
    Friendship raises cheerful mirth,
All united to refine
    Man from grosser parts of earth.

Stately temples now arise,
   And on lofty columns stand;
Mighty domes attempt the skies
   To adorn this happy land.

XLVIII.

KNIGHTS TEMPLAR SONG.

(Tune, *God save the King*).

GOD bless the royal band,
   Who grace this happy land
     With valiant knights:
May the united three
Of the blest trinity
Ever lamented be
   Of all great lights.

Twelve once were highly lov'd,
But one a Judas prov'd,
     Put out his fire;
May Simon haunt all fools
Who vary from all rules,
May the heads of such tools
   Rest high on spires.

'Gainst Turks and Jews we fight,
And in religion's right
     We'll breathe our last;
Poor pilgrims, begging, we
Will our Jerusalem see,
All steps, sir knights, have ye
   Gloriously pass'd.

Enter'd, pass'd, rais'd and arch'd,
And then like princes march'd
      Through rugged ways
  At length great lights we saw,
  And poor old Simon too,
  Also the word and law,
      Glory and praise.

God in his rainbow gave
Colours which now we have,
      Black, red, and blue,
  These colours emblems are
  Of our rights most rare,
  We are in soul sincere,
      Just, good, and true.

Sir Knights, clasp hand in hand,
None but Knights Templar stand,
      In circle round;
  May we e'er live in love,
  And ev'ry comfort prove;
  May manna from above
      Fall on this ground.

XLIX.

ROYAL ARCH SONG.

GOD caused great lights to shine,
  Moving in orbs divine,
      Which ever shall
  Banish all darkness quite,
  With such refulgent light,
  And from eternal night
      Save royals all.

SANCTUM, SANCTORUM,
Triangles——no more of 'em,
    Wisdom's revealed!
Sublimest arts refin'd,
Excellent arches bind!
No flaw in heart or mind
    Shall be conceal'd.

Few in our numbers are,
Therefore in royal chair,
    Honours abound;
We'll join hearts and hand,
Whilst truths in gospel stand,
None but the royal band
    Shall circle round.

———

L.

THE TREASURER'S SONG.

(Tune, *Near some cool shade*).

GRANT me, kind heav'n, what I request,
    In masonry let me be blest;
Direct me to that happy place,
Where friendship smiles in every face,
Where freedom and sweet innocence
Enlarge the mind and cheer the sense.

Where scepter'd reason from her throne
Surveys the lodge, and makes us one;
And harmony's delightful sway,
For ever sheds ambrosial day!
Where we blest Eden's pleasures taste.
While balmy joys are our repast.

Our lodge the social virtues grace,
And wisdom's rules we fondly trace;
Whole nature open to our view,
Points out the paths we should pursue;
Let us subsist in lasting peace,
And may our happiness increase.

No prying eye can view us here,
No fool or knave disturb our cheer;
Our well-form'd laws set mankind free,
And give relief to misery;
The poor, oppress'd with woe and grief,
Gain from our bounteous hand relief.

LI.

BY BROTHER STANFIELD.

(Tune, *Contented I am, &c.*)

GRAVE bus'ness now clos'd—and a call from the south—
    The bowl of refreshment we drain;
Yet e'en o'er our wine we reject servile sloth,
    And our rites 'midst our glasses retain.
        My brave boys, &c.

With loyalty brighten'd, we first toast the king—
    May his splendour and virtues entwine!
And, to honour his name, how we make the lodge ring,
    When the king and the craft we combine!

May the son's polish'd graces improve on the sire—
    May the arts flourish fair from his smile—
And long our grand master, with wisdom and fire,
    Give beauty and strength to the pile!

As the ruby lipp'd wine its soft spirit imparts,
    Louder strains and fresh ardours abound;
What a glow of true pleasure enlivens our hearts
    When our honour'd provincial goes round!

The absent we claim, tho' dispers'd round the ball—
    The silent and secret our friends—
And one honoured guest, at our magical call,
    From the grave of concealment ascends.

Immortal the strain, and thrice awful the hand,
    That our rites and libations control;
Like the sons of Olympus, 'midst thunders we stand,
    And with mysteries ennoble our bowl.

What a circle appears when the border entwines,
    How grapple the links to each soul!
'Tis the zodiac of friendship embellish'd with signs,
    And illum'd by the star in the pole.

Thus cemented by laws unseen and unknown,
    The universe hangs out its frame;
And thus secretly bound, shall our structure be shown
    Till creation shall be but a name.

LII.

G{REAT} Architect high,
    That rules in the sky,
And formed the great light all around;
    From chaos arose,
    The violet and rose,
And nature with plenty he's crown'd.

Our parent at first
Was form'd out of dust,
The head of creation he stood;
The command it was giv'n
By God out of heaven,
And all was pronounced very good.

Then out of his side
God made him a bride,
His happiness there to complete:
And in love's sweet solace,
With social embrace,
Enjoy'd Eden's happy retreat.

But how soon did the crown
From their heads tumble down,
Which caused them both much to mourn;
They lost that was good,
And naked they stood,
'Till aprons of leaves they put on.

Let our conduct express
What we each do profess,
By rule and by compass to steer;
And let them reflect,
Who those duties neglect,
That the walk of a mason is square.

Then bold let us stand,
And join hand in hand,
Like masons accepted and free:
For our order is good,
When right understood,
And that many can prove it to be.

LIII.

GUARDIAN genius of our art divine,
    Unto thy faithful sons appear;
Cease now o'er ruins of the East to pine,
    And smile in blooming beauty here.

Egypt, Syria, and proud Babylon,
    No more thy blissful presence claim;
In England fix'd thy ever-during throne,
    Where myriads do confess thy name.

The sciences from eastern regions brought,
    Which after shone in Greece and Rome,
Are here in several stately lodges taught,
    To which remotest brethren come.

Behold what strength our rising domes uprear,
    'Till mixing with the azure skies;
Behold what beauties through the whole appear,
    So wisely built they must surprise.

Nor are we only to these arts confin'd,
    For we the paths of virtue trace;
By us man's rugged nature is refin'd,
    And polished into love and peace.

LIV.

(Tune, *God save the King*)

Hail, Masonry divine!
   Glory of ages, shine,
     Long may'st thou reign!
Where'er thy lodges stand,
May they have great command,
And always grace the land.
   Thou art divine.

Great fabric! still arise,
And grace the azure skies,
   Great are thy schemes!
Thy noble orders are
Matchless beyond compare:
No art with thee can share;
   Thou art divine!

Hiram, the architect,
Did all the craft direct
   How they should build:
Sol'mon, great Israel's king,
Did mighty blessings bring,
And left us cause to sing,
   Hail, Royal Art!—*Chorus three times.*

LV.

A FELLOW CRAFT'S SONG.

(Tune, *Rule, Britannia*).

Hail, Masonry, thou craft divine!
   Glory of earth, from heav'n reveal'd;
Which doth with jewels precious shine,
   From all but masons' eyes conceal'd;
     Thy praises due, who can rehearse,
     In nervous prose, or flowing verse?

All craftsmen true distinguish'd are,
   Our codes all other laws excel;
And what's in knowledge choice and rare,
   Within our breasts securely dwell.
     The silent breast, the faithful heart,
     Preserve the secrets of the art.

From scorching heat and piercing cold
   From beasts whose roar the forest rends;
From the assaults of warriors bold
   The masons' art mankind defends.
     Be to this art due honour paid,
     From which mankind receives such aid.

Ensigns of state, that feed our pride,
   Distinctions troublesome and vain,
By masons true are laid aside,
   Art's free-born sons such toys disdain;
     Ennobled by the name they bear,
     Distinguish'd by the badge they wear.

Sweet fellowship, from envy free,
   Friendly converse of brotherhood,
The lodge's lasting cement be,
   Which has for ages firmly stood.
     A lodge thus built, for ages past
     Has lasted, and shall ever last.

Then let us celebrate the praise
   Of all who have enrich'd the art,
Let gratitude our voices raise,
   And each true brother bear a part.
     Let cheerful strains their fame resound,
     And living masons' healths go round.

LVI.

(Tune, In Infancy).

HAIL, Masonry! thou sacred art,
    Of origin divine!
Kind partner of each social heart,
    And fav'rite of the Nine!
By thee we're taught our acts to square,
    To measure life's short span;
And each infirmity so bear
    That's incident to man.
    Cho.—By thee, &c.

Tho' envy's tongue should blast thy fame,
    And ignorance may sneer,
Yet still thy honoured ancient name
    Is to each brother dear;
Then strike the blow, to charge prepare,
    In this we all agree,
"May freedom be each mason's care,
    And ev'ry mason free."
    Cho.—Then strike the blow, &c,

LVII.

By Brother ROBERT M'CANN, *P.M. of Lodge No. 244.*

(Tune, Can you to the battle go).

HAIL, Masonry! thou source divine,
    Of pure and solid pleasure,
With friendship's chain our hearts entwine,
    Thus prove our joy and treasure.
Thine influence shed on each freeman,
    Who walks the line of duty,
And forms his conduct on the plan
    Of wisdom, strength, and beauty.

CHORUS.

May craftsmen all, thy maxims hold
   Through life on all occasions,
In virtue's cause upright and bold,
   Like good and faithful masons.

How happy we that vot'ries are,
   How great our satisfaction,
With lights so bright, with rules so rare
   To regulate our action.—
Strict justice ought our lives to sway,
   With honour pure, in this state,
Sweet peace should bless our level way,
   And truth our words should dictate.
      Cho.—May craftsmen all, &c.

Our lodge is tyled, our minds meanwhile
   Shut out each wild intrusion,
May knowledge bright upon us smile
   To guard us from delusion.
May every brother here below,
   Who just and upright now stands,
From labour to refreshment go,
   To th' temple made without hands.

FINAL CHORUS.

Where joys eternal ever reign,
   And nought from them can sever,
With the world's Grand Master to remain
   For ever and for ever.

LVIII.

By Brother W. UTLEY, *of the Lodge of Prince George,
No. 574, Bottoms, in Stansfield.*

(Tune, *The Spotted Cow*).

HAIL, masons free! whom friendship binds
   In softest, strongest ties;
Soft be the temper of your minds,
   Bright as your shining eyes.

Check ev'ry idle passion, pray,
   And imitate the dove;
Each dirty humour throw away,
   And harmonize in love.

Then let no angry passions raise
   Bad humour in your breast,
Firm our foundation, love its base,
   Be every mason's test.

So wisdom shall our lodge adorn,
   And harmony unite
With friendship, blooming as the morn,
   To masons give delight.

Then, sons of science, now attend
   A brother's good advice,
To duty all with rev'rence bend,
   And shun each noxious vice.

Cherish a heav'nly, zealous fire,
   Which masons' hearts doth warm;
Faith, hope, and charity admire,
   Strength, beauty, wisdom's charm.

The five points ever bear in mind,
   To none but masons known.

They'll keep you gentle, good, and kind,—
   On a brother ne'er to frown.

Then ye who know the mystic tie,
   Its precepts e'er obey,
And as your fabric's raised on high,
   Beauty it will display.

Now a good will to masonry
   I give with all my heart;
And the brethren in society,
   Though ever so far apart.

Here's a health to our worthy grand,
   And worshipful likewise;
And when in lodge they give command,
   May the craft in duty rise.

LIX.

HAIL! Sacred Art, by heav'n design'd
   A gracious blessing for mankind;
Peace, joy, and love thou dost bestow
On us, thy votaries below.

Bright wisdom's footsteps here we trace,
From Solomon, that prince of peace,
Whose glorious maxims we still hold
More precious than rich Ophir's gold.

His heavenly proverbs to us tell,
How we on earth should ever dwell,
In harmony and social love,
To emulate the blest above.

Now having wisdom for our guide,
By its sweet precepts we'll abide;
Envy and hatred we'll dispel,
No wrathful fool with us shall dwell.

Vain, empty grandeur shall not find
Its dwelling in a mason's mind;
A mason who is true and wise,
All glitt'ring pomp must e'er despise.

Humility, love, joy and peace,
Within his mind shall fill their place,
Virtue and wisdom thus combin'd,
Shall beautify the mason's mind.

LX.

HAIL, secret art! by heav'n design'd
To cultivate and cheer the mind;
Thy secrets are to all unknown,
But masons just and true alone.

CHORUS.

Then let us all their praises sing,
Fellows to peasant, prince, or king.

From west to east we take our way,
To meet the bright approaching day;
That we to work may go in time,
And up the sacred ladder climb.
Cho.—Then let us all, &c.

Bright rays of glory did inspire,
Our master great who came from Tyre;

Still sacred history keeps his name,
Who did the glorious temple frame.
   Cho.—Then let us all, &c.

The noble art, divinely rear'd,
Uprightly built upon the square,
Encompass'd by the powers divine,
Shall stand until the end of time.
   Cho.—Then let us all, &c.

No human eye thy beauties see,
But masons truly just and free;
Enlighten'd by thy heavenly spark,
Whilst cowans labour in the dark.
   Cho.—Then let us all, &c.

LXI.

By BROTHER KELLY.

HARK! I hear the warden call—
   "Masons to your sports away,
Join the banquet in the hall,
   Give your hearts a holiday."

When around the festive bowl,
   We delight in song and glee;
Gay and open is the soul,
   When it feels secure and free.

Joyous as the jest goes round,
   Taunt nor jibe can masons fear;
None, by sacred pledges bound,
   Prate again of what they hear.

When we toast the fair we prize,
    Not a tongue shall slander tell;
Masons' hearts, by honour's ties,
    Guard the sex they love so well.

And though we fill our glasses high,
    Feeling still shall warm the breast;
We have not left the poor man dry,
    So the cheerful cup is blest.

LXII.

HENCE, sorrow, avaunt! you have no business here
    To dull-thinking mortals—go, furrow-fac'd care!
You've nothing to do with the free and sincere;
    Which nobody can deny.

No ill natur'd babbler with us e'er shall join,
Our free-mason art I'll prove it divine,
What you've (if I want it) shall also be mine;
    Which nobody, &c.

Fair ladies with fribbles your joys never share,
They sue but for telling;—while masons who bear
Undivulg'd their own secrets,—to you'll be sincere;
    Which nobody, &c.

We're true to our king, to our country, our Lord;
For just cause a mason will unsheath his sword,
A mason's no courtier, he ne'er breaks his word;
    Which nobody, &c.

The mightiest monarch who rules on a throne,
A brother (tho' begging) can never disown,
In this kind of friendship we're really alone;
    Which nobody, &c.

Our light, among men who're enlighten'd, shall blaze,
While those who're in darkness shall stand in amaze,
Like thunder-struck asses shall stupidly gaze;
        Which nobody, &c.

Come, here's to all freemasons under the sun,
Who e'er yet assembled to honour St. John,
May health, joy, and glory attend every one,
        Say every true brother, Amen.

LXIII.

HERE let no dull faces of business appear;
   Farewell till to-morrow hard labour and care:
This night shall be sacred to friendship and ease,
Each bosom be open, mirth dart from each face.

Consider, dear brethren, that masons grow old,
That relish abates as the blood waxes cold;
And if to be happy too long we delay,
Soon as we attempt, cries death, come away.

Then, fellows in masonry, let us rejoice,
In beautiful melody join ev'ry voice;
Time shan't overtake us before we can say,
That we have been easy, blithe, social, and gay.

Adieu, sober-thinking detraction and spleen;
You ought to be strangers where masons convene;
Come, jest, love, and laughter, ye joyful throng,
You're free of the lodge, and to masons belong.

Let monarchs run mad after riches and power,
Fat gownmen be dull, and philosophers sour,
While the claret goes round, and the company sings,
We're wiser than sages, and richer than kings.

Then fill up the goblet, and deal it about;
Each brother will see it thrice twenty times out;
Our pleasures, as well as our labours, can tell,
How free-hearted masons all mankind excel.

LXIV.

(Tune, *Entered Apprentice's Song*).

HERE'S a health to each one,
From the king on the throne
To him that is meanest in station,
If he can contend
To have lawfully gain'd
The name of an accepted mason.

The glories of kings
Are poor empty things,
Tho' empires they have in possession,
If void of the fame,
Of that noblest of names,
A free and an accepted mason.

It is ancienter far
Than other arts are,
Surpassing all other profession:
There's none can pretend
To discover a friend
Like a free and an accepted mason.

The world is amaz'd,
Their wonder is rais'd,
To see such concurring relation
Among us: they cry,
The devil is nigh,
When one is accepted a mason.

But let them say on,
To us 'tis well known
What's true or false in the relation;
Let's drink his health round
That is secret and sound,
And a faithful and accepted mason.

LXV.

HOW bless'd are we, from ignorance free,
And the base notions of mankind,
Here every virtuous moral deed
Instructs and fortifies the mind:
Hail! ancient, hallow'd, solemn ground,
Where light and masonry I found.

Hence! vile detractors, from us fly,
Far to the gloomy shades of night,
Like owls that waste the mid-day sky,
And sink with envy from its light;
With them o'er graves and ruins rot,
For hating knowledge you know not.

When we assemble on a hill,
Or in due form upon the plain,
Our master doth with learned skill,
The secret work and plan explain;
No busy eye, nor cowan's ear,
Can our grand myst'ry see or hear.

Our table deck'd with shining truth,
Sweet emblems that elate the heart;
While each attentive list'ning youth
Burns to perform his worthy part,
Resolving with religious care,
To live by compass, rule, and square.

Our master watching in the east
    The golden streaks of rising sun,
To see his men at labour plac'd,
    Who all like willing crafts do run,
Oh! may his wisdom ever be,
Honour to us and Masonry.

Not far from him as Gnomon true,
    Beauty stands with watchful eye,
Whose cheerful voice our spirits renew,
    And each his labour doth lay by;
His kind, refreshing office still
Inspires each craft in Masons' skill.

See in the west our oblong's length,
    The brave Corinthian pillar stands,
The lodge's friend and greatest strength,
    Rewarding crafts with lib'ral hands;
Sure this our lodge must lasting be
Supported by these columns three.

Each Roman chief did proudly view
    Their temples rising to the sky,
And as the nations did subdue,
    They rais'd triumphal arches high;
Which gave us Masons such a name
As vies with mighty Cæsar's fame.

The kings who raised Diana's columns,*
    With royal art, by skilful hands,
As priests accorded in their volumes,
    And poets sing to distant lands—
Th' adoring world that did them see,
Forgot th' enshrined Deity.

---

*The Temple of Diana at Ephesus.

Such is our boast, my brethren dear;
    Fellows to kings and princes too,
The master's gift were proud to wear,
    As now the great and noble do;
The great, the noble, and the sage,
Masons rever'd from age to age.

CHORUS.

Then to each brother in distress,
    Throughout all nations, parts, or climes,
Charge, brethren, to this quick redress
    As Masons did in ancient times;
From want and hardships set them free,
Bless'd with health and Masonry.

Nor once forget the lovely fair,
    Divinely made of Adam's bone;
Whose heavenly looks can banish care,
    And ease the sighing lover's moan,
To those who soft enjoyment brings
Us heroes, architects, and kings.

LXVI.

By GAVIN WILSON.

(Tune, *By the side of a murmuring stream*).

HOW doubly blest the condition
    Of brethren that live on the square!
How excellent that institution,
    No discord can germinate there.
No sallies of angry resentment,
    No sullen effect of the spleen;
No meagre-hue'd pale, discontentment
    Is e'er in the lodge to be seen.

Complacency, mirth, and good nature
   Is ev'ry Free-mason's enjoyment;
Which, by the glass rendered sweeter,
   Doth soften our harder employment.
The graces and virtues united,
   Regard us with fond admiration,
Beholding their work so completed
   In forming the heart of a Mason.

LXVII.

(Tune, *The Miller of Mansfield.*

HOW happy a Mason, whose bosom still flows
   With friendship, and who ever cheerfully goes!
The effects of the mysteries lodged in his breast,
Mysteries rever'd and by princes possest.
Our friends and our bottle we best can enjoy,
No rancour or envy our quiet annoy,
Our plumb line and compass, our square and our tools,
Direct all our actions in virtue's fair rules.

To Mars and to Venus we're equally true,
Our hearts he enlivens, her charms we subdue;
Let the enemy tell, and the ladies declare,
No class or profession with Masons compare;
To give us a lustre we ne'er need a crest,
Since honour and virtue remain in our breast;
We'll charm the rude world when we clap, laugh and
     sing,
If so happy a Mason, say, who'd be a king?

LXVIII.

IF unity be good in every degree
   What can be compar'd with that of Masonry?
In unity we meet, and in unity we part;
Let every Mason chorus—Hail! mighty art!
    Let every, &c.

The vulgar often murmur at our noble art,
   Because the great arcana we don't to them impart;
In ign'rance let them live, and in ign'rance let them die,
"Be silent and secret," let every Mason cry.
    Be silent, &c.

Let a bumper be crown'd to the art of Masonry,
And to each jovial brother that is a Mason free;
We act upon the square, on the level we'll depart,
Let every Mason sing:—Hail! glorious art!
    Let every, &c.

LXIX.

By Mr. Dibdin.

IN all thy dealings take good care,
   Instructed by the friendly square,
To be true, upright, just, and fair,
   And thou a fellow-craft shalt be.

The level so must poise thy mind,
That satisfaction thou shalt find,
When to another fortune's kind;
   And that's the drift of masonry.

The compass t'other two compounds,
And says, though anger'd on just grounds,
Keep all your passions within bounds,
   And thou a fellow-craft shalt be.

Thus symbols of our order are
The compass, level, and the square,
Which teach us to be just and fair;
And that's the drift of masonry.

LXX.

(Tune, *Belleisle March*)

IN hist'ry we're told how the lodges of old
   Arose in the east, and shone forth like the sun;
But all must agree, that divine Masonry
Commenced when the glorious creation began:
With glory divine, oh! long may'st thou shine,
Thou choicest of blessings derived from above!
Then charge bumpers high, and with shouts rend the
      sky,
To Masonry, friendship, and brotherly love.
      Cho.—With glory divine, &c.

Judea's great king, whose vast praises we sing,
With wisdom contriv'd while the temple he plann'd;
The mysterious art then took place in each heart,
And Hiram with Solomon went hand in hand:
While each royal name was recorded in fame.
Their works earth and heaven did jointly approve;
Then charge bumpers high, and with shouts rend the
      sky,
To Masonry, friendship, and brotherly love.
      Cho.—While each royal, &c.

Then masons were true, and the craft daily grew;
They liv'd within compass, and work'd by the square;
In friendship they dwelt, no ambition they felt;
Their deeds were upright, and their consciences clear;

On this noble plan Free-masons began;
To help one another they mutually strove;
Then charge bumpers high, and with shouts rend the sky,
To Masonry, friendship, and brotherly love.
        Cho.—On this noble plan, &c.

These maxims pursue, and your passions subdue,
And imitate those worthy masters of yore;
Fix a lodge in each breast, be fair virtue your guest,
Let wisdom preside, and let truth tile the door:
So shall we arise to an immortal prize
In that blissful lodge which no time can remove;
Then charge bumpers high, and with shouts rend the sky,
To masonry, friendship, and brotherly love.
        Cho.—So shall we arise, &c.

LXXI.

By Brother W. HARDMAN, *of the Lodge of Relief, No. 57, Bury, Lancashire.*

(Tune, *Queen Bess*).

IN praise of Free-masonry my muse now shall sing, sir,
  A science not degrading to subject or to king, sir.
Where friendship cements Christian, Pagan, and Turk, sir,
And plants the seeds of love where envy used to lurk, sir.
    Oh! the noble art of Masonry,
    Blessed be the science of Free-masonry.

We have had for our patrons the great, good, and wise, sir,
And princes oft divested to know our device, sir,

Their hands put forth to mortar, the royal art to learn, sir, [sir,
And by its worthy precepts great mystic truths discern,
    Cho.—Oh! the noble art, &c.

With square and with compass, with level and plumb-rule, sir,
Signs, angles, and tangents, not fitted for the fool, sir,
We fabrics erect with beauty, wisdom and strength, sir,
Contriving, supporting—adorning breadth and length,
    Cho.—Oh! the noble art, [sir.

The naked to clothe and the needy to feed, sir,
'Tis pleasure celestial when we find them in need, sir;
And like the good Samaritan, bind up their wounds, sir,
As men, and as Masons, in duty we're bound, sir.
    Cho.—Oh! the noble art, &c.

When the work of the lodge we are met to promote, sir,
Prince, peasant, or beggar, we never cast out, sir,
For the sun's splendid lustre all equally share, sir,
And death's dire summons lays all level in the grave,
    Cho.—Oh! the noble art, [sir.

LXXII.

(Tune, *Ye lads of true spirit, pay courtship to claret*).

IN times of old date, when (as stories relate)
    Good men to the gods had admission,
When those who were grieved might with ease be relieved,
    By offering an humble petition:

Some few who remain'd in their morals unstain'd,
    Submissively made application
To build a retreat, if the gods should think meet,
    To shield them from wicked invasion.

Delighted to find there was yet in mankind,
    Some laudable sentiments planted,
Without hesitation they gave approbation,
    And instant their wishes were granted.

Then for artists they sought, and fam'd architects brought,
    Who the various employments were skill'd in;
Each handled his tools, and by science and rules
    They straightway proceeded to building.

Fair Wisdom began first to sketch out the plan,
    By which they were all to be guided;
Each order she made was exactly obeyed,
    When the portions of work she divided.

The great corner-stone was by Charity done,
    But Strength was the principal builder;
When for mortar they cried 'twas by Friendship supplied,
    And Beauty was carver and gilder.

Having long persever'd a grand temple they rear'd,
    A refuge from folly and scandal,
Where all who reside are in virtue employ'd,
    Nor fear the attacks of a vandal.

But if in their rage they should ever engage
    In th' attempt, 'twould be always prevented;
The door is so high 'twould be madness to try,
    And the walls are all strongly cemented.

The gods all agreed 'twas an excellent deed,
    And to show the affection they bore them,
A treasure they gave, which the tenants still have,
    Secur'd in the sanctum sanctorum.

Thus bless'd from above with a token of love,
    Each brother with joy should receive it;
Safe lock'd in his heart, it should never depart,
    'Till call'd for by heaven that gave it.

LXXIII.
THE SQUARE, LEVEL, AND PLUMB-RULE.
By Brother PAUL THACKWELL.

IN the world, my dear brethren, we oft hear remarks,
    And wit shot at random to tease us;
From idiots profest to the most learned clerks,
Nor from jests will the ladies release us.
But we're taught by the square such attacks to deride,
If we fall on its moral dictation,
We alike can withstand wit, ill nature, or pride,
And support our well known reputation.

Let worldlings unfeeling treat merit with scorn,
And on virtuous poverty trample;
But let nobler feelings our actions adorn,
Let us show to the world an example,—
That of virtue; with us, howe'er humble the sphere
Of the man who excites our compassion,
The level instructs us to dry up the tear,
And remove the sad cause of vexation.

How bless'd is the man who in providence trusts,
And uprightly walks with his neighbour;
How clear will he steer of those wretched disgusts,
Under which foolish profligates labour.
By the plumb-rule we're taught such a course to pursue,
That with temp'rance using each blessing,
Our lives being upright, consistent, and true,
We are freed from reflections distressing.

Thus, my brethren, the lessons we're taught by the square,
With justice and honour are blended;
The level instructs us of pride to beware,
For our love must to all be extended.
By the plumb-rule we're taught to be upright and fair,
As we soberly pass through this life;
He who follows these lessons can never despair,
Nor his days be embitter'd with strife.

LXXIV.

The Glasgow Royal Arch.———For St. John's Day.

JOY to my brother Masons,
    Who are met to remember
   And think upon
   The great St. John,
This twenty-seventh December.

CHORUS,

   Fill it up
   To the top;
Let the sparkling glass go round;
   And to him
   To the brim,
For in love he doth abound:
   And to him
   To the brim;
Love and harmony abound.

My glass will be yours,
And your glass will be mine;

In token of friendship
Our hands let us join:
And with this cheering glass,
With pleasure round we'll pass
The mem'ry of the great
And the good divine.

We'll study all to follow
The great St. John's example,
   By doing well,
   And hating ill;
For the reward is ample.
Chorus.

We will behave like brothers,
Avoiding all disorder;
   Observing still
   What is the will
Of him who calleth order.
Chorus.

While we perform our duty,
We shall be respected;
   But if this place
   We do disgrace,
With shame shall be ejected.
Chorus.

May providence protect us
From all ensnaring dangers,
   That we ne'er may
   Become the prey
Of faithless friends or strangers.
Chorus.

T' our master and our wardens
With pleasure we agree,
   To wish good health,
   Success and wealth,
By honours three times three.
              Chorus.

May every loving brother
Employ his thoughts, and search
   How to improve
   In peace and love
The Glasgow Royal Arch.
              Chorus.

LXXV.

(Tune, *Come, let us prepare*).

JUST straight from his home
   See yon candidate come,
Prepared for the time and occasion;
   Of all that can harm
   We will him disarm,
That he may no ways hurt a Free-mason.

   His eyes cannot search
   Out the way of his march,
Nor yet where his steps he must place on;
   When him we receive
   He cannot perceive
How he came to be made a Free-mason.

   Then he'll danger defy,
   And on heaven rely

For strength to support the occasion;
    With the blessing of pray'r
    He banishes fear,
And undaunted is made a Free-mason.

    When he makes his demand,
    By the master's command,
To know if he's fit for the station:
    Around he is brought,
    Ere he got what he sought,
From a free and an accepted Mason.

    When girded with care,
    By the help of the square,
The emblem of truth and of reason,
    In form he is plac'd,
    While to him are rehears'd,
The mysteries of a Free-mason.

    Then full in his sight
    Doth shine the great light,
To illumine the works which we trace on;
    And now, as his due,
    He's cloth'd in full view
With the badge of an accepted Mason.

    Now hark! we enlarge
    On the duties and charge,
Where his conduct and walk he must place on;
    Then a bumper we'll fill,
    And show our goodwill
To a free and an accepted Mason.

LXXVI.

(Tune, *Come, all hands ahoy to the anchor*).

KING Solomon, that wise projector,
    In Masonry took great delight;
And Hiram, that great architector,
    Whose actions shall ever shine bright.
From the heart of a true Mason
    There's none can the secrets remove;
Our maxims are justice, morality,
    Friendship, and brotherly love.

CHORUS.

    Then who would not be a Free-mason?
        So happy and social are we;
    To lords, dukes, and princes we're brothers,
        And in ev'ry lodge we are free.

We meet like true friends on the level,
    And lovingly part on the square;
Alike we respect king and beggar,
    Provided they're just and sincere.
We scorn an ungenerous action;
    None can with Free-masons compare;
We all love to live within compass,
    By rules that are honest and fair.
        Cho.—Then who, &c.

We banish all talkative fellows,
    That will babble and prate past their wit;
They ne'er shall come into our secret,
    For they're neither worthy nor fit:
But the person that's well recommended,
    If we find him both honest and true,
When our lodge is well til'd we'll prepare him,
    And like Masons our work we'll pursue.
        Cho.—Then who, &c.

There are some foolish people reject us,
    For which they are highly to blame;
They cannot show any objection
    Or reason for doing the same:
The art shows divine inspiration,
    As all honest men will declare;
So here's to all true hearted brothers,
    That live within compass and square.
          Cho.—Then who, &c.

LXXVII.

By Brother NORTHOUCK.

LET drunkards boast the power of wine,
    And reel from side to side;
Let lovers kneel at beauty's shrine,
    The sport of female pride:
Be ours the more exalted part,
To celebrate the Mason's art,
    And spread its praises wide.

To dens and thickets dark and rude
    For shelter beasts repair;
With sticks and straws the feather'd brood
Suspend their nests in air:
And men untaught, as wild as these,
    Bind up sad huts with boughs of trees,
    And feed on wretched fare.

But science dawning in the mind,
    The quarry they explore;
And art with industry combin'd
    Improv'd all nature's store;

Thus walls were built and houses rear'd,
No storms nor tempests now are fear'd,
　　Within the well fram'd doors.

When stately palaces arise,
　　When columns grace the hall,
When towers and spires salute the skies,
　　We owe to Masons all:
Nor buildings only do they give,
But teach men how within to live,
　　And yield to reason's call.

All party quarrels they detest,
　　For virtue and the arts,
Lodg'd in each true Free-mason's breast,
　　Unite and rule their hearts:
By these, while Masons square their minds,
The state no better subjects finds,
　　None act more upright parts.

When Bucks and Albions are forgot,
　　Free-masons will remain;
Mushrooms, each day, spring up and rot,
　　While oaks stretch o'er the plain:
Let others quarrel, rant, and roar,
Their noisy revels when no more,
　　Still Masonry shall reign.

Our leather aprons we compare
　　With garters red and blue;
Princes and kings our brothers are,
　　While they our rules pursue:
Then drink success and health to all
The craft around this earthly ball,
　　May brethren still prove true.

LXXVIII.

By Brother KERTLAND.

LET light abound! Jehovah spoke,
    T' illume the rising earth;
Refulgent streams from chaos broke,
    And gave the planets birth.
The world was raised: and ever praised
    The Architect shall be,
Who caused to shine the light divine
    Of glorious, glorious Masonry.

By friendship join'd in social band,
    In light which fills the mind,
By choice selected, lo! we stand
    To love and aid mankind.
The widow's sigh, the orphan's cry,
    Each brother's care shall be,
While, arch'd in love, the light above
    Illumines glorious Masonry.

LXXIX.

LET malicious people censure,
    They're not worth a Mason's answer;
  While we drink and sing,
  With no conscience to sting,
Let their evil genius plague them,
And for Mollies devil take them,
  We'll be free and merry,
  Drink port and sherry,
'Till the stars at midnight shine,
And our eyes with them combine

The dark night to banish;
Thus we will replenish
Nature, whilst that the glass
Does with the bottle pass;
Brother Mason free,
Here's to thee, and thee!
And let it run the table round,
While envy does the Mason's foes confound!

LXXX.

GRAND WARDEN'S SONG.

LET Masonry be now my theme,
   Throughout the globe to spread its fame,
And eternize each worthy brother's name:
   Your praise shall to the skies resound,
   In lasting happiness abound,
And with sweet union all your deeds be crown'd

CHORUS.

Sing, then, my muse, to Masons' glory,
Your names are so revered in story
That all th' admiring world do now admire ye.

Let harmony divine inspire
   Your souls with love and gen'rous fire,
To copy well wise Solomon, your sire;
   Knowledge sublime shall fill each heart,
   The rules of geometry to impart,
While Wisdom, Strength, and Beauty crown the royal art.
      Cho.—Sing, then, my muse, &c.

Let ancient Masons' healths go round,
   In swelling cups all cares be drown'd,
All hearts united 'mongst the craft be found;

May everlasting scenes of joy
  Our peaceful hours of bliss employ,
Which time's all conquering hand shall ne'er destroy.
    Sing, then, my muse, &c.

My brethren, thus all cares resign,
  Your hearts let glow with thoughts divine!
And veneration show to Solomon's shrine;
  Our annual tribute thus we'll pay,
  That late posterity shall say
We've crown'd with joy this happy, happy day.
    Cho.—Sing, then, my muse, &c.

LXXXI.

(Tune, *In Infancy*).

LET Masonry from pole to pole
    Her sacred laws expand,
Far as the mighty waters roll,
    To wash remotest land:
That virtue has not left mankind,
    Her social maxims prove,
For stamped upon the Mason's mind,
    Are unity and love.

Ascending to her native sky,
    Let Masonry increase;
A glorious pillar raised on high,
    Integrity its base.
Peace adds to olive boughs, entwin'd,
    An emblematic dove,
As stamped upon the Mason's mind
    Are unity and love.

LXXXII.

LET Masons be merry each night when they meet,
And always each other most lovingly greet,
Let envy and discord be sunk in the deep,
By such as are able great secrets to keep;
Let all the world gaze on our art with surprise,
They're all in the dark till we open their eyes.

All those who are known to act on the square,
And likewise well skill'd in our secrets rare,
And always respected, whether wealthy or poor,
And ne'er yet were careless of matters most pure,
Their actions are bright, and their lives spent in love,
At length will unite in the grand lodge above.

We are brothers to princes, and fellows to kings,
Our fame through the world continually rings;
As we lovingly meet, so we lovingly part,
No Mason did ever bear malice at heart;
The fool that's conceited we'll never despise,
Let him come to the lodge and we'll make him more wise.

The sanctum sanctorum by Masons was framed,
And all the fine works which the temple contained,
By Hiram's contrivance, the pride of my song,
The noise of a tool was not heard all along;
And the number of Masons that round it did move,
By him were directed, inspired from above.

LXXXIII.

(Tune, *God save the King*).

LET Masons' fame resound,
    Through all the nations round,
  From pole to pole;
See what felicity,
Harmless simplicity,
Like electricity,
  Runs through the whole.

Such sweet variety,
Ne'er had society,
  Ever before;
Faith, hope, and charity,
Love and sincerity,
Without temerity,
  Charm more and more.

When in the lodge we're met,
And in due order set,
  Happy are we;
Our works are glorious,
Deeds meritorious,
Never censorious,
  But great and free.

When folly's sons arise,
Masonry to despise,
  Scorn at their spite;
Laugh at their ignorance,
Pity their want of sense,
Ne'er let them give offence,
  Firmer unite.

Masons have long been free,
And may they ever be
  Great as of yore;

For many ages past
Masonry has stood fast,
And may its glory last
  'Till time's no more.

LXXXIV.

LET us sing to the honour of those
    Who baseness and error oppose;
Who from sages and magi of old
Have got secrets which none can unfold:
    Whilst through life's sweet career,
    With mirth and good cheer,
      We're revelling,
      And levelling.
    The monarch says we
    In our joys far transcend
    What on thrones do attend,
And thinks it a glory with us to be free.

The wisest of kings paved the way,
And his precepts we keep to this day.
The most glorious of temples gave name
To Free-masons, who still keep their fame.
    Though no prince did arise
    So great and so wise,
      Yet, in falling,
      Our calling
    Still bore high applause;
    And though darkness o'er-run
    The face of the sun,
We, di'mond like, blaz'd to illumine the cause.

LXXXV.

(Tune, *Hail! Masonry*).

LET worthy brethren all combine
    To beautify our mystic art,
So as the Craft may ever shine,
    And cheer each faithful brother's heart.

CHORUS.

Then, brethren, all in chorus sing,
    Prosper the Craft and bless the King.

We've levell'd, plumm'd, and squar'd aright,
    The five noble orders upright stand,
Wisdom and strength, with beauty's height,
    The wonder of the world command.
        Cho.—Then, brethren, all, &c.

Ye fools and cowans all, who plot
    To penetrate our mystery,
Ye strive in vain, attempt it not,
    Such creatures never shall be free.
        Cho.—Then, brethren, all, &c.

The wise, the noble, good, and great,
    Can only be accepted here;
The knave or fool, tho' deck d in state,
    Shall ne'er approach the Master's chair.
        Cho.— Then, brethren, all, &c.

Now fill your glasses, charge them high,
    Let our Grand Master's health go round,
And let each heart o'erflow with joy,
    And love and unity abound.
        Cho.—Then, brethren, all, &c.

LXXXVI.

Composed in the year 1757, by SIR W. GRANT.

L IKE an arch well cemented together,
    We truly and firmly will stand,
And justly support one another,
    With plumb-line and level in hand.
Until this world's consumed with fire,
    And judgment is passed on us all,
Foes ne'er shall come into our secret;
    No—nor we from Free-masonry fall.

JUNIOR WARDEN'S SONG.

By Brother THOMAS ELLISTON, *of the Lodge of Unanimity, No. 509, Stockport.*

(Tune, *Jockey to the fair*).

M Y brethren all, with one accord,
    When duty calls obey the word,
Support to you I will afford
    By assisting you to-day,
In laying a foundation sure,
That will for evermore endure,
Our building then will stand secure
Upon the rock of ages sure.

CHORUS.

    Free-masonry's the way
That will bring a workman, just and true,
    To everlasting day.

Then let the plumb-rule guide this day,
That Masons truly ever may
A building make, shall not decay
    Throughout the age of time:

But stand secure against the storm
Of life, and always in due form,
And our Masonic plan adorn,
Truth, wisdom, strength, and beauty round.
    Cho.—Free-masonry's the way, &c.

Then from the east the sun doth steer,
And when th' meridian he is near
Our labour then we will lay by,
    The hour of twelve is here;
And when refreshment is your due,
I, Junior, then will call to you,
Come, my brethren, every one
From labour to refreshment come.
    Cho.—Free-masonry's the way, &c.

When sun has passed meridian blaze,
I in due order do engage
To call the men to labour on,
    Until the setting of the sun;
And if for mortar they do cry,
I then will send a 'prentice boy,
Your orders he will well supply,
For at the building he must try.
    Cho.—Free-masonry's the way, &c.

Your working tools pray now take care,
And always act upon the square,
The Junior Warden—for his care—
    May have with you an equal share
Of wages and refreshment too;
For our Grand Master will then do
Unto his workmen just and true,
That have worked well their journey through.
    Cho.—Free-masonry's the way, &c.

LXXXVII.

(Tune, *Hearts of Oak*).

No sect in the world can with Masons compare,
So ancient, so noble the badge which they wear,
That all other orders, however esteemed,
Inferior to masonry justly are deemed.

  Cho—We always are free,
   And for ever agree;
   Supporting each other,
   Brother helps brother,
  No mortals on earth are so friendly as we.

When first attic fire mortal's glory became,
Tho' small was the spark, it soon grew to a flame;
As Phœbus celestial, transcendently bright,
It spread o'er the world a fresh torrent of light.
   Cho.—We always, &c.

The greatest of monarchs, the wisest of men,
Free-masonry honoured again and again;
And nobles have quitted all other delights,
With joy to preside o'er our mystical rites.
   Cho.—We always, &c.

Tho' some may pretend we've no secrets to know,
Such idle opinions their ignorance show;
While others, with raptures, cry out, "they're revealed,"
In Free-masons' bosoms they still lie concealed.
   Cho.—We always, &c.

Coxcombical pedants may say what they can,
Abuse us, ill use us, and laugh at our plan;
We'll temper our mortar, enliven our souls,
And join in a chorus o'er full flowing bowls.
   Cho.—We always, &c.

LXXXVIII.

By J. F. STANFIELD, *Sunderland.*

(Tune, *To Anacreon in Heaven*).

NOT the fictions of Greece, nor the dreams of old Rome,
Shall with visions mislead, or with meteors consume;
No Pegasus' wings my short soarings misguide,
Nor raptures detain me on Helicon's side.
All clouds now dissolve, from the east beams the day,
Truth rises in glory, and wakens the lay.
The eagle-eyed muse sees the light, fills the grove
With the song of Free-masons, of friendship and love.

Inspired with the theme, the divinity flies,
And, throned on a rainbow, before her arise
Past, present, and future—with splendid array,
In order masonic their treasures display:
She views murder'd merit by ruffian hand fall,
And the grave gives its dead up at fellowship's call!
While the Craft, by their badges their innocence prove;
And the song of Free-masons is friendship and love.

From those ages remote see the muse speeds her way,
To join in the glories that brighten this day.
In freedom and friendship she sees the true band
With splendour and virtue illumine the land.
Religion's pure beams break the vapours of night,
And from darkness mysterious the Word gives the Light,
While the lodge here below, as the choirs from above,
Join the song of Free-masons in friendship and love!

That the future might keep what the present bestows,
In rapture prophetic the goddess arose;
And as she sang through the skies angels echo'd the sound,
And the winds bore the notes to the regions around;

The grand proclamation our song shall retain,
'Twas—"That Masonry long may its lustre maintain:
"And, till time be no more, our fraternity prove,
"That the objects we aim at are friendship and love!"

LXXXIX.
THE CANDIDATE'S SONG.

As sung at the Lodge, in Carmarthen, in South Wales.
(Tune, *O my little rolling Sailor*).

O Blandusia, (1) noble fountain,
    Pure as glass and clear as light!
Flowing from the (2) sacred mountain,
    Thou dost charm both taste and sight.

Come, brave boys, this evening (3) crown ye
    All her border round with flowers,
For to-morrow she shall drown ye
    In sweet wines and pleasant hours.

A (4) young victim shall to-morrow,
    Welcome as a milk-white kid,
Without clamour, sigh, or sorrow,
    In thy crystal basin bleed.

Mad as first year's (5) hornëd cattle,
    Or lascivious as a ram;
Pointed steel shall cool his mettle,
    And shall tame him like a lamb.

1.—The science of Masonry.
2.—Of Solomon's temple.
3.—Alluding to the clothing of the Lodge.
4.—Alluding to the form of the entered apprentice's apron, &c.
5.—Alluding to its great and undefiled solemnity, &c.

The (6) hot dog-star's persecutions
  Can't thy (7) cooling shades inflame,
Nor the (8) bear's cold revolutions
  Come to freeze thy constant stream.

Lab'ring beasts (9) here find when weary,
  Cooling draughts to cure all pain.
Wand'ring (10) flocks here meet, and merry
  Drink, and never thirst again.

Now shall I and sacred Horace
  Both alike immortal be
By thy noble fountain; for as
  Long as thou art, so are we.

This the (11) rock thy (12) lymph while giving,
  Into voice melodious breaks;
This the (13) cov'ring oak, as living,
  And the (14) stony cavern, speaks.

XC.

(Tune, *By Jove, I'll be Free*).

OF all institutions for forming the mind,
  And making us ever to virtue inclin'd;
None can with the craft of Free-masons compare,
Nor teach us so truly our actions to square.
For know 'twas ordained, by our founder's decree,
That we should be loyal, be loving, and free.

6.—By the Romans, Catholicks, Turks, Barbarians, &c.
7.—The Patrons of Free-masonry.
8.—Nor the overflowings of the Goths, nor Calvinists, nor Lutherans, &c.
9.—Teachers.   10.—Societies.   11.—The literal word.
12.—The Metaphor. 13.—Alluding to the expressive forms both of the Jewels and of   14.—The Lodge itself.

In harmony, friendship, and concord we meet,
And every brother most lovingly greet;
To him in distress, we gladly impart
Some comfort to cheer and enliven his heart;
Thus we always live, and for ever agree,
Resolved to be loyal, most loving, and free.

By points of good fellowship we still accord,
Observing each brother's true sign, grip, and word,
Which from our great architect was handed down,
And ne'er will to any but Masons be known;
Then here's to our brethren of every degree,
Who always are loyal, and loving, and free.

Thus we interchangeably hold one another,
To let mankind see how we're link'd to each brother;
No monarch the mystical knot can untie,
Nor may prying mortals the reason know why:
For our hearts, like our hands, united shall be;
Still secret, still loyal, still loving, and free.

XCI.

(Tune, *A begging we will go.*)

OF all the places in the town
  That's for instruction good,
There is none like a Mason's lodge,
  If rightly understood.
   And to the lodge we'll go, &c.

There what is good is to be learnt
  From brethren just and true;
In harmony we all agree,
  And deference pay where due.
   And to the lodge we'll go, &c.

The master, he is in the east,
 Due homage to him pay;
The wardens sitting east and west,
 His will well pleased obey.
  And to the lodge we'll go, &c.

The Craft and 'prentices around
 Their orders always take,
And in the rules of Masonry
 Due progress daily make.
  And to the lodge we'll go, &c.

And after we've our bus'ness done,
 Then we rejoice and sing;
To our Grand Master take a glass,
 And George the Third, our King.
  And to the lodge we'll go, &c.

Then, if the Master will permit,
 Dear brethren, join with me,
To all Free-masons drink a health,
 And give them three times three.
  And to the lodge we'll go, &c.

XCII.

BY A YOUNG LADY.

(Tune, *Come, let us prepare.*)

OF your hearts to take care, now, ladies prepare;
 Be silent! I'll tell you the reason:
Sly Cupid, they say, as the most certain way
 To conquer the fair, is made Mason.

The music you hear will ravish your ear;
　　Your eye will be pleas'd past expression;
But think on the smart that follows the dart,
　　When thrown by the hand of a Mason.

The nymph may pretend her heart to defend,
　　But let her from me take a lesson;
She's surely undone though her heart were of stone,
　　It will melt at one glance from a Mason.

By the apron and glove Cupid reigns god of love,
　　His empire to doubt is now treason;
Then I humbly agree soon married to be,
　　And answer each call of my Mason.

Heaven prosper the youth for honour and truth,
　　And secrecy famed by all nations;
I'll ne'er be ashamed, nor fear to be blamed,
　　While I write in the praise of Free-masons.

XCIII.

OH! glorious days for Masons wise,
　　O'er all the Roman empire, when,
Their fame resounding to the skies,
　　Proclaim'd them good and useful men;
For many ages thus employ'd,
　　Until the Goths, with warlike rage,
And brutal ignorance, destroy'd
　　The toil of many a learned age.

But when the conqu'ring Goths were brought
　　T' embrace the Christian faith, they found
The folly that their fathers wrought,
　　In loss of architecture sound;

At length their zeal for stately fanes,
    And wealthy grandeur, when at peace,
Made them exert their utmost pains,
    Their Gothic buildings to upraise.

Thus many a lofty, sumptuous pile
    Was rais'd in every Christian land,
Tho' not confined to Roman style,
    Yet which did reverence command;
The King and Craft agreeing still,
    In well form'd lodges, to supply
The mournful want of Roman skill
    With their new form of Masonry.

For many ages this prevails,
    Their work is architecture deemed;
In England, Ireland, Scotland, Wales,
    The Craftsmen highly are esteemed,
By Kings, as Master of the lodge,
    By many a wealthy, noble peer,
By lord and laird, by priest and judge,
    By all the people everywhere.

To Masons, ancient records tell,
    King Athelstan, of Saxon blood,
Gave a broad charter, free to dwell
    In lofty lodge, with orders good;
Drawn from old writings by his son,
    Prince Edwin, their Grand Master bright,
Who met at York the brethren soon,
    And to that lodge did all recite.

Thence were their laws and charges fine,
    In every reign observed with care,
Of Saxon, Danish, Norman line,
    Till British crowns united were:

The monarch first of this whole isle,
   Was learned James, a Mason King,
Who first of kings revived the style
   Of great Augustus: therefore sing:

CHORUS.

Who can unfold the royal art,
   Or sing its secrets in a song?
They're safely kept in Masons' heart,
   And to the ancient lodge belong.

XCIV.

ROYAL ARCH SONG.

OH! grant me, kind heaven, the powers to others giv'n,
   Freemasonry's praise to rehearse;
Whilst we sing of the three, who in blest masonry,
   Are recorded in loftiest verse.
     Cho.—Oh! bless that day, and hail that morn,
       Whereon these three great men were born,
       Who Isr'el's temple did adorn
         With wisdom, strength, and beauty.

We sing of the three who first did agree,
   The Royal Arch secret to keep;
And the same to disclose unto none but to those
   The Grand Master should lovingly greet.
     Cho.—Oh! bless, &c.

Long lay it concealed, and all efforts failed,
   To bring forth the secret word;
Till in lodge secure, with three keys tiled the door,
   The grand word was held on record.
     Cho.—Oh! bless, &c.

'Till by heaven's decree, it was found out by three
    Fellow-crafts who knew nought of the same,
Who pulled up a key by a secret way,
    And to a jambed pedestal came.
        Cho.—Oh! bless, &c.

At noon they contend to know who should descend,
    And lots they did equally draw;
When fixing on one, they let him safe down,
    But first bound him fast by a law.
        Cho.—Oh! bless, &c.

His orders were clear, to check without fear,
    If aught should obstruct his design;
He with diligence sought, and up with him brought
    The logos which ever shall shine.
        Cho.—Oh! bless, &c.

Then with hands and eyes uprais'd to the skies,
    On their knees they offered praise
To Jehovah on high, that His All-seeing Eye,
    Might direct all the Craft in their ways.
        Cho.—Oh! bless, &c.

Then straightway they came unto Jerusalem,
    Where the Grand Master sat on his throne,
And delivered the same, with due homage to him;
    And by him to us 'tis made known.
        Cho.—Oh! bless, &c.

Then with jewels possessed he them did invest,
    And placed them in royal estate,
And presenting them wands, with some secret
        commands,
    Three Crafts were made Royal and Great.
        Cho.—Oh! bless, &c.

Each Royal Arch Mason, of every nation,
  Draw near and give ear to my song:
Toast a health unto those who ne'er did disclose
  To a cowan the arts which to us do belong.
  Cho.—O blest be that morn these three did agree,
  With wisdom endow'd from on high,
  A temple to raise to Jehovah's high praise,
  Whose glory doth reach to the sky.

XCV.

Composed and sung by Brother SAMUEL PORTER, *Master of the Lodges of St. John, No. 492, Henly, in Arden, and of the Shakespear, No. 516, Stratford on Avon, at the Dedication of the Shakespear Lodge.*

(Tune, *Mulberry Tree*).

ON Avon's sweet banks, where the silver streams
    glide,
The beauties in Stratford oft Shakespear would pride,
And say, when enraptur'd by the juice of the vine,
He would there raise a lodge to his favourite nine.
  Cho.—To honour now his country
    Do honour to his memory,
    And toast him round with three times three.

A few sons of science his name to revere,
Agreed to his mem'ry a pillar to rear,
In true antique order, immense in its size,
From earth's hallow'd surface, to heaven should rise.
  Cho.—For so build we o'er earth and sea,
    With beauty and true symmetry
    A sacred pile to Masonry.

From the north to the south pole its width be exprest,
Its length full extending between east and west;

To make it immortal they gave it a name,
And call'd it the Shakespear, to Warwickshire's fame.
   Cho.—And thus build we o'er earth and sea,
      With beauty and true symmetry,
      Such sacred piles to Masonry.

In Jehosophat's vale the foundation was laid,
By our Royal Grand Master, the prince of the trade,
And to keep up in concord a grand jubilee
Ordain'd it a lodge of Free-masons should be.
   Cho.—Ye sons, born free, with me agree,
      The King and Craft let our toast be,
      And toast him round with three times three.

May heaven's Grand Architect bless the design,
And health, peace, and concord its members conjoin;
May they flourish in harmony, friendship, and love,
'Till they're summon'd to join in the grand lodge above.
   Cho.—And so build we o'er earth and sea,
      Such sacred piles to Masonry,
      Through time to all eternity.

XCVI.

BY GAVIN WILSON.

(Tune, *Old Sir Simon the King*).

ON a whimsical frolic, fair Venus
   Invited the gods to a ball;
The occasion was Chloe the coquette
Surrendered to Damon, that's all.
A special request was committed
To Mercury, nimble of wing,
That Apollo, with all his nine daughters,
Would come at their revels to sing.

When Mercury presented his card,
Apollo smiled at the occasion:
But, friend Mercury, said he, I'm debar'd,
You don't recollect I'm a Mason,
And this night, by express invitation,
I go to the feast of St. John;
Let the gods quaff their goblets of nectar,
And strum o'er a song as they can.

XCVII.

(Tune, *Sailor Jack*).

ONCE I was blind and could not see,
    And all was dark around,
But providence protected me,
    And soon a friend I found:
Through hidden paths my friend me led,
Such paths as babblers never tread.
    With a fa, la, la, la, la, la, &c.

He took all stumbling blocks away,
    That I might walk secure;
And brought me, long e'er break of day,
    To Sol's bright temple door,
Where soon we both admittance found,
By help of magic spell and sound.
    With a fa, la, &c.

The curber of my rash attempt
    Did then my breast alarm,
And hinted I was not exempt
    Nor free from double harm,
Which put a stop to rising pride,
And made me trust more to my guide.
    With a fa, la, &c.

With sober pace I then was led,
    And brought to Sol's bright throne;
And there I was compelled to stop,
    Till I myself made known:
With mighty sound I round was brought,
That to obtain which much I sought.
      With a fa, la, &c.

In humble posture and due form,
    I list'ned with good will;
Instead of mighty noise and storm,
    All then was calm and still;
Such charming sounds I then did hear,
As quite expelled all doubt and fear.
      With a fa, la, &c.

The mighty monarch from his throne,
    Bade darkness then withdraw;
No sooner said than it was done,
    And then great things I saw;
But what they were I'll not now tell,
But such they were as here shall dwell.
      With a fa, la, &c.

Then round and round me he did tie
    A noble ancient charm,
All future darkness to defy,
    And ward off cowans' harm:
So I returned from whence I came,
Not what I was, but what I am.
      With a fa, la, &c.

XCVIII.

THE DEPUTY GRAND MASTER'S SONG.

N.B.—The third and fourth lines of each verse is the Chorus.

ON, on, my dear brethren, pursue your great lecture,
    And refine on the rules of old architecture;
High honour to masons the craft daily brings,
To those brothers of princes, and fellows of kings,

We've driven the Vandals and Goths off the stage,
Reviving the arts of Augustus' fam'd age;
Vespasian destroy'd the vast temple in vain,
Since so many now rise in great George's mild reign.

The noble five orders, composed with such art,
Will amaze the fixed eye and engage the whole heart;
Proportion's sweet harmony gracing the whole,
Gives our work, like the glorious creation, a soul.

Then master and brethren preserve your great name,
This lodge, so majestic will purchase your fame;
Rever'd it shall stand till all nature expire,
And its glories ne'er fade till the world is on fire.

See! see! behold here what rewards all our toil,
Enlivens our genius, and bids labour smile;
To our noble Grand Master let a bumper be crown'd,
To all Masons a bumper, so let it go round.

Again, my lov'd brethren, again let it pass,
Our ancient firm union cements with the glass;
And all the contentions 'mongst Masons shall be,
Who better can work, or who best can agree.

XCIX.

(Tune, *To all you ladies now on land*).

ON you who Masonry despise,
  This counsel I bestow,
Don't ridicule, if you are wise,
  A secret you don't know:
Yourselves you banter, but not it;
You shew your spleen but not your wit.
  With a fa, la, &c.

Inspiring virtues by our rules,
  And in ourselves secure,
We have compassion for those fools
  Who think our acts impure:
We know from ignorance proceeds
Such mean opinions of our deeds.
  With a fa, la, &c.

If union and sincerity
  Have a pretence to please,
We brothers of Free-masonry
  Lay justly claim to these:
To state disputes we ne'er give birth,
Our motto friendship is, and mirth.
  With a fa, la, &c.

Some of our rules I will impart,
  But must conceal the rest;
They're safely lodg'd in Masons' hearts,
  Within each honest breast:
We love our country and our king;
We toast the ladies, laugh and sing.
  With a fa, la, &c.

C.

OPEN, ye gates, receive the fair, who shares
  With equal sense our happiness and cares:
Then, charming females, there behold,
What massy stores of burnish'd gold,
  Yet richer is our art;
Not all the orient gems that shine,
Nor treasures of rich Ophir's mine,
  Excel the Mason's heart.

True to the fair, he honours more
Than glitt'ring gems, or priceless ore,
  The plighted pledge of love:
To every tie of honour bound,
In love and friendship constant found,
  And favoured from above.

CI.

By Brother JOHN RICHARDSON, *of the Royal Brunswick Lodge, Sheffield.*

(Tune, *A Rose tree in full bearing*).

"OWHAT a happy thing it is,
  Brethren to dwell in unity!"
Whilst every action's squar'd by this,
  The true base line of Masonry,
Our plumb-rule fixed to the point,
  The angle of uprightness shows;
From side to side, from joint to joint,
  By steps the stately mansion rose.

Whate'er the order or the plan,
    The parts will with the whole agree,
For, by a geometric man,
    The work is done in symmetry.
From east to west, from north to south,
    Far as the foaming billows roll,
Faith, hope, and silver-braided truth,
    Shall stamp with worth the Mason's soul.

But, chiefest, come, sweet Charity,
    Meek, tender, hospitable guest;
Aided by those, inspired by thee,
    How tranquil is the Mason's breast!
An olive branch thy forehead binds,
    The gift that peerless Prudence gave,
An emblem of congenial minds,
    And such Masonic brethren have.

CII.

PRAY don't sleep or think,
    But give us some drink,
For 'faith I'm most plaguily dry.
    Wine cheers up the soul,
    Then fill up the bowl,
For e'er long you all know we must die.

    Yesterday's gone,
    This day is our own;
To-morrow we never may see:
    Thought causes us smart,
    And eats up the heart;
Then let us be jovial and free.

The world is a cheat,
With a face counterfeit,
And freedom and mirth discommends:
But here we may quaff,
Speak our thoughts, sing, and laugh,
For all here are Masons and friends.

CIII.

A return to a compliment from the Chair.

BY GAVIN WILSON.

(Tune, *On, on, my dear Brethren*).

RIGHT worshipful Master, and worshipful wardens,
Dear kind worthy brethren, true secrecy's guardians,
The friendship, the honour, so kindly conferred,
With gratitude, thanks, and respect I regard.

Then kindly permit me the toast to return,
From a heart that for ever with friendship shall burn;
To all worthy brethren of every degree,
Craving aid with the honours, and by three times three.

CIV.

By Brother JOHN JACKSON, S.G.W.

SEE in the east the Master plac'd,
How grateful unto us the sight;
His wardens just he doth intrust
His noble orders to set right;
Wheree'er he list his deacons straightway run,
To see the lodge well til'd and work begun.

Like Tyre's sons we then pursue
    The noble science we profess,
Each Mason to his calling true,
    Down to the lowest from the best.
Square, plumb, and level, we do all maintain,
Emblems of justice are, and shall remain.

King Solomon, the great Free-mason,
    Honour unto the craft did raise;
The Tyrian prince and Widow's Son,
    Let every brother jointly praise:
Drink to the memory of all the three,
    And toast their names in glasses charg'd full high.

CV.

THE MASON'S PROGRESS.

By J. Evans.

(Tune, *The high mettled Racer*).

SEE the lodge fill'd with Masons, the rites are begun,
    The Master calls "order" and quickly 'tis done;
Now silence prevails: hark! a candidate's near,
He's honest, he's worthy, then let him appear.
On the sharp point of conscience behold him receiv'd,
From terror and danger now see him relieved;
Secure, but yet careful, he treads the still dome,
And though whelm'd in thick darkness he fears not to
    roam.

In posture quite humble, behold on the square,
He reverently bows with intentions sincere;
He firmly resolves he'll our secrets conceal.
And to none but Free-masons will ever reveal.

His darkness withdraws and the light shines full bright,
See emblems of virtue display'd to his sight;
With innocence clothed, and with fortitude armed,
The honest apprentice no longer's alarmed.

A craftsman next see him with plumb, maul and square,
With pulleys and levers great fabrics to rear;
With hands that are clean, and with mem'ry correct,
A heart that is pure and a judgment exact,
His conduct he plumbs, and actions he squares,
And the temple of knowledge divinely rears;
Where faith, hope, and charity fix their abode,
For a Free-mason's heart is a temple for God.

A wise master builder next see him become,
Who carefully levels the great corner stone;
His craftsmen instructs both by precept and line,
The work to perform and complete his design.
His orders so just are with pleasure obeyed,
His wisdom profound to each brother's conveyed;
By actions most worthy we nobly do prove
The cap-stone of masonry is brotherly love.

Now in regions of darkness next see him descend,
Two faithful companions his steps do attend,
They boldly press forward, resolved to explore
What those arches contain, and to Masons restore.
What terrors and dangers around them do wait,
The passages rough and the arches most strait;
Now, from dangers secure, by a glorious light
The long hidden myst'ries are revealed to their sight.

A pilgrim next see him with staff in his hand,
Sword, sandals, and scrip, in Emanuel's land.
The sepulchre to guard and defend,
From Turks, Jews, and Pagans old Salem to rend;

'Gainst all their attempts he his trusty sword draws,
And manfully fights in his great Master's cause;
Having finished his warfare, and fought the good fight,
The faithful Knight Templar claims mansions of light.

CVI.

(Tune, *Which nobody can deny*).

SOME folks have with curious impertinence strove
From Free-masons' bosoms their secrets to move,
I'll tell them in vain their endeavours must prove,
    Which nobody can deny, &c.

Of that happy secret when we are possessed,
The tongue can't explain what is lodg'd in the breast,
For the blessing's so great it can ne'er be expressed,
    Which nobody can deny, &c.

By friendship's strict ties we brothers are joined,
With mirth in each heart, and content in each mind,
And this is a difficult secret to find,
    Which nobody can deny, &c.

But you who would fain our grand secret expose,
One thing best conceal'd to the world you disclose,
Much folly in blaming what none of you knows,
    Which nobody can deny, &c.

Truth, charity, justice, our principles are;
What one doth possess the other may share;
All these in the world are secrets most rare,
    Which nobody can deny, &c.

While then we are met, the world's wonder and boast,
And all do enjoy that which pleases each most,
I'll give you the best and most glorious toast,
  Which nobody can deny, &c.

Here's a health to the generous, brave and the good,
To all those who think and who act as they should,
In all this the Free-mason's health's understood,
  Which nobody can deny, &c.

CVII.

The following song was composed and sung upon the occasion, by MR. JAMES BISSETT, *Steward of the St. Alban's Lodge, Birmingham.*

  (Tune, *Vicar of Bray*).

THE corner stone, this day, we have,
  By solemn dedication,
Of Stratford Lodge, most firmly laid,
  On our most grand foundation.
Great Shakespear's name the pile shall boast,
  A name so much renowned, sir;
With flowing bumpers let this toast
  Then cheerfully go round, sir.
  Cho.—May this new lodge for ever stand,
    To grace Masonic story,
    The wonder of this happy land,
    And raise old Shakespear's glory.

The mystic arts of Masonry,
  From east to west extending,
From pole to pole expands apace
  A gift of heaven's own sending.

Blest light divine, sent from above
    To cheer the discontented,
To make mankind unite in love,
    Like Masons thus cemented.
        Cho.—Blest light, &c.

Great honours have been paid before;
    But Shakespear's name to blazon,
Or give him fame, none can do more
    Than say—he was a Mason!
Upon the square he firmly stood,
    Such lovely structures rear'd, sir,
That ne'er before nor since the flood,
    Have buildings such appear'd, sir.
        Cho.—Upon the square, &c.

All nature's secrets he explored,
    With wonder struck she view'd him;
She "never saw his like before,"
    And all her works she show'd him,
The child of fancy, e'en in youth,
    In knowledge he surpassed her;
None ever could with him compare,
    But Hiram, our Grand Master.

    Cho.—May Shakespear's lodge for ever stand,
        And grace Masonic story,
    The wonder of this happy land,
        Old Stratford's boast and glory.

CVIII.

(Tune, *On, on, my dear Brethren.*)

THE curious vulgar could never devise,
    What social Free-masons so highly do prize;
No human conjecture, no study in schools—
Such fruitless attempts are the actions of fools.

Sublime are our maxims, our plan from above,
Old as the creation, cemented by love,
To promote all the virtues adorning man's life,
Subduing our passions, preventing all strife.

Pursue, my dear brethren, embrace with great care,
A system adapted our actions to square;
Whose origin clearly appeareth divine,
Observe how its precepts to virtue incline.

The secrets of nature King Solomon knew,
The names of all trees in the forest that grew;
Architecture his study, Free-masons' sole guide,
Thus finished his temple, antiquity's pride.

True, ancient Free-masons our art did conceal,
Their hearts were sincere, and not prone to reveal;
Here's the Widow's Son's mem'ry, that mighty great sage,
Who skilfully handled plumb, level, and gauge.

Toast next our Grand Master of noble repute,
No brother presuming his laws to dispute:
No discord, no faction our lodge shall divide!
Here truth, love, and friendship shall always abide.

Cease, cease, ye vain rebels, your country's disgrace!
To ravage, like Vandals, our arts to deface;
Learn how to grow loyal, our King to defend,
And live as Free-masons, your lives to amend.

CIX.

THE Great Architect of heaven above
  Has ordained of His great love
That we all should brethren be
And dwell together in unity;
Then, brethren all, with one accord,
Pay great attention to His word,
    With sincerity.

Now let brotherly affection
Unite us all together as one,
That peace and love may with us dwell,
And future ages may it tell,
That all of us with one accord
Pay great attention to His word,
    With sincerity.

If a brother, in adversity
Should apply for help to thee,
Thou in mercy dost him relieve,
'Tis better to give than to receive;
Then may we all have pow'r to give
An indigent brother relief,
    Without injury.

When from th' lodge we depart this night,
May we consider our ties aright,
That at each succeeding time
Our deeds of love may brighter shine;
Then would the art become more bright
To all those who are so upright
    In Masonry.

CX.

Composed for the Carberry Lodge, No. 504.

(Tune, *Nancy Dawson*).

THERE is a lodge in Skibbereen,
    As truly good as e'er was seen;
Compos'd of upright honest men,
    Men who are fit for Masons:
No coxcombs pert shall ever join,
Nor bloated swabs, replete with wine;
Our secrets truly are divine,
    We're the enlighten'd Masons.

Knights Templar, all of worth immense,
Of wit, of humour, and of sense,
Without a tinge of impudence,
    A health to all such Masons:
The poor ne'er feel from us neglect,
But always meet with due respect;
The needy brother we'll protect,
    And prove ourselves good Masons.

Our Tyler's good as any lord,
If to our tenets he'll accord,
And firmly mind the secret word,
    Unknown to all but Masons:
Nor is there one amongst us all,
Who on a summons or a call,
Would not with resolution fall,
    Defending a Free-mason.

From this our lodge we'll never stray,
'Tis here that Sol's diffusive ray
Has beam'd from high perpetual day,
    On us true constant Masons.

A solemn tie to never part,
Imprinted on each Templar's heart,
Without equivocating art,
   But like staunch honest Masons.

Our sweet * high-priest we will revere,
And †governor who fills the chair,
Both ever gay and debonair,
   The men to rule o'er Masons:
Two thousand chosen men upright,
Have been by them restor'd to sight,
And usher'd into glorious light,
   Let's toast ‡ Cymonic Masons.

CXI.

By Gavin Wilson.

(Tune, *A Cobbler there was, and he liv'd in a stall*).

THERE once was a Mason who lov'd a long drink,
   And a fop of a cowan, who fondly did think,
Could he get him fuddl'd, and find out this wonder,
He'd make all the Masons of Scotland knock under.
   Derry down, down, down, derry down.

He went to the Mason, and told him his tale,
A bargain was struck for three dozen strong ale;
He told him some nonsense, and gave him in fine
What the cowan thought truly the Free-masons' sign.
   Derry down, &c.

---

* The Presiding Officer in a Royal Arch Excellent and Knights' Templar Encampment.

† The Master of that lodge, who really presided at the making of some thousands of Free and Accepted Masons in different parts of this Kingdom.

‡ Vide the Knights' Templar song.

Brimful of his learning, next day in the street
With two or three Masons he happened to meet,
And, impatient to be recogniz'd a Free-mason,
Gave signs, words, and tokens without hesitation.
    Derry down, &c.

They saw he was bubbl'd, but wanting some fun,
They adjourned to a tavern, where, being sat down,
They told the young brother it was not discreet
To expose Masons' signs in the public street.
    Derry down, &c.

And for this indiscretion he must pay a fine,
If I rightly remember, three bottles of wine,
Which he willingly paid, and e'en call'd for another;
For he firmly believed that he was a true brother.
    Derry down, &c.

But, presuming on this, to a lodge he did go,
Where alas! he soon found he was *in statue quo;*
For they told him, to his no small mortification,
He had neither the face nor the heart of a Mason.
    Derry down, &c.

CXII.

By Mr. Dibden.

THE Sun's a Free-mason, he works all the day,
  Village, city, and town to adorn;
   Then from labour at rest,
   At his lodge in the west,
Takes with good brother Neptune a glass on his way.
   Thence ripe for the fair,
   He flies from all care,

To dame Thetis' charms,
'Till rous'd from her arms
By the morn.

Cho.—So do we, our labour done,
　　First the glass,
　　And then the lass,
　　And then
　　Sweet slumbers give fresh force,
　　To run our course,
　　Thus with the rising sun.

The course of the sun all our mysteries defines;
　　First Masonry rose in the east,
　　Then, to no point confined,
　　His rays cheer mankind;
Besides, who'll deny but he well knows the signs?
　　The Grand Master he
　　Then of Masons shall be,
　　Nor shall aught the craft harm,
　　'Till to shine and to warm
　　He has ceased.

Cho.—Then like him, our labour done,
　　First the glass,
　　And then the lass,
　　And then
　　Sweet slumbers give fresh force,
　　To run our course,
　　Thus with the rising sun.

CXIII.
THE MASON'S ALLEGORY.
By G. S. Cary.

THE trade of a Mason's a good moral school,
    Where the measures of life are establish'd by rule;
When affairs go awry let your judgment incline,
To make matters even by drawing the line.

Should your paths, being crooked, bewilder the mind,
Or, encircled by care, no alternative find,
Ne'er let your guide, reason, give way to despair,
Old Time, with exertion, your troubles may square.

Should you meet with a brother in craft too profound,
Make use of your plummet, his subtlety sound;
And if you no bottom should find in his heart,
When his hand he presents you, then bid him depart.

Let your converse be level, your life not too gay,
But just within compass, the moderate way;
When you're crippled by age, infirm, and oppress'd,
Let Faith lend a pillar on which you may rest.

CXIV.
THE FELLOW CRAFT'S SONG.
(Tune, *Sailor Jack*).

THO' millions 'gainst the craft unite,
    Their union is but vain,
In vain they ridicule that light
    Which they can ne'er obtain;
Our secrets we can keep with ease,
For they're lock'd up with iv'ry keys.
    Fa, la, la, la, la, la, la.

We never fail to show respect,
    To whom respect is due;
The indigent we ne'er neglect,
    We're to each brother true:
Mankind distress'd partake our store,
And want goes smiling from our door.

Our charity, quite unconfined,
    Spreads east, west, north, and south;
Expressions tender, good, and kind,
    Proceed from every mouth;
And men may make, by means of these,
Five talents ten, whene'er they please.

We're always pleas'd when vice does smart,
    Yet feel for others' woe;
But doubly pleas'd when the proud heart
    Is humbled and brought low;
We always pity where we can,
Abhor the guilt, but love the man.

Malicious men may still conspire,
    In vain they shoot their darts;
We know they see, and must admire
    The goodness of our hearts:
Their schemes to blast the Mason's name,
Serve only to increase his fame.

We're open, gen'rous, and sincere,
    We mean to do no wrong;
Our guides, the compass and the square,
    Yet don't to us belong;
By one we live, by t'other move,
And all our lives are spent in love.

> May every brother here agree
>   To take his glass in hand,
> And drink a health, with three times three,
>   Unto our Master Grand;
> With pens of gold record his name,
> In that great book, the book of fame.

CXV.

A new occasional Lyric, Masonic Eulogium, sung by Messrs. DAVIS, HELME, *and* BLANCHARD, *at* JONES'S *Royal Circus, St. George's Fields, on Saturday Evening, May 21st, 1796, for the benefit of the Royal Cumberland Free-masons' School.*

Written by J. C. CROSS. *The Music by* MR. SHIELD.

THO' my voice can't enchant like the syrens of old.
   I'll venture your ears to assail;
The attempt do not deem too intruding or bold,
   Good humour 'tis meant to exhale.
Of the compact that binds proud ambition and pow'r,
   My poor simple lays never dream;
But that which for ages true friendship has wore,
   Free-masonry's compact's my theme.

Cho.—Then join my song, brothers, the sentiment pass,
      No harm's in an honest endeavour;
   Fill higher—affection presides o'er the glass,
      "May Free-masonry flourish for ever."

Their pillars of rectitude ne'er will decay,
   Honour's temple's erected on high;
And architect Truth does a building display
   Of virtue, can't moulder or die.

I flattery scorn, it to falsehood gives birth;
    But rapture the deed must impart
Which bids soft humanity patronize worth,
    And light make the sad orphan's heart.
        Cho.—Then join, &c.

Let sensual drones to rich viands invite,
    Or tempt to gay Bacchus's board,
One moment of feeling will give more delight
    Than ages of mirth can afford:
To wipe from the eye the big tear of distress!
    Infant gratitude view, fondly shown!
To blessings bestow, sure the donor must bless,
    Whose heart is humanity's throne.
        Cho.—Then join, &c.

CXVI.

By Brother BLACKLOCK, *of the Lodge at Dumfries.*

THOUGH bigots storm, and fools declaim,
    And Masons some through ign'rance blame,
The good, the just, the learn'd the wise,
Free-masonry will ne'er despise.

    Cho.—O'er all the earth let Masons join,
        To execute one grand design,
        And strike amazement into fools,
        Who laugh at Masons and their tools.

On justice, truth, and charity,
This edifice shall founded be;
And we'll combine to rear the whole,
By wisdom's just, unerring rule.
        Cho.—O'er all, &c.

Let every Mason then prepare
By virtue's mould his work to square;
And ev'ry task adjusted be,
By the level of equality.
   Cho.—O'er all, &c.

Let jollity and freedom then
For ever in our lodge remain,
And still our work cemented be
By universal harmony.
   Cho.—O'er all, &c.

This structure we will fortify,
With the barrier of secrecy;
A Mason-barrier we may boast
Shall e'er impenetrable last.
   Cho.—O'er all, &c.

To mutual love and friendship rais'd,
This fabric shall by all be prais'd,
And those who strive to ridicule
Our craft, shall but themselves befool.
   Cho—Then o'er the earth, &c.

CXVII.

THUS happily met, united and free,
 A foretaste of heaven we prove;
Then join heart and hand, and firmly agree
 To cultivate brotherly love.

With corn, wine, and oil, our table replete,
 The altar of friendship divine;
Each virtue and grace the circle complete,
 With aid of the musical Nine.

Thus blest, and thus blessing, employment supreme!
  May Masonry daily increase,
Its grand scheme of morals our fav'rite theme,
  The source of contentment and peace.

CXVIII.

THE GRAND MASTER'S SONG.

THUS mighty eastern Kings, and some
    Of Abram's race, and monarchs good
Of Egypt, Syria, Greece, and Rome,
    True architecture understood;
No wonder, then, if Masons join
    To celebrate those Mason Kings
With solemn note and flowing wine,
    Whilst ev'ry brother jointly sings:

CHORUS.

Who can unfurl the royal art,
    Or show its secrets in a song;
They're safely kept in Masons' hearts,
    And to the ancient lodge belong.

CXIX.

THUS, though in Italy the art,
    From Gothic rubbish first was rais'd;
And great Palladio did impart
    A style by Masons justly prais'd;
Yet here his mighty rival Jones,
    Of British architects the prime,
Did build such glorious heaps of stones,
    As ne'er were matched since Cæsar's time.

King Charles the First, a Mason too,
  With several peers and wealthy men,
Employ'd him and his craftsmen true,
  Till wretched civil wars began:
But after peace and crown restored,
  Tho' London was in ashes laid,
By Masons' art, and good accord,
  A finer London rear'd its head.

King Charles the Second raised then,
  The finest column upon earth,
Founded St. Paul's, that stately fane,
  And Royal 'Change, with joy and mirth;
But afterwards the lodges failed
Till great Nassau the taste reviv'd,
Whose bright example so prevailed,
  That ever since the art has thriv'd.

Let other nations boast at will,
  Great Britain now will yield to none
For true geometry, and skill
  In building timber, brick, and stone;
For architecture of each sort,
  For curious lodges, where we find
The noble and the wise resort,
  And drink with craftsmen true and kind.

Then let good brethren all rejoice,
  And fill their glass with cheerful heart;
Let them express with grateful voice
  The praises of the wondrous art;
Let ev'ry brother's health go round,
  Who proves a Mason just and wise:
And let our Master's fame resound
  The noble Antrim to the skies.

CHORUS.

Who can unfurl the royal art,
    Or sing its secrets in a song?
They're safely kept in Masons' heart,
    And to the ancient lodge belong.

CXX.

'TIS Masonry unites mankind,
    To gen'rous actions forms the soul;
In friendly converse all conjoin'd,
    One spirit animates the whole.

Where'er aspiring domes arise,
    Wherever sacred altars stand;
Those altars blaze unto the skies,
    Those domes proclaim the Mason's hand.

As passions rough the soul disguise,
    Till science cultivates the mind;
So the rude stone unshapen lies,
    Till by the Mason's art refin'd.

Though still our chief concern and care
    Be to deserve a brother's name;
Yet, ever mindful of the fair,
    Their kindest influence we claim.

Let wretches at our manhood rail;
    But they who once our order prove,
Will own that we who build so well,
    With equal energy can love.

Sing, brethren, then the craft divine,
    Blest band of social joy and mirth;
With choral sound and cheerful wine,
    Proclaim its virtues o'er the earth.

CXXI.

(Tune, *Rule Britannia*).

TO Masonry, that gem divine,
 Which sparkles on creation's breast,
 The willing homage of the tuneful Nine
 Shall be in grateful strains express'd.
Hail, with rapture, the Mason's mystic art,
Which swells with joy each brother's heart.

 O'er every region of the earth,
  Our social banners are unfurl'd,
 And each proclaims of Masonry the worth,
  Which with its arms infolds the world.
   Hail, &c.

 Philanthropy each bosom warms,
  Where the Masonic treasure lies;
 And Charity, with her benignant charms,
  Our base and ornament supplies.
   Hail, &c.

 The Mason, friend to all mankind,
  To all his free assistance gives;
 Nor is to the human race confin'd,
  For lo, he feels for all that lives.
   Hail, &c.

CXXII.

By Brother JOHN CARTWRIGHT, *of Cheadle, Lancashire.*

(Tune, *The bonny broom.*)

TO Masonry your voices raise,
 Ye brethren of the craft;
To that and our great Master's praise,
 Let bumpers now be quaff'd:

True friendship, love, and concord join'd,
    Possess a Mason's heart;
Those virtues beautify the mind,
    And still adorn the art.

CHORUS.

Hail! all hail! my brethren dear,
    All hail to ye alway;
Regard the art while ye have life,
    Revere it every day.

While thus in unity we join,
    Our hearts still good and true;
Inspired by the grace divine,
    And no base ends in view;
We friendly meet, ourselves employ
    T' improve the fruitful mind
With blessings which can never cloy,
    But dignify mankind.
        Cho.—Hail! all hail! &c.

No flinty hearts amongst us are,
    We're gen'rous and kind;
The needy oft our fortune share,
    If them we worthy find:
Our charity, from east to west,
    To worthy objects we
Diffuse, as is the great behest,
    To every man that's free.
        Cho.—Hail! all hail! &c.

Thus blest and blessing, well we know
    Our joys can never end;
For long as vital spirits flow
    A Mason finds a friend.

Then join your heart and tongue with mine,
   Our glorious art to praise;
Discreetly take the gen'rous wine,
   Let reason rule your ways.
            Cho.—Hail! all hail! &c.

CXXIII.

(Tune, *Heaving the Lead*).

TO raise the great and noble pile,
   Each Mason free to work prepares;
While marching to their much lov'd toil,
   The beauteous rising sun appears.
To mark the work the Master hies,
And to his craftsmen cheerly cries,
         "Masons, work true!"

And when they are with heat oppress'd,
   By Sol's bright beams at noon-tide shed;
Then Junior Warden bids refresh,
   Thus cheer our hearts beneath the shade:
The Wardens then, with flowing bowls,
Cry out aloud, ye jovial souls,
         "Drink and be free."

But when the air with heat declines,
   The lab'rers, well refreshed and fed,
The watchful Warden still enjoins,
   And bids to work and quit the shade:
Again to toil the Wardens bring,
To work all then cheerful sings,
         "Masons, work well."

With cheerful hearts the brethren dear
    Perform the Master's well form'd plan;
And truly act upon the square,
    Firmly united man to man.
To lay the work the Warden springs,
And to his watchful Master sings,
       "Plumb, level, and square."

But see, the Warden in the west,
    Careful observes the setting sun;
The labourers pay, and send to rest,
    The business of the day is done:
The Warden then with cheerful heart,
Freely bids every man depart,
       And part in peace.

With cordial hearts, united hands,
    And cheerful concord let us join,
And drink to every mystic band
    Of Masons free who keep the line.
May Masons all, from east to west,
Their tasks perform, then seek for rest,
       Secure of bliss.

CXXIV.

(Tune, *By Jove, I'll be free*).

TO the science that virtue and art do maintain,
  Let the muse pay her tribute in soft gliding strain;
Those mystic perfections so fond to display,
As far as allow'd to poetical lay;
Each profession and class of mankind must agree,
That Masons alone are the men who are free.
        The men who are free, &c.

Their origin they with great honour can trace,
From the sons of religion and singular grace;
Great Hiram and Solomon, virtue to prove,
Made this the grand secret of friendship and love;
Each profession and class of mankind must agree,
That Masons, of all men, are certainly free.
       Are certainly free, &c.

The smart and the beau, the coquette and the prude,
The dull and the comic, the heavy and rude,
In vain may enquire, then fret and despise
An art that's still secret 'gainst all they devise;
Each profession and class of mankind must agree,
That Masons, tho' secret, are loyal and free.
       Are loyal and free, &c.

Commit it to thousands of different mind,
And this golden precept you'll certainly find,
Nor interest nor terror can make them reveal,
Without just admittance, what they should conceal;
Each profession and class of mankind must agree,
That Masons alone are both secret and free.
       Both secret and free, &c.

Fair virtue and friendship, religion and love,
The cement of this noble science still prove;
'Tis the lock and the key of the most godly rules,
And not to be trusted to knaves or to fools;
Each profession and class of mankind must agree,
That ancient Free-masons are steady and free.
       Are steady and free. &c.

Th' Israelites distinguish'd their friends from their foes
By signs and by characters; then why should those
Of vice and unbelief be permitted to pry
Into secrets that Masons alone should descry?

Each profession and class of mankind must agree,
That Masons, of all men, are secret and free.
Are secret and free, &c.

The dunce, he imagines that science and art
Depend on some compact, or magical part;
Thus men are so stupid to think that the cause
Of our constitution's against divine laws;
Each profession and class of mankind must agree,
That Masons are jovial, religious, and free.
Religious and free, &c.

Push about the brisk bowl, and let it circling pass,
Let each chosen brother lay hold on a glass,
And drink to the heart that will always conceal,
And the tongue that our secrets will never reveal;
Each profession and class of mankind must agree,
That the sons of Old Hiram are certainly free.
Are certainly free, &c.

CXXV.

THE COMPASS AND SQUARE.

Adapted to the New Instructions.

By Brother JOSEPH THORNTON, *of the Lodge of Candour, No. 642, Bell Inn, Delph, in Saddleworth.*

'TWAS heaven's injunction, when nature began,
That "man should be social and friendly with
Free-masons observing its precepts with care, [man;"
Adhere to the rules of the compass and square.

By the great architect the grand fabric was form'd,
By wisdom contrived, and with beauty adorn'd;
Supported by strength, all its parts shall declare
The order resulting from compass and square.

United and bound by the cement of love,
Those true sons of nature and science shall prove;
No mortals with Masons can justly compare,
Who act on the rules of the compass and square.

Three lights emblematic unerring will show,
What to God, to ourselves, and our neighbours we owe;
How to act to each other,—in memory bear
Five points—best explain'd by the compass and square.

Fidelity owns we her dictates obey,
Disdaining as Masons our trust to betray:
Benevolence teaches our hand not to spare,
When required by a brother o'th' compass and square.

With temp'rance to chasten, and prudence to guide,
And justice and truth o'er our acts to preside;
Forgetting their envy our foes must declare,
We are worthy our emblems, the compass and square.

Then fill up your glasses, let pleasure abound,
And this toast with good will and good humour go
      round;
"Success to each brother whose principles are,
"To be guided and govern'd by compass and square."

CXXVI.

THE JUNIOR WARDEN'S SONG.

(Tune, *He comes, &c*).

UNITE, unite, your voices raise,
    Loud, loudly sing Free-masons' praise;
Spread far and wide their spotless fame,
And glory in the sacred name.
    Glory, &c.

Behold, behold the upright band,
In virtue's paths go hand in hand;
They shun each ill, they do no wrong,
Strict honour does to them belong.
   Honour, &c.

How just, how just are all their ways,
Superior to all mortal praise;
Their worth description far exceeds,
For matchless are Free-masons' deeds.
   Matchless, &c.

Go on, go on, ye just and true,
Still, still the same bright path pursue;
Th' admiring world shall on you gaze,
And friendship's altar ever blaze.
   Friendship, &c,

Begone, begone, fly, Discord! hence
With party rage and insolence!
Sweet peace shall bless this happy band,
And freedom smile throughout the land.
   Freedom, &c.

CXXVII.

(Tune, *Rule Britannia*).

URANIA, sing the art divine,
 Beauty, strength, and wisdom grace each line;
Soar higher than Jove's famed bird can go,
Tho' out of sight, his flight's too low;
Boast Ubiquarians from this your pedigree,
But we from Jove take Masonry.

When the Great Architect design'd
Brooding nature's plan, and made mankind;
Then He ordained the Masons' orders fair,
For Masonry was all His care;
By omniscience and Free-masonry,
The jarring elements He made agree.

The Almighty by Masonry did scheme
His holy dwelling place, and heaven did name;
Made many mansions, which He supplied with light
Proceeding from His essence bright;
With shining stars adorn'd the vaulted skies,
To raise our wonder and surprise.

By Masonry this stupendous ball
He pois'd on geometry, and measured all
With line east and west; also from north to south:
This spacious lodge He measured out,
And adorned with precious jewels three,
As useful light to Masonry.

To rule the day th' Almighty made the sun,
To rule the night He also made the moon;
And God-like Adam, a Master Mason free,
To rule and teach posterity;
Sanctity of reason, and majesty of thought,
Amongst Free-masons should be sought.

In the deluge where mortals lost their lives,
God sav'd four worthy Masons and their wives;
And in the ark great Noah a lodge did hold,
Shem and Japheth his wardens, we are told,
And Ham, as tyler, was ordered to secure
From all their wives the sacred door.[*]

---

[*] And so soon as ever the day began to break, Noah stood up towards the body of Adam; and before the Lord, he, and his sons Shem, Ham, and Japheth, and Noah prayed, &c. And the women answered, from another part of the ark, Amen, Lord.—Vide Caten. Arab. C. XXV. Fol. 56. B.

When Israel's sons were held in slavery,
God sent His word and sign to set them free:
Nightly by fire, and in a cloud by day,
He pav'd His lov'd Free-masons' way,
Through the Red Sea, with wond'rous mystery,
From Pharaoh's yoke He set them free.

On Horeb's mount great Moses did stand,
With wardens twain, and rod of God in hand;
Devoutly prayed by word and sign to heaven;
While to his deputy conquest was given;
When on Mount Nebo he saw and died,
Jehovah did his time provide.

The world's great wonders, mankind agree,
Their beauties owe the art of Masonry;
Ephesus' temple, the walls of Babylon,
And labyrinths wond'rous works unknown;
The Pyramids, Mausoleum, and fam'd Colossus high,
And Olympus greeting the azure sky.

By God's command and Free-masonry,
The Temple had most exact symmetry;
In order raised by Hiram's mighty art,
From nature's rude materials start;
The world's wonders before were deemed but seven,
'Till this grand fabric made them even.

Come, charge, charge your glasses speedily,
To all true brothers skill'd in Masonry;
Likewise the King, long happy may he reign,
Old England's glory to maintain;
In order stand, you know the ancient charge,
Pay due respect to mighty George.

CXXVIII.

(Tune, *On, on, my dear Brethren*).

WE brethren Free-masons, let's mark the great name,
    Most ancient and loyal recorded by fame;
In unity met, let us merrily sing,
The life of a Mason's like that of a king.

No discord, no envy, amongst us shall be,
No confusion of tongues, but always agree;
Not like building of Babel, confound one another,
But fill up your glasses, and drink to each brother.
A tower they wanted to lead them to bliss,
I hope there's no brother but knows what it is;
Three principal steps in our ladder there be;
A mystery to all but to those that are free.

Let the strength of our reason keep th' square of our heart,
And virtue adorn ev'ry man in his part:
The name of a cowan, we'll not ridicule,
But pity his folly, and count him a fool.
Let's lead a good life, whilst power we have,
And when that our bodies are laid in the grave,
We hope with good conscience to heaven to climb,
And give Peter the pass-word, the token and sign.

Saint Peter he opens, and so we pass in,
To a place that's prepared for those free from sin;
To that heav'nly lodge which is tyl'd most secure,
A place that's prepared for all Mason's who're pure.

CXXIX.

(Tune, *The Steward's Song*).

WE have no idle prating
   Of either Whig or Tory;
      But each agrees
      To live at ease,
And sing or tell a story.
                CHORUS.
      Fill to him
      To the brim,
   Let it round the table roll;
      The divine
      Tells us, wine
   Cheers the body and the soul.

We will be men of pleasure,
Despising pride and party;
   Whilst knaves and fools
   Prescribe us rules,
We are sincere and hearty.
         Cho—Fill to him, &c.

If any are so foolish
To whine for courtiers' favour,
   We'll bind him o'er
   To drink no more,
Till he has a better favour.
         Cho.—Fill to him, &c.

If an accepted Mason
Should talk of high or low church,
   We'll set him down
   A shallow clown,
As understanding no church.
         Cho.—Fill to him, &c.

The world is all in darkness,
About us they conjecture;
   But little think
   A song and drink
Succeed the Mason's lecture.
        Cho.—Fill to him, &c.

Then, landlord, bring a hogshead,
And in the corner place it;
   'Till it rebound
   With hollow sound
Each Mason here will face it.
        Cho.—Fill to him, &c.

CXXX.

THE GRAND MASTER'S SONG.

WE sing of Masons' ancient fame!
   Lo! eighty thousand craftsmen rise
Under the Masters of great name,
   More than three thousand just and wise,
Employed by Solomon the sire,
   And general Master Mason too,
As Hiram was in stately Tyre,
   Like Salem built by Masons true.

The royal art was then divine,
   The craftsmen counselled from above,
The temple was the grand design
   The wond'ring world did all approve.
Ingenious men from every place
   Came to survey the glorious pile;
And, when returned, began to trace
   And imitate its lofty style.

At length the Grecians came to know
    Geometry, and learn'd the art
Pythagoras was rais'd to show,
    And glorious Euclid to impart:
Great Archimedes, too, appear'd,
    And Carthaginian masters bright;
Till Roman citizens uprear'd
    The art with wisdom and delight.

But when proud Asia they had quell'd,
    And Greece and Egypt overcome,
In architecture they excell'd,
    And brought the learning all to Rome;
Where wise Vitruvius, warden prime
    Of architects, the art improved
In great Augustus' peaceful time,
    When arts and artists were belov'd.

They brought the knowledge from the east,
    And as they made the nations yield,
They spread it thro' the north and west,
    And taught the world the art to build.
Witness their citadels and tow'rs,
    To fortify their legions fine;
Their temples, palaces, and bow'rs,
    That spoke the Masons' grand design.

Thus mighty eastern kings, and some
    Of Abram's race, and monarchs good
Of Egypt, Syria, Greece, and Rome,
    True architecture understood:
No wonder, then, if Masons join
    To celebrate those Mason Kings,
With solemn note and flowing wine,
    Whilst every brother jointly sings:

CHORUS.

Who can unfold the royal art,
 Or sing its secrets in a song?
They're safely kept in Masons' heart,
 And to the ancient craft belong.

CXXXI.

(Tune, What tho' they call me Country Lass).

WHAT tho' they call us mason fools?
 We prove by geometry our rules
 Surpass the arts they teach in schools;
They charge us falsely, then:
We make it plainly to appear,
By our behaviour everywhere,
That when you meet with Masons, there
 You meet with gentlemen.

'Tis true we once have charged been,
With disobedience to our Queen,*
But after-monarchs plain have seen
 The secrets she had sought:

---

* Queen Elizabeth hearing the Masons had certain secrets that could not be revealed to her (for that she could not be Grand Master) and being jealous of all secret assemblies, &c., she sent an armed force to break up their Annual Grand Lodge, at York, on St. John's Day, the 27th of December, 1561. Sir Thomas Sackville, then Grand Master, instead of being dismayed at such an unexpected visit, gallantly told the officers that nothing could give him greater pleasure than seeing them in the Grand Lodge, as it would give him an opportunity of convincing them that Free-masonry was the most useful system that ever was founded on divine and moral laws. The consequence of his arguments were, that he made the chief men

We hatch no plot against the state,
Nor 'gainst great men in power prate,
But all that's noble, good, and great,
    Is daily by us taught.

These noble structures which we see,
Rais'd by our fam'd society,
Surprise the world; then shall not we
    Give praise to Masonry:
Let those who do despise the art,
Live in a cave on some desert,
To herd with beasts, from men apart,
    For their stupidity.

But view those savage nations, where
Free-masonry did ne'er appear,
What strange, unpolished brutes they are;
    Then think on Masonry.
It makes us courteous men alway,
Gen'rous, hospitable, gay;
What other art the like can say?
    Then drink to Masons free.

Free-masons, who, on their return, made an honourable report to the Queen, so that she never more attempted to dislodge or disturb them, but esteemed them as a peculiar sort of men, that cultivated peace and friendship, arts and sciences, without meddling in the affairs of church and state.

CXXXII.

By Gavin Wilson.

(Tune, *Fair Flora, beautiful and gay*).

WHEN Adam started from the ground,
    And found himself a man,
  With judgment solid, clear and sound,
    T' explore the wond'rous plan;
All Eden smiled, each balmy grove
    Perfum'd the ambient air,
And fruits and flowers conjunctly strove
    To deck the landscape fair.

Beasts of the land, fowls of the spray,
    Came all with one accord,
To get new names, and homage pay
    Unto their new made lord.
Fair Eve the partner of his soul,
    To nuptial bower he led;
Then feasted on the richest spoil
    That Eden's garden had.

In silent visions of the night,
    Angelic skill prepared,
To give the patriarch's mind delight,
    A Mason lodge uprear'd,
Where each congenial soul inspir'd
    With every social charm;
Each heart with gen'rous friendship fir'd,
    Each other's bosom warm.

Sweet music's charms did please his ear,
    Their order pleas'd his eye;
Delighted with their social cheer,
    Indulg'd a heart-felt joy.

The grandeur of the hallow'd scene
    Did glad his honest soul:
He cry'd, my sons, come, charge again;
    Stewards, make another bowl.

To all my sons of each degree
    The gen'rous patriarch spoke;
Then took his glass, and drank like me,
    And clapt, and so awoke.
Eve wak'd, but to disturb him loth,
    Much wish'd to know the cause;
He told his dream, which pleas'd them both,
    Eve sweetly smiled applause.

CXXXIII.

By Brother BRICE *of Exeter.*

(Tune, *Roast Beef of Old England*).

WHEN a lodge, just and perfect, is form'd all a right,
    The sun-beams celestial (altho' it be night)
Refulgent and glorious appear to the sight
    Of hearty and faithful true Masons,
    True Masons in heart, word, and act.

Their eastern mild ruler then lays the first stone;
The craftsmen, obedient, united as one,
Him copy, and cheerfully work till high noon,
    As hearty and faithful true Masons, &c.

Rough ashlar they hew, and form by the square,
By the level lay solids, and by the plumb rear
Their uprights: strength beautiful being the care
    Of hearty and faithful true Masons, &c.

Hence a building, by wisdom contriv'd, does arise,
Well fix'd in the centre, sublime to the skies,
Which storms, thunder, war, and time's envy defies,
    Blest labour of faithful true Masons, &c.

Strong net-work they carve—its emblem they know—
Where lilies milk-white, and rich fruits seem to grow;
Concord, peace, and plenty,—how lovely the show
    To all hearty and faithful true Masons! &c.

No Babel distraction is heard, no debate;
The cock's crow they need not, the dog's barking hate;
Decorum they keep, and avoid idle prate,
    Being hearty and faithful true Masons, &c.

Intent on their task, their labour's their pleasure,
Nor seems it, however prolonged, beyond measure;
But all appear tir'd most, when most at leisure;
    Such trusty true workmen are Masons, &c.

When dismiss'd—wages paid,—and all satisfied,
As loth to depart, they yet social abide,
Join hands, with join'd hearts, toasting,—Joy e'er
    betide
    All hearty and faithful true Masons, &c.

Then, brothers, well met, charge right and let's sing,
Like ourselves, trebly thrice, to the craft and the king,
And crowning three cheers, make the happy lodge ring,
    Proclaiming us happy true Masons, &c.

CXXXIV.

(Tune, *Ye lads of true spirit, pay courtship to claret*).

WHEN a lodge of Free-masons are cloth'd in their
 In order to make a new brother, [aprons,
With firm hearts and clean hands they repair to their
 And justly support one another. [stands,

Trusty brother, take care, of eaves-droppers beware,
 'Tis a just and a solemn occasion;
Give the word and the blow, that workmen may know
 You are going to make a Free-mason.

The Master stands due, and his officers too,
 While craftsmen are plying their station;
The deacons do stand right for the command
 Of a free and an accepted Mason.

Now traverse your grounds, as in duty you're bound,
 And revere the authentic oration,
That leads to the way, and proves the first ray
 Of the light of an accepted Mason.

Here are words, here are signs, here are problems and
 And room, too, for deep speculation; [lines,
Here virtue and truth are taught to the youth
 When first he is bound to a Mason.

Hieroglyphics shine bright, and light reverts light,
 On rules and the tools of vocation;
We work and we sing, the craft and the king,
 'Tis both duty and choice in a Mason.

What's said or is done, is here truly laid down,
 In this form of our high installation;
Yet I challenge all men to know what I mean,
 Unless he's an accepted Mason.

The ladies claim right to come into our light,
    Since the apron they say is their bearing;
Can they subject their will, can they keep their tongues
    And let talking be changed into hearing?   [still?

This difficult task is the least we can ask,
    To secure us on sundry occasions,
When with this they comply, our utmost we'll try
    To raise lodges for lady Free-masons.

Till this can be done, must each brother be mum,
    Tho' the fair one should wheedle and tease on;
Be just, true, and kind, but still bear in mind
    At all times that you are a Free-mason.

CXXXV.

WHEN chaos and night were both dispers'd,
    The Almighty the great work survey'd;
Being pleased with what He had done, He said,
    Now let one earthly lord be made:
Straight at the royal mandate rose
    Enliven'd man, that lord to be;
All innocence his mind disclosed,
    And his first thoughts were Masonry.

Great Solomon, for wisdom fam'd,
    The world and all its secrets knew;
Yet nothing wisdom ever nam'd
    Save what from Masonry he drew.
The Urim and Thummin he disclosed
    To all those who were made free,
And sable clouds around inclosed
    All such as knew not Masonry.

To the bright temple's awful dome,
    Where glorious knights in armour dress'd;
To this place I slowly came,
    Sincerity within my breast,
A pilgrim to this house I came,
    With sandals, scrip, and staff that's white;
By rugged ways, my feet were lame,
    All this I bore to become a knight.

With trembling hand I gently smote
    At this bright temple's awful gate;
What I beheld when it was ope'd
    Was splendid, elegant, and great;
Twelve dazzling lights I plainly saw,
    Enlisted for the cross to fight;
But in one of those I found a flaw,
    So hastily put out his light.

With weapon I pierced the air,
    Enlisted for a glorious work,
For it's in this war I would take share,
    Against an Infidel, Jew, or Turk;
In regimental red I dress'd,
    Trimm'd with a glorious black and blue,
And a blazing star fixed to my breast,
    Conceals a heart that is most true.

CXXXVI.
(Tune, *Rule Britannia*).

WHEN earth's foundation first was laid
    By the Almighty Artist's hand,
'Twas then our perfect laws were made,
    Which soon prevailed throughout the land.
    Cho.—Hail, mysterious! hail, glorious masonry!
        That mak'st thy vot'ries good and free.

In vain mankind for shelter sought,
   From place to place in vain did roam,
Until by heaven they were taught
   To plan, to build, t' adorn a home.
          Cho.—Hail, mysterious! &c.

Illustrious hence we date our art,
   And now its beauteous piles appear,
Which shall to endless time impart
   How favoured and how free we are.
          Cho.—Hail, mysterious! &c.

Nor yet less fam'd for ev'ry tie
   Whereby the human thought is bound;
Love, truth, and boundless charity,
   Join all our hearts and hands around.
          Cho.—Hail, mysterious! &c.

Our deeds approv'd by virtue's test,
   And to our precepts ever true,
The world, admiring, shall request
   To learn, and all our paths pursue.
          Cho.—Hail, mysterious! &c.

CXXXVII.

(Tune, *Attic Fire*).

WHEN first a Mason I was made,
   What terrors then did me invade,
Oh! how I was alarmed!
But when the solemn scene was o'er,
My fears and terrors were no more,
   I found myself unharmed.

For since a brother I'm become,
A member of the social room,
   The scene is alter'd quite:
With pleasure now my hours pass;
With brethren free, and temp'rate glass,
   I spend the cheerful night.

My grateful thanks I now return,
And will with emulation burn,
   Such favours to deserve;
From Masons' ancient mystic rites,
Which truth with friendship e'er unites,
   From such I'll never swerve.

Hail, Masonry! thou glorious art!
Which to thy vot'ries dost impart
   Truth, honour, justice, love.
Thy sacred name rever'd shall stand
In foreign climes, and distant land,
   Which slander shall not move.

CXXXVIII.
FRIENDSHIP, LOVE, AND TRUTH.

WHEN "friendship, love, and truth" abound
   Among a band of brothers,
The cup of joy goes gaily round,
   Each shares the bliss of others;
Sweet roses grace the thorny way,
   Along this vale of sorrow;
The flowers that shed their leaves to-day
   Shall bloom again to-morrow:

CHORUS.
   How grand in age, how fair in youth,
   Are holy "friendship, love, and truth."

On halycon wings our moments pass,
    Life's cruel cares beguiling;
Old Time lays down his scythe and glass,
    In gay good humour smiling;
With ermine beard, and forelock gray,
    His reverend front adorning,
He looks like Winter turn'd to May,
    Night soften'd into morning!
        Cho.—How grand in age, &c.

From these delightful fountains flow
    Ambrosial rills of pleasure:
Can man desire, can heaven bestow,
    A more resplendent treasure?
Adorn'd with gems so richly bright,
    We'll form a constellation,
Where every star, with modest light,
    Shall gild his proper station.
        Cho.—How grand in age, &c.

CXXXIX.

By Bro. W. T. Harding,

Nile Lodge, Batley.

WHEN evening dim is ushered in,
    And the night wind softly blows;
When the lunar Queen, in beauty's mien,
    Her light to the wide world shows;
Like a widow'd bride, in her youthful pride,
    Who muses in silence alone;
Her night-watch keeps, while the weary sleeps,
    At the foot of her starlit throne.

Oh! bewitching hour of enchanting power,
    The inciter of friendship and love;
When the goddess of Truth, to age and youth,
    Descends from the realms of above.
'Tis then we meet, in love to greet,
    And the joys of fraternity share;
In order sublime, at a Mason's shrine,
    At the hierophant compass and square.

Our bosoms confide, and their secrets hide,
    From all Anti-masons and foes;
For on His sacred laws we've founded our cause,
    As Free-masonry's potency shows.
Our heaven-born order will know not disorder,
    While love warms the heart of each other,
If ills e'er betide, we find by our side,
    A Mason, a friend, and a brother.

CXL.

FAITH, HOPE, AND CHARITY.

Music from BRO. GEORGE LENG, Humber Lodge, 65, Hull.

WHEN Faith left her mansion celestial for earth,
    On Seraphin's plumes she was borne thro' the sky;
A crown o'er her temples betoken'd her birth,
    The gem on her breast show'd her mission from high:
Softly gliding thro' clouds by her radiancy clear'd,
Sweet Hope, her fair sister, in smiles now appear'd;
As friends they approach'd, interchanging the sign,
On earth thus cementing a union divine.

To join this loved pair, while discoursing below,
    Mild Charity came her best gifts to divide,
All the blessings of life she resolved to bestow
    Where honour with Virtue and Truth should preside.
Faith this world supported, Hope promised another,
While Charity bound man to man as his brother;
By signs, words, and tokens, this system began,
The eye of the Deity sanctioned the plan.

These heavenly strangers now sought to obtain
    A spot free from guile, for their earthly abode;
A threshold where folly had ne'er left a stain,
    Nor the footsteps of vice a dark taint to corrode:
Despairing they droop'd, led in darkness astray,
Till a light in the east clearly pointed the way;
They entered a Lodge, all their wishes were crown'd,
Here Faith, Hope, and Charity ever are found.

To Masons presiding these virtues combine,—
    Faith beckons to join the Grand Master above,
While Hope, through the Arch, points to regions divine,
    And Charity teaches peace, friendship and love:
To all who deserve be those principles shown,
The Craft is most honoured when most it is known;
May Truth's sacred records to man be unfurl'd,
And Faith, Hope, and Charity govern the world.

CXLI.

By Bro. W. MILTON, *No. 386, Stansfield.*

(Tune, *Old Adam*).

WHEN heaven at first had ordain'd it
    That man should be happy and free,
Then to us was made known the blest secret
    And science of Free-masonry:

Arts, learning, and myst'ries are good, then,
    Which virtue and love do impart;
Geometry's a science most noble,
    A gem in a Masonic heart.

Now architecture to all Masons
    Doth beautiful orders display;
Its emblems to us are good lessons
    Through every part of the day;
For man, he is but a rough ashlar
    If wisdom his heart doth not bind,
Then put on this true badge of a Mason,—
    Strength, beauty, and wisdom you'll find.

Fidelity's found in the lodge, then,
    While our secrets are never betray'd;
For Faith, Hope, and Charity reign here,
    And Prudence doth lend us her aid:
The goddess, Dame Justice, presides here,
    Whilst Fortitude stands by her side,
And Temperance, ready assisting,
    Doth blessed Free-masonry guide.

In the lodge we are what men should be,
    We are happy, and social, and free,
And tyranny ne'er can be raised here,
    To control divine Masonry.
Then, join hand in hand, all true brothers,
    In harmony, concord, and love;
Like pillars immutable stand firm,
    Till summoned to the grand lodge above.

CXLII.

(Tune, *Rule Britannia*).

The two last lines of each verse are Chorus.

WHEN heav'n design'd that man should know
All that was good and great below,
This was the happy, choice decree,
The blessings of Free-masonry.

Hence peace and friendship deign to smile,
Instructive rules the hours beguile:
In social joy and harmony
Are spent the hours of Masonry.

To beauty's shrine they homage pay,
Its power they know, and own its sway;
And this their toast will always be,
Success to love and Masonry.

Of modern learning, ancient lore,
Masons possess an ample store;
At faction spurn, but loyalty
Congenial is with Masonry.
When taste and genius both combine
To shape the stone or draw the line,
In fair proportion, just and free,
All own the power of Masonry.

Whate'er in sculptur'd skill we prize,
Or domes are reared, or structures rise;
Such wonders ne'er mankind could see,
But from the help of Masonry.

An edifice we're proud to own,
Of wood not made, nor yet of stone,
Whose angles, squares, and symmetry,
Are emblems of Free-masonry.

'Tis founded on a brother's love,
Relief and Truth its pillars prove;
Its corner-stone is Charity;
The building's then Free-masonry.

By nature rear'd, improv'd by art,
The mansion view—a Mason's heart!
Which ne'er was equalled, all agree,
When modelled by Free-masonry.

CXLIII.

WHEN Masonry by heaven's design
    Did enter first into great Hiram's brain,
A choir of angels did rejoice,
And this chorus sung with united voice:—

CHORUS.

Hail! ye happy, happy sons that be,
Brothers of Freemasonry.

Great Hiram he did then repair,
And went to work with rule and square;
With his level and plumb he form'd a plan,
And did the glorious temple frame.
        Cho—Then hail! &c.

When Solomon beheld the same,
He then set forth great Hiram's fame:
Oh! excellent Mason! he did say,
Above all others you bear the sway.
        Cho.—Then hail! &c.

Now to great Hiram's memory
Let's fill a glass most pleasantly,
Including St. John, who light did bring,
Not forgetting George our King.
        Cho.—Then hail! &c.

Then next to our Grand Master pass,
My brethren dear, a flowing glass,
Including ourselves, so pass it round,
And with a clap make the lodge resound.
   Cho.—Then hail! &c.

CXLIV.

ON THE REVIVAL OF MASONRY IN CORNWALL.

(Tune, *Vicar of Bray*).

WHEN Masonry expiring lay,
 By knaves and fools rejected,
Without one hope, one cheering ray,
 By worthless fools neglected;
  Fair Virtue fled,
  Truth hung her head,
 O'erwhelmed in deep confusion;
  Sweet Friendship too
  Her smiles withdrew
 From this blest institution.
   Cho.—Fair Virtue fled, &c.

Cornubia's sons determin'd then
 Free-masonry to cherish;
They roused her into life again,
 And bid fair science flourish.
  Now Virtue bright,
  Truth, rob'd in white,
 With Friendship hither hastens;
  All go in hand
  To bless the band
 Of upright Cornish Masons.
   Cho.—Now Virtue bright, &c.

Since Masonry's revived once more,
   Pursue her wise directions;
Let Circumspection go before,
   And Virtue square your actions:
      Unite your hands
      In friendship's bands,
   Supporting one another;
      With honest heart
      Fair truth impart
   To every faithful brother.
      Cho.—Unite your hands, &c.

Let coxcombs grin, and critics sneer,
   While we are blithe and jolly;
Let fops despise the badge we wear,
   We laugh at all their folly:
      Let empty fools
      Despise our rules,—
   By Jove we ne'er will heed 'em;
      Say what they will,
      We're Masons still,
   And will support our freedom.
      Cho—Let empty fools, &c.

But may kind heaven's gracious hand
   Still regulate each action;
May every lodge securely stand
   Against the storms of faction;
      May love and peace
      Each day increase
   Throughout this happy nation;
      May they extend
      Till all shall end
   In one great conflagration.
      Cho.—*May love and peace*, &c.

CXLV.
A ROYAL ARCH SONG.
The words by BRO. J. F. STANFIELD.
Set to Music, with a grand chorus, by Bro. HUQUIER.

WHEN orient Wisdom beam'd serene,
  And pillar'd Strength arose;
When Beauty ting'd the glowing scene,
  And Faith her mansion chose;
Exulting bands the fabric view'd;
  Mysterious powers ador'd;
And high the triple union stood,
  That gave the Mystic Word.

Pale Envy wither'd at the sight,
  And, frowning o'er the pile,
Call'd Murder up from realms of night,
  To blast the glorious toil.
With ruffian outrage, join'd in woe,
  They form'd the league abhorr'd;
And wounded Science felt the blow
  That crush'd the Mystic Word.

Concealment, from sequester'd cave,
  On sable pinions flew;
And o'er the sacrilegious grave
  Her veil impervious threw.
Th' associate band in solemn state
  The awful loss deplor'd;
And Wisdom mourn'd the ruthless fate
  That whelm'd the Mystic Word.

At length, thro' time's expanded sphere,
  Fair Science speeds her way;
And, warm'd by Truth's refulgence clear,
  Reflects the kindred ray.

A second fabric's towering height
    Proclaims the sign restor'd;
From whose foundation—brought to light,
    Is drawn the Mystic Word.

To depths obscure the favoured trine
    A dreary course engage,
Till thro' the Arch the ray divine
    Illumes the sacred page!
From the wide wonders of this blaze
    Our ancient signs restor'd;
The Royal Arch alone displays
    The long-lost Mystic Word.

CXLVI.

HIRAM'S DREAM.

WHEN Sol from high meridian had finished his
    career,
A lively vermilion in the west there did appear,
With a dark shady mantle the globe all round was
    dress'd,
In the azure blue canopy the stars were interspers'd.

It is then unto my chamber immediately I came,
And in my silent slumbers I fell into a dream;
I thought four men, in ancient dress, presented me a plan,
How that I might admittance find to the Order of St. John.

They told me that they brethren were, and from Jerusalem
    came,
In Solomon's reign they porters were about the temple of
    fame;

There were Solomon, Hiram, and Abif, whose names I did inquire,
And Tolman, that sojourner was, and came from Mount Moriah.
They bade me to prepare with speed, all with a comely grace,
They led me to Mount Horeb to view that holy place,
Where Tolman gave the orders, and bade me not refuse,
But on that holy mountain then to take off my shoes.
Then orders from the altar came that I examain'd be,
And on a point I entrance found by being born free;
I heard a voice come from the east which had a heav'nly sound,
And from my eyes a veil did drop and soon great light I found.
Straightway to Mount Moriah a pilgrim I did repair,
With cherubims and palm trees the walls all covered were.
And in a trembling posture I knocked at the door,
Resolv'd if I admittance found to see Ornan's threshing floor.
I saw two pillars in the east that were twelve cubits round,
And in each of their altitudes were eighteen cubits found;
They were hollow, made of brass, as history doth maintain,
Cast by Hiram, the widow's son, upon bright Jordan's plain.
To Enoch's buildings then I came, to view that pleasant town.
He being a son to Samuel, that Craft of great renown;

To me his friendship was so great I thought myself
  secure,
A Master builder I was made on Ornan's threshing
  floor.

Around the circle I was brought towards the temple
  door,
Conducted was unto the east of Ornan's threshing
  floor;
Five noble orders I was taught, all in the temple of
  fame,
But suddenly, as I awoke, I found 'twas all a dream.

CXLVII.

(Tune, *From the East breaks the morn.*)

WHEN the Deity's word
  Through all chaos was heard,
And the universe rose at the sound,
Trembling night skulk'd away,
Bursting light hail'd the day,
  And the spheres did in concert resound.

Then the Grand Architect,
In omnipotence deck'd,
  In order the mass did compound;
Deem'd the Sun King of Light,
Crown'd the Moon Queen of Night,
  And the earth with an atmosphere bound.

Mighty man then was form'd,
With five senses adorn'd,
  Which the noble five orders expound:

With the birth of the sun
Architecture begun,
   And 'till nature expires 'twill abound.

Bible, compass, and square,
As our ensigns we wear,
   The bright symbols of wisdom profound;
And while these are our guide,
Ev'ry mystery beside
   As a foil to our art will be found.

———

CXLVIII.

WHEN quite a young spark,
   I was in the dark,
And wanted to alter my station;
   I went to friend,
   Who prov'd in the end,
A free and an accepted Mason.

   At a door he then knock'd,
   Which quickly unlock'd,
When he bid me put a good face on;
   And not be afraid,
   For I should be made
A free and an accepted Mason.

   My wishes were crown'd,
   And a Master I found,
Who made a most solemn oration;
   Then showed me the light,
   And gave me the right
Sign, token, and word of a Mason.

How great my amaze
When I first saw the blaze,
And how struck with the mystic occasion!
Astonished, I found,
Though free, I was bound
To a free and an accepted Mason.

When cloth'd in white,
I took great delight
In the work of this noble vocation;
And knowledge I gained
When the lodge he explained
Of a free and an accepted Mason.

I was bound, it appears,
For seven long years,
Which to me is of trifling duration;
With freedom I serve,
And strain every nerve
To acquit myself like a good Mason.

A bumper then fill,
With a hearty goodwill,—
To our Master pay due veneration;
Who taught us the art
We ne'er will impart,
Unless to an accepted Mason.

CXLIX.

(Tune, *Balance a Straw*).

WHEN the sun from the east first salutes mortal eyes,
And the sky-lark melodiously bids us arise;
With our hearts full of joy we the summons obey,
Straight repair to our work, and to moisten our clay,

On the tressel our master draws angles and lines,
There with freedom and fervency forms his designs;
Not a picture on earth is so lovely to view,
All his lines are so perfect, his angles so true.

In the west see the warden submissively stand,
The Master to aid and obey his command;
The intent of his signal we perfectly know,
And we ne'er take offence when he gives us a blow.

In the lodge sloth and dulness we always avoid,
Fellow-crafts and apprentices, all are employed;
Perfect ashlar some finish, some make the rough plain,
All are pleased with their work, and are pleased with their gain.

When my Master I've serv'd seven years, perhaps more,
Some secrets he'll tell me I ne'er knew before;
In my bosom I'll keep them as long as I live,
And pursue the directions his wisdom shall give.

I'll attend to his call both by night and by day;
It is his to command, and 'tis mine to obey:
Whensoe'er we are met, I'll attend to his nod,
And I'll work till high twelve, then I'll lay down my hod.

CL.

(Tune, *Arno's Vale*).

WHEN my divine Althæa's charms
    No more shall kindle soft alarms,
And the keen lightning of her eye
Passes unfelt, unheeded by;
When moral beauty's heavenly form
Shall cease the frozen soul to warm;
When manners thus corrupt we see,
Farewell the sweets of Masonry!

When Science shall withdraw her light,
And Error spread a Gothic night;
When Pity's sacred source is dry,
No pearly drop to melt the eye;
When Truth shall hide her blushing head,
And famish'd Virtue beg her bread;
When manners thus corrupt we see,
Farewell the sweets of Masonry!

But while the fair transports our sight,
And moral Beauty's charms delight;
While Science lifts her torch on high,
And Pity shows the melting eye;
While Truth maintains despotic power,
And Virtue charms without a dower;
While manners thus unstrain'd we see,
All hail! the sweets of Masonry!

CLI.

WHILE science yields a thousand lights
To irradiate the mind,
Let us that noblest art pursue
    Which dignifies mankind.
        Cho.—So to Masonry, huzza!
            So to Masonry, huzza!
            Whose art and mystery coincide
            With gospel and with law.

The pompous dome, the gorgeous hall,
    The temple's cloud-capt tower,[*]
The Mason's glory shall proclaim,
    Till time's remotest hour.
        Cho.—Then to Masonry, &c.

Yet he who thinks our art confined
    To mere domestic laws,
As well might judge great nature's works,
    Sprung up without a cause.
        Cho.—Then to Masonry, &c.

Ideal fabrics to uprear,
    Some fools think all our art;
But little dream what plans we draw
    To form an upright heart.
        Cho.—*Then* to Masonry, &c.

---

  * Alluding to the following well known inscription on Shakespear's Monument:—

        "The cloud-capt Towers,
        The gorgeous Palaces,
        The solemn Temples,
        The great Globe itself,
        Yea, all which it inherit,
            Shall dissolve,
        And, like the baseless fabric of a vision,
        Leave not a wreck behind!"

The plumb we poise, and clear each log
    Which hangs about the string;
And each unruly passion's flight
    Within due compass bring.
        Cho.—Then to Masonry, &c.

Religion's all enlightened page
    We spread before our eyes,
By which we're taught those steps to trace,
    Which lead us to the skies.
        Cho.—Then to Masonry, &c.

The *summum bonum* then we learn,
    To which true Masonry tends,
Our brethren as ourselves to love,
    And all mankind as friends.
        Cho.—Then to Masonry, &c.

The good Samaritan to prove
    To all, and everywhere;
Upon the level still to meet,
    And part upon the square.
        Cho.—Then to Masonry, &c.

Upon this rock we'll stand, when worlds
    To oblivion are consigned,
And vision's baseless fabric like,
    Leave not a wreck behind.
        Cho.—Then to Masonry, &c.

CLII.

(Tune, *The First of August*).

WITH cordial hearts let's drink a health
    To ev'ry faithful brother,
Whose candid hearts, whilst breath endures,
    Are faithful to each other:

Whose precious jewels are so rare,
　　Likewise their hearts so framed are,
And levell'd with the truest square
　　That nature can discover.

The greatest monarch in the land,
　　Or in any other nation,
Would take a brother by the hand,
　　And greet him in his station.
Neither king nor prince, tho' e'er so great,
　　Nor any emperor of state,
But with great candour would relate
　　To ev'ry faithful brother.

The world shall still remain in pain
　　And at our secrets wonder,
No cowan shall it e'er obtain,
　　Tho' all their lives they ponder:
Still aiming at the chiefest light,
　　In which Free-masons take delight,
They never can obtain that light,
　　Tho' all their lives they ponder.

King Solomon, the great and wise,
　　He was a faithful brother;
Free-masonry he ne'er despised,
　　No secrets he discovered;
But he was always frank and free,
　　Professing such sincerity
To all of that fraternity,
　　He loved them 'bove all others.

Come, let us build on firm ground,
　　Still aiding of each other,
And lay a foundation that's most sound,
　　That no arts-man can discover;

Nor ever shall revealed be,
    But to bright stars in Masonry;
Here is to them where'er they be,
    I am their faithful brother.

Come, let us join our hearts and hands
    In this most glorious manner,
And to each other firmly stand,
    Under Great George's banner;
That God may bless him still I pray,
    And o'er his enemies bear the sway,
And for ever win the day,
    And crown his reign with honour.

CLIII.
(Tune, *The Dusky Night*).

WHILE cowans preach up their vile rules.
Strange liberty to define,
The precepts taught in Hiram's schools,
    We Masons hold divine.
    Cho.—Success to Masons all,
        Success to Masons all,
    The King, the craft, the mystic bands,
        Of happy Masons all.

When in the lodge we all are met,
    We work, refresh, and sing;
Dull politics we soon forget,
    Yet drink to our good King.
        Cho.—Success, &c.

From us protection you'll receive,
    Ye ladies kind and fair;
Due satisfaction we will give,
    So banish all your care.
        Cho.—Success, &c.

The bible, square, and compass too,
 With lights refulgent shine;
Pure friendship from its sacred clue,
 Does round our hearts entwine.
  Cho.—Success, &c.

Then join your hands, my brethren dear,
 Let Masons be the toast;
Long may they all exist on earth,
 And wives their order boast.
  Cho.—*Success, &c.*

CLIV.

Written by Brother NOORTHOUCK, *and sung in the Provincial Grand Lodge, at Margate, in Kent, June 12, 1786, by Brother* ROBSON.

(Tune, *Rule Britannia.*)

WHILE trifles lead the world astray,
 And vice seduces giddy youth,
Rejoice, my brethren, in this auspicious day,
 That guides a steady few to truth:
Raise, raise your voices, ye Kentish Masons all,
'Tis Sawbridge rules, obey his call.

Shall Masonry through Britain spread,
 And flourish every where but here?
Forbid it, Virtue! while you our footsteps lead,
 Kent foremost shall in worth appear:
Huzza, my brethren! to Sawbridge raise the song,
Our grateful strains to him belong.

When Harold's crown the Norman gain'd,
    In Kent a hardy race he found;
Whose sons, to cherish their ancient fame unstrain'd,
    Preserve it on Masonic ground:
True to your duty, your ancestors, and land,
Let Sawbridge lead a worthy band.

Away with politics and news,
    Away with controversies all;
We are here united above all party views,
    And gladly hail the social call:
Fill, fill your glasses; let Sawbridge be the toast,
Long may we his protection boast!

CLV.

(Tune, *From the East breaks the morn.*)

WHILST each poet sings of great princes and kings,
To no such does my ditty belong;
'Tis freedom I praise, that demands all my lays,
And Masonry honours my song.
    Cho.—'Tis freedom I praise, &c.

Within compass to live, is a lesson we give,
Which none can deny to be true;
All our actions to square, to the time we take care,
And virtue we ever pursue;
    Cho.—All our actions, &c.

On a level we are, all true brothers share
The gifts which kind heaven bestows;
In friendship we dwell; none but masons can tell
What bliss from such harmony flows;
    Cho.—In friendship we, &c.

In our mystical school we must all work by rule,
And our secrets we always conceal;
Then let's sing and rejoice, and unite every voice,
With fervency, freedom, and zeal;
    Cho.—*Then let's sing, &c.*

Then each fill a glass, let the circling toast pass,
And merrily send it around;
Let us Masonry hail, may it ever prevail,
With success may it ever be crown'd!
    Cho.—Let us Masonry, &c.

CLVI.
By Brother FOOTE.
(Tune, *Green Sleeves.*)

WHILST some sing of love and its powerful flame,
    Whilst others the king or the ministry blame,
We glory to chant the immortaliz'd fame
                      Of Masonry.

Tho' titles and orders do greatly abound,
Examine each herald thro' Christendom round,
Not the fleece, star, nor garter, so ancient is found
                      As Masonry.

Tho' malice has oft-times misconstru'd our rules,
Spite of villainous lies or the ign'rance of fools,
Strict honour and justice are taught in the schools
                      Of Masonry.

Should any but dare from these precepts to stray,
Or decline the bright path where the sun lights the way,
Our gavel should hack the excrescence away
                      From Masonry.

Geometry, chief of all science, we trace,
Where Doric, Corinthian, Composit, find place;
The Ionic and Tuscan, too, each adds a grace
                              To Masonry.

The use of these orders not those can divine
Who ne'er had the light, or the word, or the sign,
And cannot most truly a letter define
                              In Masonry.

We labour most cheerful in hill or in dale,
At Moriah's fam'd mount, or Jehosaphat's vale,
And whene'er 'tis high twelve with due order regale
                              In Masonry.

No noise, no disorder, no riot we know,
But strictest decorum and harmony show,
Whilst the graces on each do their favours bestow,
                              In Masonry.
Whilst Phœbus with spendour shall govern the day,
Or pale Luna the night with her absolute sway,
So long, could we live, we would walk in the way
                              Of Masonry.

Whilst the sea ebbs and flows, or the stars shed their
    light;
'Till all nature dissolves like the visions of night;
So long will true brothers in friendship unite
                              In Masonry.

CLVII.

By Gavin Wilson.

(Tune, *Sweet are the charms of her I love*).

WHILE arts and sciences did lie
    In embryo in the human mind,
'Twas then the rough inclement sky
    Made men employ their wits to find
A shelter from the piercing cold:
    Hence caves and dens were dug of old.

But Masonry, with generous skill,
    Bade cities, castles, temples rise;
With influence superior still,
    Form'd Masons in societies,
Where friendship in perfection shines,
    And harmony unceasing reigns.

Thus chaos wrapt in darkness lay,
    When it th' omnific fiat heard:
From womb of night sprang new-born day,
    And thus the worlds grand lodge was rear'd.
With joy angelic harps were strung,
    From pole to pole creation sung.

CLVIII.

WHILST poets of old have in verses sublime,
    Rehearsed the deeds of great men in their time:
Be these to record in a few ardent lays.
A song of Free-masons in Combermere's praise.

The Hero of Cheshire renowned is in fame!
In Masonry, Loyalty, Friendship the same;

His country he's served, and the hearty huzzas
Of Old England ring forth in Combermere's praise!

In his country's cause he is faithful and true,
Blest peace to preserve and dire war to subdue;
May his efforts succeed, and long be his days,
And Free-masons will join in Combermere's praise.

To Masonry true—to its precepts and laws
He is firm and sincere, and just to the cause:
Free-masons of Cheshire! withold not the lays
Which are due from you all in Combermere's praise!

To Charity's call his kind heart does expand,
To Masons, and all who are poor in the land;
God's blessing attend him on earth all his days,
And Free-masons respond in Combermere's praise.

While Combermere rules, let all Masons take part
In singing a chorus of joy from the heart;
When death calls him hence may Free-masons still raise
Their voices united in Combermere's praise.

CLIX.
(Tune, *When Phœbus the tops, &c*).

WHILE princes and heroes promiscuously fight,
    And for the world's empire exert all their might,
We sit in our lodges, from danger secure,
No hardships we meet with, no pains we endure;
    But each brother cheerfully joins in a song:
        Our rites we renew,
        Our pleasures pursue;
    Thus we waft time along.

To restless ambition we never give way,
Our friends and our secrets we never betray:
Henceforth, O ye heroes, your ravages cease,
And the laurels ye wear to Free-masons release;
Tho'ye won them by warfare, we claim them by peace,
    They are ours, they are still ours.
Tho' ye won them by warfare, we claim them by peace.

CLX.

(Tune, *Derry Down*).

WHOEVER wants wisdom must with some delight
    Read, ponder, and pore noon, morning, and night;
Must turn over volumes of monstrous size,
Enlighten his mind, tho he put out his eyes.
    Derry down, down, down, derry down.

If a general would know how to muster his men,
By a thousand, a hundred, by fifty, by ten;
Or level his siege on high castle or town,
He must borrow his precepts from men of renown.
    Derry down, &c.

Would a wry-fac'd physician or lawyer excel,
In haranguing a court, or the sick making well;
He first must read Galen or Littleton through,
Ere he get his credentials, or business to do.
    Derry down, &c.

But these are all follies, Free-masons can prove,
In the lodge they find knowledge, fair virtue and love;
Without deafening their ears, without blinding their eyes,
They find the compendious way to be wise.
    Derry down, &c.

CLXI.

WITH plumb, level, and square, let us prepare,
 And join in a sweet harmony;
Then fill up each glass, and round let it pass,
 To all honest men that are free.

CHORUS.

 A fig for those who are Free-masons' foes,
  Our secrets we'll never impart;
 But in unity let's always agree,
  And chorus it—Prosper our Art.

Being properly clothed, the Master discloses
 The secret that's lodged in his breast;
Firm to the cause that deserves such applause,
 In which we are happily blest.
    Cho.—A fig for those, &c.

The bible's our guide, and by that we abide,
 Which shows that our actions are pure;
The compass and square are emblems most rare
 Of justice, our cause to ensure.
    Cho.—A fig for those, &c.

True brotherly love we always approve,
 Which makes us all mortals excel;
Should knaves then, by chance, to this science advance,
 Such men with one voice we'll expel.
    Cho.—A fig for those, &c.

Our lodge that's so pure to the end will endure,
 In virtue and true secrecy;
Then toast a good health, that honour and wealth,
 May attend him whose hands made us free.
    Cho.—Then a fig for all those, &c.

CLXII.

(Tune, *Ye mortals that love drinking*).

YE ancient sons of Tyre,
    In chorus join with me,
And imitate your sire,
    Who was fam'd for Masonry!
His ancient dictates follow,
    And from them never part;
Let each sing like Apollo,
    And praise the royal art.

Like Salem's second story,
    We raise the Craft again,
Which still retains its glory;
    The secrets here remain
Amongst true ancient Masons,
    Who always will disdain
Those new invented fashions
    Which we all know are vain.

Our temples now rebuilding,
    You see grand columns rise,
The Magi they resembling,
    They are both good and wise;
Each seems as firm as Atlas,
    Who on his shoulders bore
The starry frame of heaven,
    What mortals can do more?

Come, now, my loving brethren,
    In chorus join all round,
With flowing wine, full bumpers,
    Let Masons' healths be crowned;
And let each envious cowan
    By our good actions see,
That we're made free and friendly
    By art of Masonry.

CLXIII.

THE SECRETARY'S SONG.

(Tune, *To all ye ladies now on land*).

YE brethren of the ancient Craft,
    Ye fav'rite sons of fame,
Let bumpers cheerfully be quaff'd
    To each good Mason's name:
Happy, long happy may he be,
Who loves and honours Masonry.
        With a fa, la, la, la, &c.

Ye British fair, for beauty fam'd,
    Your slaves we wish to be;
Let none for charms like yours be nam'd,
    That loves not Masonry.
This maxim has been proved full well,
That Masons never kiss and tell.
        With a fa, la, &c.

Free-masons, no offences give,
    Let fame your worth declare;
Within your compass wisely live,
    And act upon the square.
May Peace and Friendship e'er abound,
And ev'ry Mason's health go round.
        With a fa, la, &c.

CLXIV.

(Tune, *Rural Felicity*).

YE dull stupid mortals, give o'er your conjectures,
    Since Free-masons' secrets ye ne'er can obtain;
The bible and compasses are our directors,
    And shall be as long as this world doth remain:
Here friendship inviting, here freedom delighting,
    Our moments in innocent mirth we employ.

CHORUS.

Come, see Masons' felicity,
    Working and singing with hearts full of joy.

No other society that you can mention,
    Which has been, is now, or hereafter shall be,
However commendable be its intention,
    Can ever compare with divine Masonry.
No envy, no quarrels, can here blast our laurels,
    No passion our pleasure can ever annoy.
              Cho.—Come, see, &c.

To aid one another we always are ready,
    Our rites and our secrets we carefully guard;
The lodge to support, we like pillars are steady,
    No Babel confusion our work can retard.
YE mortals, come hither, assemble together,
    And taste of those pleasures which never can cloy.
              Cho.—*Come, see,* &c.

We are to the Master for ever obedient,
    Whenever he calls to the lodge we repair;
Experience has taught us that 'tis most expedient
    To live within compass and act on the square;
Let mutual agreement be Free-masons' cement
    Until the whole universe Time shall destroy.
              Cho.—*Come, see,* &c.

CLXV.

By Bro. Samuel Porter, *Henley-in Arden.*

(Tune, *A Rose-tree in full bearing*).

YE free-born sons of Britain's isle,
    Attend while I the truth impart,
And show that you are in exile,
    'Till science guides you by our art;
Uncultivated paths you tread,
    Unlevell'd, barren, blindfold be,
'Till by a mystery you are led
    Into the light of Masonry.

From chaos this round globe was form'd,
    A pedestal for us to be,
A mighty column it adorn'd,
    In just proportion raised were we;
When our Grand Architect above,
    An arch soon rais'd by His decree,
And placed the sun the arch key-stone,
    The whole was formed by Masonry.

It pleased our Sov'reign Master then
    This glorious fabric to erect,
Upon the square let us, as men,
    Never the noble work neglect;
But still in friendship's bonds unite
    Unbounded as infinity;
'Tis a sure corner-stone fix'd right,
    And worthy of Free-masonry.

In ancient times, before the flood,
    And since, in friendship we've adher'd,
From pole to pole have firmly stood,
    And by all nations been rever'd.

When rolling years shall cease to move,
    We from oblivion raised shall be;
Then, since we're met in peace and love,
    Let's sing "All hail to Masonry!"

CLXVI.

(Tune, *I'll weave him a garland*).

YE Masons, come, join with a friend and true brother,
    The praise of Free-masonry loud to proclaim;
May charity reign in the breast of each other,
    As long as the Masons their freedom maintain.

CHORUS.

Let justice direct you, and prudence correct you,
    May faith, hope, and charity, in pure sincerity,
    For ever unite you in brotherly love.

A Mason's a friend to the naked and needy,
    The orphan he clothes, and the widow relieves;
To assist in all wants no one is more speedy,
    To each worthy object his mite freely gives.
        Cho.—Let justice direct you, &c.

May no party faction nor discord e'er enter
    In Free-masons' lodges, so ancient and pure,
But may virtue always be fix'd in the centre,
    'Twill bind you so firm, and will link you secure.
        Cho.—Let justice direct you, &c.

Here's a health to all Masons, wherever dispers'd,
    May they find both comfort and speedy relief;
If they ever know sorrow, may they soon be releas'd
    From danger, from trouble, from affliction or grief.
        Cho.—Let justice direct you, &c.

CLXVII.

(Tune, *O Polly, you might have toy'd and kiss'd*).

YE people who laugh at Masons, draw near,
    Attend to my ballad without any sneer,
And if you'll have patience, you shall soon see
What a fine art is Masonry.

There's none but an atheist can ever deny
But that this art came first from on high;
    The Almighty Architect I'll prove to be,
    The first great Master of Masonry.

He took up His compass with masterly hand,
He stretch'd out His rule, and He measur'd the land;
    He laid the foundation of earth and sea,
    By His known rules of Masonry.

Our first father, Adam, deny it who can,
A Mason was made as soon as a man;
    And a fig-leaf apron at first wore he,
    In token of love to Masonry.

The principal laws our lodge does approve,
Is, that we still live in brotherly love;
    Thus Cain was banish'd by heaven's decree,
    For breaking the rules of Masonry.

The temple that wise King Solomon rais'd,
For beauty, for order, for elegance prais'd,
   To what did it owe all its elegancy?
   To the just form'd rules of Masonry.

But should I pretend in this humble verse
The merits of Free-masons' art to rehearse,
   Years yet to come too little would be
   To sing the praises of Masonry.

Then, hoping I have not detained you too long,
I here shall take leave to finish my song,
   With a health to the Master, and those who are free,
   That live by the rules of Masonry.

CLXVIII.

(Tune, *Mulberry tree*).

YE Sons of fair Science, impatient to learn,
   What's meant by a Mason you here may discern;
He strengthens the weak, he gives light to the blind,
And the naked he clothes—is a friend to mankind.

   All shall yield to Masonry;
     Bend to thee,
     Blest Masonry;
  Matchless was he who founded thee,
  And thou, like him, immortal shalt be.

He walks on the level of honour and truth,
And spurns the wild passions of folly and youth;
The compass and square all his frailties reprove,
And his ultimate oblect is brotherly love.

The temple of knowledge he nobly doth raise,
Supported by wisdom, and learning its base;
When rear'd and adorn'd, strength and beauty unite,
And he views the fair structure with conscious delight.

With fortitude bless'd, he's a stranger to fears;
And, govern'd by prudence, he cautiously steers;
Till Temperance shows him the port of content,
And Justice, unask'd, gives the sign of consent.

Inspired by his feelings, he bounty imparts,
For charity ranges at large in our hearts;
And an indigent brother, relieved from his woes,
Feels a pleasure inferior to him who bestows.

Thus a Mason I've drawn and exposed to your view;
And truth must acknowledge the figure is true;
Then members become, let's be brothers and friends,
There's a secret remaining will make you amends.

CLXIX.

YE thrice happy few
    Whose hearts have been true,
In concord and unity found;
    Let us sing and rejoice,
    And unite every voice
To send the gay chorus around.

CHORUS.

    Like pillars we stand,
    An immoveable band,
Cemented by power from above;
    Then freely let pass
    The generous glass,
To Masonry, friendship, and love.

The Grand Architect,
Whose word did erect
Eternity, measure and space,
First laid the fair plan
Whereon He began
The cement of friendship and peace.
   Cho.—Like pillars, &c.

Whose firmness of hearts,
Fair treasure of arts,
To the eye of the vulgar unknown;
Whose lustre can beam
New splendour and fame
To the pulpit, the bar, and the throne.
   Cho.—Like pillars, &c.

The great David's son,
The wise Solomon,
As written in scripture's bright page,
A Mason became,
The fav'rite of fame,
The wonder and pride of his age.
   Cho.—Like pillars, &c.

Indissoluble bands
Our hearts and our hands
In social benevolence bind;
For true to his cause,
By immutable laws,
A Mason's a friend to mankind.
   Cho—Like pillars, &c.

Let joy flow around,
And peace, olive bound,
Preside at our mystical rites;

  Whose conduct maintains
  Our auspicious domains,
And freedom with order unites.
    Cho.—Like pillars, &c.

  Nor let the dear maid
  Our mysteries dread,
Or think them repugnant to love;
  To beauty we bend,
  Her empire defend,
An empire deriv'd from above.
    Cho.—Like pillars, &c.

  Then let us unite,
  Sincere and upright,
On the level of virtue to stand;
  No mortal can be
  So happy as we,
With a brother and friend in each hand.
    Cho.—Like pillars, &c.

CLXX.

(Tune, *By Jove, we'll be free*).

YOUR slumber is over, now cheerfully view,
 What monarchs hold secret is conveyed to you;
What Noah preserved in a world of sea,
You have in perfection, for ever obey.

CHORUS.

Rejoice, my dear brother, remember the love
We Masons enjoy from our Guardian above.

The seeds of old darkness encumber the mind,
And keep in subjection th' unwilling and blind:
A part from that portion of darkness you have seen,
You're elected and chosen as th' prophets have been.
                    Cho.—Rejoice, &c.

There ne'er was a secret in council or trade
But time and corruption a conquest have made;
But what Free-masons in union conceal,
No mortal yet living can find or reveal.
                    Cho.—Rejoice, &c.

What pleasure can equal the pleasures we have?
In the secrets we honour none can us deceive;
It's a breast-plate of wisdom, undivided and pure,
To remain with Free-masons while time shall endure.
                    Cho.—Rejoice, &c.

All Greece did admire, and the Hebrews of old,
Bezeleel's great knowledge and wisdom in gold;
The surprising performance of Hiram the brave,
Both Masons endued with the secrets you have.
                    Cho.—Rejoice, &c.

With raptures unconquered let your praise ascend,
And loudly applaud both your Maker and Friend;
All hail to JEHOVAH! who elected you one,
Belov'd and respected like the Widow's Son.
                    Cho.—Rejoice, &c.

CANTATAS.

I.

Set to Music by HIGHMORE SKEATS.

RECITATIVE.

ONCE on earth immortal Jove
　　Descended from the realms above,
To seek the virtues, and to find
Their estimation 'mongst mankind;
The court, the cottage, he surveyed;
No graces found, th' immortal said.

AIR.

Morality, return to Jove;
　　And bring with thee
　　Sweet secrecy,
Morality, brotherly love,
And all the other virtues too;
　　For here below
　　There are few that know
That happiness consists in you.

RECITATIVE.

Jove had sung on, if he'd not seen
Morality, bright virtue's queen,
Attended by her social train
Come tripping o'er the verdant plain.
Jove flew to press them to his breast;
The Virtues thus the god request:—

AIR.

Immortal Jove! resign thy throne,
    And with us go
    Where thou wilt know
One very far excels thy own;
Where real pleasures always flow,
    And we are blest,
    By all caressed,
And happy in our state below.

RECITATIVE.

The god consents, and soon was found
Within the lodge's sacred ground,
A lodge of Masons, just and free;
He heard their lectures, saw their glee:
The god, surprised, with joy possess'd,
In raptures thus the lodge address'd:—

AIR.

Happy mortals! thus possessing
    Just employment,
    True enjoyment,
Crown'd with every earthly blessing:
From hence the virtues can't depart;
    For here alone
    I'll fix their throne,
In every Mason's faithful heart,

II.

By Brother WILLIAM STOKES.

RECITATIVE.

SILENT the pipe had lain, neglected long,
The muse uncourted, and the lyre unstrung;
Poetic fire sunk to a latent spark,
'Till rais'd by *Rancliffe*—for its theme the Ark;
(The Ark to whom we all existence owe)
And gracious promise of the varied bow.

AIR.

When, in his ark of gopher-wood,
Noah rode buoyant on the flood,
O'erwhelm'd with sad despair and woe,
A guilty race sunk down below.
With blest omnipotence its guide,
The mastless ark did safely ride,
And on the mount, from danger free,
Did rest the whole fraternity.

RECITATIVE.

The floods decrease, and now with joy are seen
The hills and valleys in their wonted green :
The altar smokes, the fervent prayer ascends,
And heav'n, well pleas'd, to man's request attends!
The grand ethereal bow is form'd above,
Sure token of beneficence and love.

AIR.

Look round the gay parterre,
 Where fragrant scents arise,
And beauteous flowrets there
 Enchanting meet your eyes:

    Delightful streak or shade
        In native colours glow;
    Yet is no hue display'd
        That shines not in the bow.

    In leafy umbrage green,
        Sweet blows the violet;
    And in the hyacine
        With deeper blue is met.
    How various are the shades
        That in our gardens blow!
    Yet not a tint's display'd
        That shines not in the bow.

DUETS.

I.

Written by MR. PECK, *and introduced by Brother* JOHN COLE, P.M.

(Tune, *Begone dull care!*).

ALL hail, blest Craft! hail Masonry divine!
All hail, blest Craft! how bright thy glories shine!
  Tho' fools against our order prate,
   And stigmatize our skill;
  I hold it one of the wisest things,
   To be a good Mason still.

All hail, blest Craft! while by thy light inspired,
We live by square—by all wise men admir'd;
  Let those who know not our designs,
   Abuse us if they will;
  We hold it one of the wisest things
   To be good Masons still.

All hail, blest Craft! long may thy glories shine
Thro' all the world, and prove the art divine;
  From east to west may all mankind,
   Thy dictates mild fulfil;
  And ev'ry brother hold it wise,
   To be a good Mason still.

II.

CHECK the growing, idle passion,
    Only built on inclination;
Then alone it reigns complete,
When mutual love and prudence meet.

CHORUS.

    Wisdom shall o'er this lodge preside,
    While Harmony our actions guide;
    Friendship is here, a sacred tie,
    And Masonry shall never die.

Curb each thriving perturbation,
Issuing from a base foundation:
Cherish ye that zealous fire,
Which here true Masons' hearts inspire.
        Cho.—Wisdom shall o'er, &c.

Those revere who do their duty,
In this lodge of Strength and Beauty,
Where unerring Wisdom reigns,
And where true Friendship still remains.
        Cho.—Wisdom shall o'er, &c.

III.

(Tune, *In Infancy*).

HAIL, Masonry! thou sacred art,
    Of origin divine!
Kind partner of each social heart,
    And fav'rite of the Nine!

By thee we're taught our acts to square,
  To measure life's short span,
And each infirmity to bear
  That's incident to man.
            Cho.—By thee, &c.

Tho' envy's tongue should blast thy fame,
  And ignorance may sneer,
Yet still thy ancient, honour'd name
  Is to each brother dear.
Then strike the blow, to charge prepare!
  In this we all agree,
"May freedom be each Mason's care,
  "And every Mason free."
            Cho.—Then strike the blow, &c.

IV.

Written by MR. CUNNINGHAM.

(Tune, *In Infancy*).

LET Masonry from pole to pole
    Her sacred laws expand,
Far as the mighty waters roll,
    To wash remotest land.
That virtue has not left mankind
    Her social maxims prove:
For stamp'd upon the Mason's mind
    Are unity and love.

Ascending to her native sky,
    Let Masonry increase;
A glorious pillar rais'd on high,
    Integrity its base.

Peace adds to olive bows, entwin'd,
   An emblematic dove,
As stamp'd upon the Mason's mind
   Are unity and love.

V.

ALL'S RIGHT.

A Masonic Parody on the Duet of "All's Well." Written by Bro. HENRY LEE, *author of "Poetic Impressions," "Caleb Quotem," &c.*

PROTECTED by the master power,
   In life's high noon, or final hour,
As one grand lodge the world is found,
And all mankind as brothers bound;
Their secrets form a moral store,
The Tyler, silence, guards the door.
Who comes there?—a stranger seeks the light,
The sign?—Your hand—The word?—All's right.

Depending on Masonic aid,
By line and compass level made,
The Master draws the social plan,
And calls to labour every man;
While Truth her great foundation lays,
And, by degrees, we merit raise.
Who's there?—A brother claims the light
In hand and heart.—The word?—All's right.
Both high and low—All's right.

VI.

By Brother JOHN COLE.

THE lodge being form'd,
    Each heart now is warm'd
For improvement—a Mason's first care;
    Let each brother and friend
    To the lecture attend,
Then for social enjoyment prepare.
    Then cheerful the Craft all agree,
    For union and order pervade Masonry.

    See the ladder arise
    From the earth to the skies,
Which to mount every true Mason strives;
    By fresh excellence crown'd,
    As they climb every round,
While by compass they quadrate their lives.
    For order by heav'n is design'd
    To give joy to the heart, and improvement the
      mind.

    Each lodge is a seat
    Where the virtues retreat;
Where the muses in harmony join;
    Where discord ne'er treads,
    Nor its influence sheds;
While of order we keep to the line.
    For order supports every plan;
    'Tis the first law of heav'n, and the comfort of man.

VII.

(Tune, *When Phœbus the tops, &c.*)

WHILE princes and heroes promiscuously fight,
    And for the world's empire exert all their might,
We sit in our lodges, from danger secure,
No hardships we meet with, no pains we endure;
    But each brother cheerfully joins in a song:
        Our rites we renew,
        Our pleasures pursue;
    Thus we waft time along.

To restless ambition we never give way,
Our friends and our secrets we never betray:
Henceforth, O ye heroes, your ravages cease,
And the laurels ye wear to Free-masons release;
Tho' ye won them by warfare, we claim them by peace,
    They are ours, ours, ours, ours, ours:
Tho' ye won them by warfare, we claim them by peace.

ANTHEMS.

I.

Composed by Brother WESLEY.

BEHOLD! how good a thing it is,
    And how becoming well,
For brethren, such as Masons are,
    In unity to dwell.

Oh! 'tis like ointment on the head;
    Or dew on Sion's hill!
For then, the Lord of Hosts hath said,
    Peace shall be with you still.

II.

Sung at the Consecration of St. Andrew's Lodge, Kilmarnock.

(Tune, *Birks of Invermay*).

BLEST Masonry! thy arts divine,
    With light and truth inform the mind,
The virtues in thy temples shine,
    To polish and adorn mankind;
Sprightly pleasures, social love,
    In thy triumphant domes unite;
'Tis these thy gallant sons improve,
    And gild the day, and cheer the night.

Dark bigots may with anger gaze,
    And fools pretend thy rites to blame,
But worth is still deserving praise,
    And Pallas' self will speak thy fame.
Apollo bids the tuneful choir
    Prepare their songs, and sweetly sing;
The music sounds from every lyre,
    And all the hills with pæans ring.

The pure, unrivall'd joys of life,
    Love and friendship 'mongst us reign;
We banish discord far, and strife
    From Masonry! thy blest domain.
As in fair nature's works, the whole
    Is mov'd with harmony and art,
So order sanctifies the soul,
    And truth and candour warm the heart.

This night another dome we raise,
    And consecrate to Hiram's laws;
Let all unite, your voices raise,
    Sing triumph to the glorious cause.
We scorn the blind's censorious pride,
    Masons united ever stand;
Nor guilt nor faction can divide
    The faithful and illustrious band.

III.

Sung by Brother OATES, *in "The Generous Freemason," 1731.*

BY Masons' art the aspiring dome
    On stately columns shall arise;
All climates are their native home,
    Their godlike actions reach the skies.

Heroes and kings revere their name,
While poets sing their lasting fame.

Great, noble, generous, good, and brave,
    Are titles they may justly claim;
Their deeds shall live beyond the grave,
    And those unborn their praise proclaim.
Time shall their glorious acts enrol,
While love and friendship charm the soul.

IV.

GRANT us, kind heav'n, what we request,
    In Masonry let us be blest;
Direct us to that happy place
Where friendship smiles in every face;
    Where freedom and sweet innocence
    Enlarge the mind and cheer the sense.

Where sceptred reason, from her throne,
Surveys the lodge, and makes us one;
And harmony's delightful sway
For ever sheds ambrosial day:
    Where we blest Eden's pleasure taste,
    Whilst balmy joys are our repast.

No prying eye can view us here,
No fool or knave disturb our cheer;
Our well-form'd laws set mankind free,
And give relief to misery:
    The poor, oppressed with woe and grief,
    Gain from our bounteous hands relief.

Our lodge the social virtues grace,
And wisdom's rules we fondly trace;
Whole nature, open to our view,
Points out the paths we should pursue.
    Let us subsist in lasting peace,
    And may our happiness increase.

V.

"LET there be Light"—the Almighty spoke,
    Refulgent streams from chaos broke,
    To illume the rising earth!
Well pleas'd the great Jehovah stood—
The power supreme pronounc'd it good,
    And gave the planets birth!

    CHORUS.

    In choral numbers Masons join,
    To bless and praise this Light Divine.

Parent of Light! accept our praise!
Who shedd'st on us Thy brightest rays,
    The light that fills his mind.
By choice selected, lo! we stand,
By friendship join'd, a social band
    That love—that aid mankind!
        Cho.—In choral numbers, &c.

The widow's tear—the orphan's cry—
All wants our ready hands supply,
    As far as power is given!
The naked clothe—the prisoner free—
These are thy works sweet Charity!
    Reveal'd to us from heaven!
        Cho.—In choral numbers, &c.

VI.

O MASONRY! our hearts inspire,
And warm us with thy sacred fire;
Make us obedient to thy laws,
And zealous to support thy cause;
    For thou and virtue are the same,
    And only differ in the name.

Pluck narrow notions from the mind,
And plant the love of human kind:
Teach us to feel a brother's woe,
And, feeling, comfort to bestow;
    Let none unheeded draw the sigh,
    No grief unnotic'd pass us by.

Let swelling Pride a stranger be,
Our friend, composed Humility.
Our hands let steady Justice guide,
And Temp'rance at our boards preside;
    Let Secrecy our steps attend,
    And injured worth our tongues defend.

Drive meanness from us, fly deceit,
And calumny, and rigid hate:
Oh! may our highest pleasure be
To add to man's felicity:
    And may we, as thy votaries true,
    Thy paths, O Masonry, pursue.

VII.

FUNERAL HYMN.

By Brother PAUL THACKWELL *of the Vitruvian Lodge, Ross, No 644.*

O MIGHTY Architect of heaven and earth!
    To Thee united heart and voice we raise;
Thou who preserv'st us from our earliest birth,
    To Thee we sing our mournful hymn of praise.
        With sacred reverence to Thy awful nod,
        We prostrate fall before Thy throne, O God!

With downcast eyes, while bending o'er the bier,
    That shrouds our much lov'd brother from our view,
Let faith, which only sanctifies the tear,
    Enrich the drops that his remains bedew;
        Ever rememb'ring who 'twas gave the blow,
        The Mighty Ruler of all things below.

The valued friend, and the companion dear,
    May justly claim the sympathetic sigh;
But Thou bast taught us never to despair,
    Thou hast decreed that all of us must die.
        Then to Thy holy name all praise be given,
        Praise to the Lord of earth and highest heaven.

Since sorrow for the dead will prove but vain,
    Our love by resignation let us prove,
In hope that we shall sometime meet again,
    In realms of endless happiness above.
        Then let us to our God our voices raise,
        To whom belongs all glory, might, and praise.

VIII.

By HENRY DAGGE, ESQ., *sung at the Founding of Freemasons' Hall.*

(Tune, *Rule, Britannia*).

TO heaven's high Architect all praise,
    All praise, all gratitude be given;
Who deign'd the human soul to raise,
    By mystic secrets sprung from heaven.

CHORUS.

Sound aloud the great Jehovah's praise,
To Him the dome, the temple raise.

IX.

Meter—THE tooth PSALM.

WITH friendly aid let us unite
    Our souls, and give our Maker praise,
Who gave us this superior light,
    Let us to Him our voices raise.

Then, great Jehovah! God and Lord!
    Divine Immanuel! send us down
Thy chiefest blessings to accord
    And worship Thee—and Thee alone.

Let all Thy servants here on earth,
    In love and friendship ever dwell;
Thou King of Worlds, great Source of Birth;
    Can finite man Thy bounties tell?

Thou Architect of worlds unknown,
    Great Builder of ten thousand orbs,
Who with a fiat made the sun,
    And with a nod the ocean curbs.

Thy blessings sure on us will wait,
    Who live like brethren—free and good;
True social harmony's a state
    By few but Masons understood.

Unless we love our brethren—know and see;
    Whom we converse with—know and see;
Can we frail creatures love afford,
    Or worship—or due praise to Thee?

All hallelujahs to Thy name,
    While on this earth we'll raise on high!
And then that heavenly lodge we'll claim,
    Far—far remov'd beyond the sky.

To Thee, the true and living Lord,
    Whom heaven and every world adore,
All hail! ye brethren—and accord
    In praising Him for evermore.

ODES.

I.

For an Exaltation of Royal Arch Masons.

By Brother DUNCKERLEY.

(Tune, *Rule, Britannia*).

ALMIGHTY Sire! our heavenly King,
   Before whose sacred name we bend,
Accept the praises which we sing,
   And to our humble prayer attend!

CHORUS.

   All hail, great Architect divine!
   This universal frame is Thine.

Thou who did'st Persia's king command,
   A proclamation to extend,
That Israel's sons might quit his land,
   Their holy temple to attend.
        Cho.—All hail! &c.

That sacred place where three in one
   Comprised Thy comprehensive name;
And where the bright meridian sun
   Was soon Thy glory to proclaim.
        Cho.—All hail! &c.

Thy watchful eye, a length of time
    The wond'rous circle did attend;
The glory and the power be Thine,
    Which shall from age to age descend.
        Cho.—All hail! &c.

On Thy omnipotence we rest,
    Secure of Thy protection here;
And hope hereafter to be blest,
    When we have left this world of care.
        Cho.—*All hail! &c.*

Grant us, great God! Thy powerful aid,
    To guide us through this vale of tears;
For where Thy goodness is display'd,
    Peace soothes the mind, and pleasure cheers.
        Cho.—*All hail! &c.*

Inspire us with Thy grace divine,
    Thy sacred law our guide shall be;
To every good our hearts incline,
    From every evil keep us free.
        Cho.—All hail! &c.

II.

(Tune, *My fond Shepherd*).

ASSIST me, ye fair tuneful Nine,
    Euphrosyne, grant me thy aid,
While the honours. I sing of the trine,
    Preside o'er my numbers, blithe maid!
Cease, clamour and faction, oh cease!
    Fly hence all ye cynical train;
Disturb not the lodge's sweet peace,
    Where silence and secrecy reign.

Religion untainted here dwells,
    Here the morals of Athens are taught;
Great Hiram's tradition here tells
    How the world out of chaos was brought.
With fervency, freedom, and zeal,
    Our Master's commands we obey;
No cowan our secrets can steal,
    No babbler our myst'ries betray.

Here Wisdom her standard displays,
    Here nobly the sciences shine;
Here the temple's vast column we raise,
    And finish a work that's divine.
Illum'd from the east with pure light,
    Here arts do their blessings bestow;
And, all perfect, unfold to the sight
    What none but a Mason can know.

If on earth any praise can be found,
    Any virtue unnam'd in my song,
Any grace in the universe round,
    May these to a Mason belong!
May each brother his passions subdue,
    Proclaim charity, concord, and love;
And be hail'd by the thrice happy few
    Who preside in the grand lodge above!

III.

By Brother JOHN CARTWRIGHT, *of Cheadle, in Lancashire.*

RECITATIVE.

BLEST be the day that gave to me
  The secrets of Free-masonry;
In that alone my pleasure's plac'd,
In that alone let me be grac'd;
No greater titles let me bear,
Than those pertaining to the square.

AIR.

Tho' envious mortals vainly try
On us to call absurdity,
  We laugh at all their spleen;
The levell'd man, the upright heart,
Shall still adorn our glorious art,
  Nor mind their vile chagrin:
The ermin'd robe, the reverend crozier too,
Have proved us noble, honest, just, and true.

CHORUS.

In vain then let prejudiced mortals declare
Their hate of us Masons, we're truly sincere;
If for that they despise us, their folly they prove,
For a Mason's grand maxim is brotherly love:
But yet, after all, if they'd fain be thought wise,
Let them enter the lodge, and we'll open their eyes.

IV.

Performed by Brothers MEREDITH, EVANCE, &c., *at the Dedication of the Phœnix Lodge, in Sunderland, April 5, 1785. The words by* DR. BROWN. *The music by Brother* SHIELD.

RECITATIVO.

BRING me, ye sacred choir, the deep ton'd shell,
  To which sublime Isaiah sung so well;
To Masonry exalt the strain sublime,
And waft her praises on the wings of time.
Thy lore to sing shall be the care of fame—
And, hark! she gives assent, and chants each honour'd name.

AIR.

I.

Sound the full harmonious song:
To Masonry divine the strain prolong:
And first the grateful tribute bring
To the great, the sapient king,
Who, inspir'd by power divine,
Made wisdom, strength, and beauty all combine
To frame, confirm, and deck the vast design!

II.

And now we mourn, alas! too late
The sad, the melancholy fate
Of him whom virtue could not save!
Cloth'd in virgin innocence,
Attend, ye craftsmen, and dispense
Your choicest flowers around the Tyrian's grave.

RECITATIVO SECUNDO.

Hail, social science! eldest born of heaven,
To soothe the brow of sad misfortune given;
To raise the soul, and gen'rous warmth impart;
To fix the noblest purpose in the heart;
To thee we owe, in this degenerate age,
Those mystic links which hearts engage.

AIR.
I.

Band of friendship! best cement
   Of social minds in brothers' love,
Far hence be envy, discontent,
   And every ill which mortals prove.

No dark suspicion harbours here,
But all is open, all sincere:
No base informer listens to betray,
But all is sunshine, all is day.

CHORUS.

No base informer listens to betray,
But all is sunshine, all is day.

II.

But now to thee, fair pity's child,
Sweet Charity, of aspect mild,
   Thy tributary lay is due:
Vain are the joys of hoarded wealth
To thine; thou giv'st the rosy bloom of health
   To sad affliction's pallid hue!
These blessings, Masonry, are thine;
Hail, sacred science!—mystery divine!

CHORUS.

These blessings, Masonry, are thine;
Hail, sacred science!—mystery divine!

GRAND CHORUS.

Thou holy mystery! first Almighty cause!
To thee the great Creator fram'd His laws,
When chaos heard th' Almighty fiat rung,
And sacred order from confusion sprung!
    The waters, now collected, flow'd,
    And as they murmur'd own'd the God.
    The mighty planets now He plac'd,
        Which, still revolving, speak His praise;
    This earth He fram'd, with seasons grac'd,
        With heat inform'd, each useful plant to raise.

The sun He fix'd, the central soul,
To animate the mighty whole,
Harmonious, regular they move,
Just emblem of fraternal love.
The laws of Masonry are nature's laws:
Hail, sacred mystery!—first Almighty cause!

V.

By Brother J. BANKS.

(Tune, *Goddess of Ease*).

GENIUS of Masonry! descend
    In mystic numbers while we sing;
Enlarge our souls, the craft defend,
    And hither all thy influence bring.
Cho.—With social thoughts our bosoms fill,
    And give thy turn to ev'ry will.

While yet Batavia's wealthy pow'rs
    Neglect thy beauties to explore;

And winding Seine, adorn'd with towers,
    Laments thee wand'ring from his shore;
Cho.—Here spread thy wings, and glad these isles,
    Where arts reside, and freedom smiles.

Behold the lodge rise into view,
    The work of industry and art;
'Tis grand, and regular, and true,
    For so is each good Mason's heart.
Cho.—Friendship cements it from the ground,
    And secrecy shall fence it round.

A stately dome o'erlooks our east,
    Like orient Phœbus in the morn;
And two tall pillars in the west
    At once support us and adorn.
Cho.—Upholden thus the structure stands,
    Untouched by sacrilegious hands.

For concord form'd, our souls agree,
    Nor fate this union shall destroy:
Our toils and sports alike are free,
    And all is harmony and joy.
Cho—So Salem's temple rose by rule,
    Without the noise of noxious tool.

As when Amphion tun'd his song,
    E'en rugged rocks the music knew;
Smooth'd into form they glide along,
    And to a Thebes the desert grew.
Cho.—So at the sound of Hiram's voice
    We rise, we join, and we rejoice.

Then may our voice to virtue move,
    To virtue own'd in all her parts:

Come, candour, innocence, and love,
    Come and possess our faithful hearts.
Cho.—Mercy, who feeds the hungry poor,

    And silence, guardian of the door.
And thou, Astrea, (tho' from earth
    When men on men began to prey,
Thou fledd'st to claim celestial birth)
    Down from Olympus wing thy way;
Cho.—And, mindful of thy ancient seat,
    Be present still where Masons meet.

Immortal Science, be thou near,
    (We own thy empire o'er the mind);
Dress'd in thy radiant robes appear,
    With all thy beauteous train behind;
Cho.—Invention young and blooming there,
    Here geometry with rule and square.

In Egypt's fabric* learning dwelt,
    And Roman breasts could virtue hide:
But Vulcan's rage the building felt,
    And Brutus, last of Romans, died:
Cho.—Since when, dispers'd, the sisters rove,
    Or fill paternal thrones above.

But, lost to half the human race,
    With us the virtues shall revive;
And, driv'n no more from place to place,
    Here science shall be kept alive:
Cho.—And manly taste, the child of sense,
    Shall banish vice and dulness hence.

---

*The Ptolomæan Library.

United thus, and for these ends,
    Let scorn deride, and envy rail;
From age to age the craft descends,
    And what we build shall never fail.
Cho.—Nor shall the world our works survey;
    But every brother keeps the key!

VI.

On certain Grand Lights in Masonry.

HAIL! beauteous lights, supremely fair!
    Whose smiles can calm the horrors of despair;
Bid in each breast unusual transport flow,
And wipe the tears that stain the cheek of woe:
How blest the man who quits each meaner scene,
Like thee exalted, smiling and serene!
Whose rising soul pursues a nobler flight;
Whose bosom melts with more refin'd delight;
Whose mind, elate with transports all sublime,
Can soar at once beyond the views of time;
'Till loos'd from earth, as angels unconfin'd,
It flies aërial on the darting wind;
Free as the keen-eyed eagle, bears away,
And mounts the regions of eternal day.

VII.
ON CHARITY.

By the REV. H. C. C. NEWMAN.

HAIL, brightest attribute of God above!
    Hail, purest essence of celestial love,!
Hail, sacred fountain of each bliss below!
Whose streams in sympathy unbounded flow.
'Tis thine, fair Charity, with lenient pow'r
To sooth distress, and cheer the gloomy hour;
To reconcile the dire, embitter'd foe,
And bid the heart of gall with friendship glow;
To smooth the rugged paths of thorny life,
And still the voice of dissonance and strife;
Abash'd, the vices at thy presence fly,
Nor stand the awful menace of that eye;
Hate, Envy, and Revenge in anguish bleed,
And all the virtues in their room succeed:
Attemper'd to the bloom of virgin grace,
See modest Innocence adorn that face:
To failings mild, to merit ever true,
See Candour each ungen'rous thought subdue!
See Patience smiling in severest grief,
See tender Pity stretching forth relief!
See meek Forgiveness bless the hostile mind,
See Faith and Hope in every state resign'd!
Happy! to whom indulgent heav'n may give
In such society as this to live.

VIII.

By Mr. Cunningham.

Hail to the craft! at whose serene command
    The gentle arts in glad obedience stand:
Hail, sacred Masonry! of source divine,
Unerring sov'reign of th' unerring line:
Whose plumb of truth, with never-failing sway,
Makes the join'd parts of symmetry obey:
Whose magic stroke bids fell confusion cease,
And to the finish'd orders gives a place:
Who rears vast structures from the womb of earth,
And gives imperial cities glorious birth.
    To works of Art her merit not confin'd,
She regulates the morals, squares the mind;
Corrects with care the sallies of the soul,
And points the tide of passion where to roll:
On virtue's tablet marks her moral rule,
And forms her lodge an universal school;
Where nature's mystic laws unfolded stand,
And sense and science, join'd, go hand in hand.
    O may her social rules instructive spread,
Till Truth erect her long neglected head!
Till through deceitful night she dart her ray,
And beam full glorious in the blaze of day!
Till men by virtuous maxims learn to move,
Till all the peopled world her laws approve,
And Adam's race are bound in brother's love.

IX.

By Brother DUNCKERLEY.   *For Solemn Ceremonies.*

(Tune, *God Save the King*).

HAIL, universal Lord!
By heaven and earth ador'd;
All hail, great God!
Before Thy name we bend,
To us Thy grace extend,
And to our prayer attend.
All hail, great God!

X.

LONG has the curious world, with prying eye,
Tried to find out the Mason's mystery,
But tried in vain, abortive thus their aim,
They join with one consent to damn our fame;
As fancy dictates each declares his thoughts,
And thus in various forms attack our faults:
The prudish matron vows 'tis strange, 'tis rude,
The ladies from our lodges to exclude.
What can it mean?—why sure there's something done
Which we should blush to see, and they to own;
The stuttering blockhead, aiming at grimace,
With mouth distorted, and unmeaning face,
Exclaims with transport he has got a hint,
And is convinc'd, egad! there's nothing in't.
Another, wiser than the rest, conjectures,
That though these Masons boast of private lectures,
He, for his part, believes it all a jest;
This and much more, too tedious to relate,
The talking gossips ignorantly prate;

While we, secure, on innocence rely,
And all their satire, wit, and spleen defy;
Conscious of this, we've no opprobious ends,
Are to the fair, to truth, and virtue friends;
And after all their wise conceits are weigh'd
Spite of the tales of Pritchard, Plot, and Slaid,
They ne'er can know how a Free-mason's made.

XI.

THE MASONS' LODGE.

LET others in exalted strains relate
 The baleful wars of some ambitious state,
By regal pride, or state intrigues begun,
With loss of each best subject carried on,
And which at last, with dreadful success crown'd,
Involve in ruin every state around;
Me, should the sacred Nine deign to inspire,
Amphion-like, to touch the warbling lyre,
Such themes unworthy of the muse I'd judge;
My peaceful muse should sing the Masons' Lodge,
Where friendship and benevolence combine,
T' enlarge the soul, and manners to refine;
Where cheerfulness beams forth in ev'ry face,
Upheld by joys that ne'er can feel decrease;
Whose happy and well regulated sway
Without compulsion Masons all obey.
Such happy themes with joy my muse should sing;
Earth, sea, and air, with loud acclaims should ring.
Nor would I e'er vain-gloriously pretend
To what I sung eternity to lend;
But rather hope for e'er to found my fame
On this my virtuous and well-chosen theme,

Whose ties shall last when nature shall decay,
Rocks be consumed, and mountains melt away;
States, empires, kingdoms, in confusion hurl'd,
All! all! shall perish with an ending world.

XII.

Ode to raising a Hall sacred to Masonry.

By Brother JOHN WILLIAMSON, *of London.*

NO more of trifling themes or vain
    My muse inwrapt shall sing,
Urania claims a nobler strain,
    A more expanded wing.
To Masonry exalt the joyful song,
Soft as the infant morn—yet as the subject—strong.

    Behold the sacred structure rise!
        On firm foundation laid,
    Where Solomon, the great and wise,
        His bounty first display'd:
    The Tyrian King materials brought,
        To aid the grand design,
    And Hiram Abiff's happy thought
        Completed it divine.
In wisdom, strength, and beauty see
The three grand orders happily agree.
    From hence, what blessings may arise
        By ev'ry brother's friendly aid!
    The fairest offspring of the skies,
        Kind Charity! all charming maid!
    Shall stretch her hand the poor to bless,
    And raise them up from deep distress;
    Banish each sorrow from the heart,
    And, like the good Samaritan, balm impart.

Hail, Masonry! to thee we raise
The song of triumph and of praise;
For surely unto thee belong
The highest note, the noblest song,
Whose arts with happiness delight,
And all like brethren unite.
    To noble Peter raise the strain,
    He bids the temple rise again,
    Him future Grands shall joyful own,
    Who laid the great foundation stone:
    Let us hands together join,
    Masonry's an art divine;
    Harmony supports the whole,
    Expands the heart, exalts the soul.
Thrice hail again, thou noble art!
That canst such mystic joys impart;
The sun which shines supreme on high,
The stars that glisten in the sky,
The moon that yields her silver light,
And vivifies the lonely night,
Must by the course of nature fade away,
And all the earth alike in time decay:
But while they last shall Masonry endure,
Built on such pillars, solid and secure;
And, at the last, sublime shall rise,
And seek its origin beyond the skies.

XIII.

Written by WALLER RODWELL WRIGHT, ESQ., *and Recited by Brother* POPE.

STROPHE I.

OH for a hand, whose magic pow'r
   Might wake the lyre of other days
To lofty and immortal lays,
  Such as in bold majestic swell
  Burst from the Theban's classic shell,
Where through Olympia's consecrated shade,
  Alpheus rolls his turbid course,
    That linger'd oft those shades among,
    And listen'd to the mighty song;
Or those melodious strains,
  Whose gentle but resistless force
Botia's very rocks obey'd,
What time amidst her wild and desert plains,
    The sacred dome and high embattled tow'r
    In self compacted order rose,
   And taught the wand'ring sons of Greece,
    Unfelt before, the happiness that flows
   From social union, harmony, and peace.

ANTISTROPHE I.

Or, rather, for that holy ecstacy,
  Which bade the royal bard of Jesse's line
Attune his harp's inspired minstrelsy
  To songs of seraphim, and themes divine.
    For, while in this auspicious hour,
  Our hands and hearts we thus unite,
And seek in closer folds to bind
    The compact of fraternal love,—
    The vow which angels might approve,—
Of peace and charity to all mankind;

While taught by faith, before the throne
    Of heaven's High Architect we bend,
With hope that rests on Him alone,
    While stars like these their radiance blend,
Their genial influence deign to pour
    On this, our high and solemn rite;
Like Sion's hallow'd strain the song should rise
That wafts our grateful tribute to the skies.

Epode I.

Vain is the hope! No master's hand
    To-day explores the breathing lyre;
    No gifted bard, whose heaven-imparted fire
Subdues the yielding soul to his command;
      But simple are the votive lays
      That breathe our gratitude and praise
      To that creative pow'r,
    Whose wisdom sketched the vast design
Of nature's universal plan;
    Whose mighty fiat o'er the realms of night,
    Shed the first glories of eternal light;
      Whose spirit, hov'ring on the vast profound,
    Laid the foundations sure and wide,
    By truth's unerring, geometric line,
    Above, below, on every side,
      Life, harmony, and beauty breath'd around;
The orbs of heaven their circling course began;
      And angels hail'd creation's natal hour.

Strophe II.

One last and greatest work remain'd—
    Hush'd was the strain: in silent awe
    The host of heaven with wonder saw
    The cold and senseless mass that lay,
    Unform'd, amidst its native clay,

    Now kindling with a spark divine,
   True to the laws of that mysterious spell,
Which binds in one concordant chain
The earth, the air, the ambient main,
      Its latent powers unfold—
   Each limb in due proportion swell,
      In beauteous symmetry combine
      To frame a structure of immortal mould.
But when in this fair form its Maker deign'd
   To breathe an intellectual soul;
      Then first the angelic hymn began,
Which the bright spheres still echo as they roll,
   Glory to God in heav'n, and peace to man.

            ANTISTROPHE II.

And shall the heir of immortality,
   Alone regardless of this high behest,
Quench the celestial glow of charity
      Which heav'nly love hath kindled in his breast?
         Perverting reason's holy light
         Deny the pow'r by which 'twas given?
      Or arrogantly deem it just,
         To close, with wild, fanatic hate,
         Fair mercy's everlasting gate
         Against his erring brother of the dust?
Far, far, from such unhallow'd strife,
   In man a kindred soul we view,
To all who share the ills of life,
   Our pity and relief are due:
Nor ask we what religious rite
Conveys his orisons to heaven,
      Enough for us if comfort we impart,
      Or soothe the anguish of a broken heart.

Epode II

Lo! where our silent emblems breathe
    Their sacred influence o'er the soul,
    In mystic order ranged: while round the whole
A starry zone the sister virtues wreathe.
    Ye, who by compass, square, and line,
    Those hidden truths can well divine,—
        To all besides unknown—
In each symbolic form pourtray'd:
Ye, who with firm, undaunted mind,
Have pierc'd the vaulted cavern's awful gloom,
And mark'd the holy secrets of the tomb;
Still let your actions to the world proclaim
The secret lessons of our art,
By whatsoever mystic rite convey'd,
The rules of moral life impart;—
Nourish bright charity's æthereal flame;
And, breathing love and peace to all mankind,
Like incense rise at heaven's eternal throne.

Strophe III.—Irregular.

    Fair queen of Science, nurse of ev'ry art,
        That crowns the happiness of social life,
        Whose dictates from the desolating strife
    Of warring passions, purify the heart:
        In ev'ry clime, through ev'ry age,
        The prince, the poet, and the sage
        Have knelt before thy hallow'd shrine;
        And nations own'd thy origin divine.
Great Hermes, founder of the Memphic rite;
And Mithras, erst through Persia's realm rever'd;
        And he who to Eleusis bore
        The treasures of thy mystic lore;

But chiefly those by holy truths inspir'd;
　　The chosen servant of the living God,
　　Who Sinai's holy precinct trod,
And he, with love of sacred wisdom fir'd,
　　The mighty prince, whose pious hand,
To the eternal fount of truth and light
That holy temple rear'd,
　　The pride and wonder of Judea's land!
　　　His great and comprehensive mind
　　　A nobler edifice design'd,
　　That time and envy should defy;
　　　Founded on truth's eternal base,
　　　Vast as the ample bounds of space,
　　And sacred to fraternal unity.

ANTISTROPHE III.—IRREGULAR.

Long were the task, and arduous to recount
　　What streams deriving from the sacred source
Of Sion's pure and unpolluted fount,
　　Through ev'ry clime have roll'd their devious course,
　　　From where Phœnicia greets the eastern tide,
　　　To fair Crotona's western towers;
　　　Or where, amidst Athenian bowers,
　　Ilissus bids his waters glide
In gentle course to meet th' Ægean main;
　　Or how, in later times, 'midst dire alarms,
　　When fierce contending nations rush'd to arms,
And deluged Palestine's ensanguin'd plain,
The vanquish'd victor cast aside his sword,
　　Yielding his stubborn pride to thy command,
With humble soul the God of Peace ador'd,
　　And turn'd, repentant, to his native land.
　　　Yes, from that memorable hour,
　　　The western world has own'd thy pow'r;

And tho' ambition's frantic strife
Will sometimes blast the joys of life,
Thy influence bade her feudal discords cease,
And taught her sons the nobler arts of peace.
Before the brightness of thine orient ray,
The shades of prejudice and error fled,
And languid Science rais'd her drooping head,
To greet the fervid blaze of thy advancing day.

Epode III.—Irregular.

Alas! that e'er a cloud should rise,
To dim the glories of thy name;
Or little jealousies divide
The souls by kindred vows allied;—
But see! while thus our rites we blend,
The mingled sacrifice ascend,
And, borne to heaven in one united flame,
Chase every ling'ring shadow from the skies.
And, as the sea-worn mariner,
When darkness shrouds each guiding star,
With transport greets the polar orb of light,
Piercing the murky veil of night;
Or those twin stars, whose milder beams assuage
The tempest in its wildest rage,
And pours his tributary strain
To the propitious rulers of the main;
Such joy is ours; be such the lay
That celebrates this happy day.
Join then, ye sons of art, in triumph join!
To hail the ruling star of Brunswick's royal line.
And ye fraternal stars, whose gentle sway
Our sever'd powers have gloried to obey,
Edward! Augustus! hail, illustrious names!
Whose princely souls confess a nearer tie
Than birch and kindred blood alone supply,
Accept the tribute each so justly claims;

While thus our former pledges we renew,
Of grateful homage, and affection true.
    And though to one alone be giv'n
To bear the ensign of supreme command,
And rule our free, united band;
    In all our orisons to heav'n
Your blended names shall still be found,
To both the votive goblet shall be crown'd;
And both, while life and memory remain,
Hold in our grateful hearts your undivided reign.

XIV.
TO HARMONY.
By Dr. Wm. Perfect.

OFFSPRING of Light! cherubic fair!
    Whose charms can never fade,
Attune the poet's humble air,
    His artless serenade.

When first from chaos nature sprung,
    And lovely order rose,
With thy own notes the regions rung,
    Or sunk to soft repose.

'T was thine, pervading land and sea,
    To animate each scene,
Diffusing wide the Deity,
    Celestial and terrene.

As Phœbus through the vernal store
    Sheds young creation's rays,
Embellishing from shore to shore
    The spring-extended days—

So thou, enthusiastic maid,
    Canst all our thoughts inspire,
And warm the muse-frequented shade
    With all the seraph's fire.

'Tis thine to soothe the human breast,
    When harrow'd deep with care;
And lull the captive into rest,
    Though fettered with despair.

To Sympathy, thy sister bland,
    Thou giv'st the power to heal;
And stay'st assassination's hand,
    When lifting murder's steel.

Does maniac passion quick subside
    To peace without alloy,
With orient reason coincide,
    And feel the bosom's joy!

Thy voice subdues the mental storm,
    And wakes the silver string,
At once to charm, instruct, and warm
    Beneath composure's wing.

And might a mason's wish inspire
    Thy philanthropic ray,
To peace thy notes should tune the lyre,
    And stop war's sanguine sway.

My muse her humble smile of praise
    Should pour in rustic song,
And cheerfully thine altar raise
    Amidst our village throng.

XV.

Performed at every meeting of the Grand Chapter of HARODIM. *Written by Brother* NOORTHOUCK.

Set to music by Companion WEBBE.

Sung by Companions WEBBE, GORE, *and* PAGE.

OPENING.

ORDER is heaven's first law: through boundless space
Unnumber'd orbs roll round their destin'd race;
On earth as strict arrangements still appear,
Suiting the varying seasons of the year:
Beneficence divine presents to view
Its plenteous gifts to man, in order true;
But chief a mind, these blessings to improve,
By arts, by science, by fraternal love.

DIVISION.

When men exalt their views to heaven's high will,
With steady aim their duty to fulfil,
    The mind expands, its strength appears,
    Growing with their growing years,
Mounting the apex of Masonic skill.
Be this the earnest purpose of our lives,
Success must crown the man who nobly strives!

CONCLUSION.

Loud let us raise our swelling strains,
    And Harodim proclaim,
    Of excellence the name;
    Goodwill to all, love to each other,
    The due of every skilful brother,
Who worthily our ancient lore maintains.

    Indulgence in pleasure
    By prudence we measure;
And, cheerfully parting, exchange an adieu,
Till we meet with fresh vigour our tasks to renew.

XVI.

An irregular Ode on the moral principles of Masonry, designed for the Consecration of the King George's Lodge, in Sunderland, on the Fourth day of June, 1778; being the Birthday of his Majesty George the Third. By J. CAWDEL, *Comedian.*

CHORUS PRIMO.

SOUND! sound aloud your instruments of joy!
    Let cheerful strains abound!
    From pole to pole resound!
And may no hostile cares our social mirth annoy!
  Raise! raise the voice of harmony, all raise!
    To hail this festive day
    Your vocal strength display,
  And charm the list'ning world with jocund songs of praise.

May this new consecration thro' ages shine secure,
A monument of social love, till time shall be no more.
    Ye powers persuasive, now inspire
    My tongue with bold, resistless fire!
    Let sacred zeal combine!
    May magic sweetness crown my lays,
    To sing aloud Masonic praise,
    And urge a theme divine!
  May swelling numbers flow without control,
  And all be music, ecstacy of soul!

Confess'd unequal to the trembling task,
    To touch the lyre so oft superior strung,
Your candour, patience, justice bids me ask,
    And for a lab'ring heart excuse a fault'ring tongue.
Behold a social train in friendship's bands
    Assembled, cheerful, eager to display
Their panting joy, to raise their willing hands,
    And hail triumphant this auspicious day!
A day which Britons e'er must hold divine;
    To sound its glories Fame expands her wings;
This day, selected for your fair design,
    Has lent our favour'd isle the best of kings.
May heaven, propitious, your endeavours crown,
    Which, like the present, virtue's basis claim!
May perfect goodness here erect her throne,
    And coward vice be only known by name!
May moral virtue meet no savage foes
    Within these walls, made sacred to your cause!
Scorn each reviler who would truth oppose,
    And learn that good are still Masonic laws.

BROTHERLY LOVE.

Hail! first grand principle of Masonry, for ever hail!
    Thou gracious attribute descending from above,
O'er each corroding passion of the soul prevail,
    And show the social charms of brotherly love
May thy bright virtues e'er resplendent shine
    Through ages yet unborn—worlds unexplor'd;
Till even rancour falls before thy shrine,
    And malice, blushing, owns thee for her lord.
This happy union of each generous mind
    Would nobly give to peace eternal birth;
Implicit confidence would bless mankind,
    And perfect happiness be found on earth.

From this celestial source behold a train
Of blooming virtues, emulous to gain
    A genial warmth from each expanded breast.
Among the pleasing numbers crowding round,
(Whose looks with well meant services are crown'd),
    Relief and Truth superior stand confess'd.

RELIEF.

Relief! of Charity the soul!
Whose lib'ral hands from pole to pole extend,
    Scorns mean restraint, disdains control,
And gives alike to enemy and friend.
    Empty distinctions here contemned fall,
    For true Relief is bounteous to all.

TRUTH.

Nor is with paler glory Truth array'd,
    In bright simplicity she shines, caress'd:
She conquers fraud, dispels its gloomy shade,
    And brings conviction to the doubtful breast.
Should e'er duplicity our ears assail,
And, fluent, forge an artful, specious tale,
    It may our easy faith awhile deceive,
But when this radiant goddess silence breaks,
Decision follows, 'tis fair Truth who speaks,
    And banish'd falsehood can no longer live.

FAITH, HOPE, AND CHARITY.

When first kind heav'n to th' astonished view
    Of mortal sight its realms of joy display'd,
Mankind enraptur'd with the prospect grew,
    And to attain this bliss devoutly pray'd.

Agreeing, all this sacred truth allow,
    (And we its force with zealous warmth increase)
That Faith, Hope, Charity, possess'd, bestow
    The fairest claim to everlasting peace.

FAITH.

By Faith what miracles in distant times were done!
    The leper cleans'd — to sight restor'd the blind—
By that the widow saved her darling son—
    And death his fruitless dart to Faith resign'd.

HOPE.

O fairest, sweetest harbinger of joy!
    Whose aid supreme with gratitude we own;
Cheer'd with thy smiles, we human ills defy,
    And drive despair in shackles from thy throne.

AIR I.

Tho' throbbing griefs the soul oppress,
And fill the heart with deep distress,
    Whilst each fond joy's withheld;
Yet when fair Hope her visage shows,
The mind inspir'd with rapture glows,
    And ev'ry pang's expell'd!

When conscious sin the dying wretch reproves,
    Whilst from his quiv'ring lip the doubtful prayer is sent;
He asks for Hope; she comes, his fear removes,
    His mind enlightens, and he dies content!

CHARITY.

Fair Charity next, Masonic patroness!
    Merits that praise which only hearts can give;
No words can her unrivall'd worth express;
    Her glowing virtues in the soul must live.

The wretched widow, plung'd in streaming woes,
    Bereft of husband, competence, and friends,
Finds no allay, no balmy quiet knows,
    Till heaven-born Charity every comfort sends.

The helpless orphan, wand'ring quite forlorn,
    Sends forth his little soul in piteous moan;
In lisping murmurs rues he e'er was born,
    And thinks in infant griefs he stands alone!

Thus, plaintive wailing, he relief despairs,
    No tender parent to assuage his pain;
No friend but Charity—she dispels his cares—
    Father and mother both in her remain.

AIR II.

An Allegory on Charity.

AS Poverty late, in a fit of despair,
Was beating her bosom, and tearing her hair,
Smiling Hope came to ask—what her countenance told,
That she there lay expiring with hunger and cold.

Come, rise! said the sweet rosy herald of joy,
And the torments you suffer I'll quickly destroy;
Take me by the hand, all your griefs I'll dispel,
And I'll lead you for succour to Charity's cell.

On Poverty hobbled, Hope soften'd her pain,
But long did they search for the goddess in vain;
Towns, cities, and countries they travers'd around:
For Charity's lately grown hard to be found.

At length at the door of a lodge they arrived,
Where, their spirits exhausted, the tyler revived.
Who when ask'd (as 'twas late) if the dame was gone home,
Said, no; Charity always was last in the room.

The door being open'd, in Poverty came,
Was cherish'd, reliev'd, and caress'd by the dame;
Each votary, likewise, the object to save,
Obey'd his feelings, and cheerfully gave.

Then shame on the man who the science derides,
Where this soft-beaming virtue for ever presides.
In this scriptural maxim let's ever accord—
"What we give to the poor we but lend to the Lord."

THE FOUR CARDINAL VIRTUES.

JUSTICE.

Inferior virtues rise from these,
Affording pleasure, comfort, peace,
   And less'ning all our cares;
Here Justice see, at Mercy's word,
Conceals her scales, and drops her sword,
Appeas'd by her, the guilty victim spares.

FORTITUDE.

Here Fortitude, of Hope the child,
With conscious resignation fill'd,
   Displays her dauntless brow;
Sees, fearless, human ills surround,
She views them all with peace profound,
   And smiles at threaten'd woe!

TEMPERANCE.

Now ruddy Temp'rance shows her blooming face,
   Replete with health, with ease, and fair content;
Whilst pamper'd luxury mourns her sickly case,
   And finds, too late, a glutton's life's misspent.

PRUDENCE.

With cautious step and serious grace,
A form behold with hidden face,
    Veil'd o'er with modest fears;
Till Confidence, unused to doubt,
Resolves to find the goddess out,
Withdraws the veil, and Prudence, see, appears!

Without thy gifts mankind would savage turn,
    Would human nature wantonly disgrace,
Would at all bounds of due restriction spurn,
    And all the noblest works of heaven deface.

These moral virtues are by us ordain'd
    Th' unerring pilots to the heavenly shore:
By these directed, endless joys obtain'd,
    And, having their kind aid, we want no more.

Of all the mental blessings given to man,
    These are the choice of each Masonic breast;
By us enroll'd, they form the moral plan
    Of this fair science—are supreme confess'd.

DUET AND CHORUS, FINALE.

Then let us all in friendship live,
    Endearing and endear'd;
Let vice her punishment receive,
    And virtue be rever'd.

CHORUS.

May love, peace, and harmony, ever abound,
And the good man and Mason united be found.

Now let the panting heart rejoice!
The glowing mind expand!
Let echo raise her double voice,
And swell the choral band.

CHORUS.

May love, peace, and harmony ever abound,
And the good man and Mason united be found.

XVII.

BY MR. WILLIAM WALKER.

STRIKE to melodious notes the golden lyre!
Spread wide to all around the ardent flame,
Till each wrapt bosom catch the sacred fire,
And join the glorious theme!
'Tis Masonry!
The Art sublimely free,
Where majesty has bow'd, and own'd a brother's name!

Through ample domes wide let the chorus roll,
Responsive to the ardour of the soul.
Hail! inspiring Masonry!
To thy shrine do myriads bend;
Yet more glorious shalt thou be,
Till o'er the world thy power extend.
Still to the sons of earth thy light dispense,
And all shall own thy sacred influence.

Though genius fires, yet faint his rays appear
Till thy mysterious lore the soul refine;

'Tis thou to noblest heights his thoughts must rear,
    And make them doubly shine.
        O Masonry!
    Thou Art sublimely free!
'Tis thou exalt'st the man, and mak'st him half divine.
Ye Masons, favour'd men, your voices raise!
You speak your glory while you sing its praise.
              Hail, inspiring Masonry! &c.

Blest be the man, and blest he is, who bears
    With virtuous pride a Mason's sacred name!
And may each brother, who the blessing shares,
    Enrich the list of fame.
        Blest Masonry!
    Thou Art sublimely free!
Heav'n bids thy happy sons, and they thy worth
        proclaim
With loud assent! their cheerful voices raise,
Their great, immortal Masonry to praise.
              Hail, inspiring Masonry! &c.

The tower, sky-pointing, and the dome sublime,
    Rais'd by the mystic rules and forming pow'r,
Shall long withstand the iron tooth of Time,
    Yet still their fall is sure:
        But Masonry,
    The Art sublimely free,
Founded by God himself, thro' time shall firm endure:
Still shall its sons their grateful voices raise,
And joyful sound their Great Grand Master's praise.
      At thy shrine, O Masonry!
    Shall admiring nations bend;
    In future times thy sons shall see
      Thy fame from pole to pole extend.

To worlds unknown thy heav'n-born light dispense,
And systems own thy sacred influence.

XIX.

By Mr. Thomas Dermody.

THOU fairest type of excellence divine,
   Whose social links the race of man combine,
Whose awful mandates coward vice control,
And breathe through nature one enlighten'd soul;
From thy mild sway benignant virtues rise,
Pour on the heart, and emulate the skies;
From thy sage voice sublime instruction springs,
While knowledge waves her many colour'd wings,
And star-eyed truth, and conscience, holy zest,
Enthrone true feeling in the glowing breast.
Then deign the labour of thy sons to guide,
O'er each full line in nervous sense preside;
Adorn each verse, each manly thought inflame,
And what we gain from genius give to fame!

XX.

URANIA, hail! to thee we sing,
   And all with pleasure own the lay;
Which from thy sacred fountain spring,
   To glad the free-born sons of day;
O still attend our meetings here,
With peace serene, and joy sincere.

True joys unruffled, calm repose,
   In friendship's sacred band behold,

The happy recompense of those
    Who laws and liberties uphold;
Who scorn all base, unmanly views,
From vice refrain and virtue choose.

May each Free-mason, good and true,
    In Britain's isle be ever found;
And in remotest regions too,
    May love and harmony abound;
And all confess true wisdom's pow'r,
Till time and Masons are no more.

XXI.

WAKE the lute and quiv'ring strings,
    Mystic truths Urania brings;
Friendly visitant, to thee
We owe the depths of Masonry;
Fairest of the virgin choir,
Warbling to the golden lyre,
Welcome; here thy art prevail!
Hail! divine Urania, hail!

Here, in friendship's sacred bow'r,
The downy wing'd and smiling hour,
Mirth invites, and social song,
Nameless mysteries among:
Crown the bowl, and fill the glass,
To every virtue, every grace,
To the brotherhood resound
Health! and let it thrice go round!

We restore the times of old,
The blooming, glorious age of gold;
As the new creation free,
Blest with gay Euphrosyne;

We with god-like science talk,
And with fair Astræa walk;
Innocence adorns the day,
Brighter than the smiles of May.

Pour the rosy wine again,
Wake a brisker, louder strain;
Rapid zephyrs, as ye fly,
Waft our voices to the sky;
While we celebrate the Nine,
And the wonders of the trine,
While the angels sing above,
As we below, of peace and love.

XXII.

Written by MR. BROWN.

Set to Music as a Glee for Three Voices, by the REV. GEORGE OLIVER, W.M. No. 544, *and* P. G. CHAP. *for the County of Lincoln.*

WHEN first the golden morn aloft,
 With maiden breezes whisp'ring soft,
Sprung from the east with rosy wing,
To kiss the heavenly first-born spring;
Jehovah then, from hallow'd earth,
Gave Masonry immortal birth;
'Twas then the new creation rung,
And thus the host of heaven sung:—

AIR.

Hail, hail, O hail, thou Source of Love!
 Great Artist of this goodly frame!
The earth and sea, the sky above,
 Thou form'st to Thy immortal fame!

SEMI-CHORUS.

To thee, our sire,
The cherub choir
The air move with seraphic sound:
Ye breezes sweet
The cadence meet,
And waft it o'er the hallow'd ground.

AIR.

Ten thousand orbial beauties bright,
  Which long confus'd in chaos lay,
Thou brought'st them forth to give delight,
  And make the face of heaven gay.

SEMI-CHORUS.

To thee, our sire, &c.

RECITATIVE.

'Twas thus the heavens in concert rung,
While nature kind from chaos sprung,
Brought forth her tender infant green,
And flow'ry sweets to deck the scene;
To finish then the Artist's plan,
Of purest mould He form'd the man;
Then gave him an immortal soul,
And bade him live and rule the whole:
While angels from their golden shrine,
Sung with angelic strains divine.

AIR.

Happy, happy mortals, rise,
Taste with us immortal joys.

Blooming on yon sacred tree,
Planted by the deity;
The hallow'd fruit is Masonry.
Far beyond the pregnant sky,
There the hopes of Masons lie,
Masons' happy choice above,
Masons every blessing prove,
Friendship, harmony, and love.

RECITATIVE.

As perfect love and power divine
    First gave our science birth,
So friendship shall our hearts entwine,
    And harmonize the earth:
Behold the virgin hither flies,
To crown us with her blissful joys.

AIR.

Blooming as fair Eden's bower,
    Friendship, goddess! heavenly bright!
Dropping in a balmy shower,
    Breathing concord and delight;
Each Mason feels the sacred fire
    Glow with ardour in his heart;
The flame inspires him with desire
    To relieve each other's smart.

FULL CHORUS.

From heaven since such blessings flow,
Let every Mason while below
Our noble science here improve:
'Twill raise his soul to realms above,
And make his lodge a lodge of love.

XXIII.

By Brother EDWARD FENNER.

WITH grateful hearts your voices raise,
To sound the great Creator's praise,
Who by His word dispell'd the night,
And form'd the radiant beams of light;
Who fram'd the heavens, the earth the skies,
And bade the wond'rous fabric rise;
Who view'd His work, and found it just,
And then created man from dust.
  Happy in Eden was he laid,
   Nor did he go astray,
  Till Eve, by serpent guile betray'd,
   First fell and led the way.

But fallen from that happy plain,
Subject to various wants and pain,
Labour and art must now provide
What Eden freely once supplied:
Some learn'd to till th' unwilling ground;
Some bade the well-strung harp to sound;
Each different arts pursu'd and taught,
Till to perfection each was brought.
  Masons pursue the truth divine,
   We cannot go astray,
  Since three great lights conjointly shine
   To point us out the way.

Zion appears, rejoice! rejoice!
Exult, and hear, obey the voice
Of mercy and enlightening grace,
Recalling us to Eden's place;
With faith believe, and hope pursue,
And mercy still for mercy show;

Proclaim aloud, with grateful theme,
The great Redeemer's blessed name.
  The eastern star now shows us light,
   Let us not go astray;
  Let faith, hope, charity unite
   To cheer the gladsome way.

XXIV.

Written by a Member of the Alfred Lodge, at Oxford. Set to Music by DR, FISHER, *and Performed at the Dedication of Free-masons' Hall.*

STROPHE.

AIR.

WHAT solemn sounds on holy Sinai rung,
 When heav'nly lyres, by angel fingers strung,
According to th' immortal lay,
That hymn'd creation's natal day!

RECITATIVE.—*(accompanied).*

'Twas then the shouting sons of morn
 Bless'd the great omnific word;
Abash'd, hoarse, jarring atoms heard,
Forgot their pealing strife,
And softly crowded into life,
When order, law, and harmony were born.

CHORUS.

 The mighty Master's pencil warm
 Trac'd out the shadowy form,
 And bade each fair proportion grace
 Smiling nature's modest face.

AIR.

Heaven's rarest gifts were seen to join
To deck a finish'd form divine,
    And fill the sovereign Artist's plan;
Th' Almighty's image stamp'd the glowing frame,
And seal'd him with the noblest name,
    Archetype of beauty, man.

ANTISTROPHE.

SEMI-CHORUS AND CHORUS.

Ye spirits pure, that rous'd the tuneful throng,
And loos'd to rapture each triumphant tongue,
    Again, with quick, instinctive fire,
    Each harmonious lip inspire:
Again bid every vocal throat
    Dissolve in tender, votive strain.

AIR.

Now while yonder white-robed train[*]
    Before the mystic shrine
    In lowly adoration join,
Now sweep the living lyre, and swell the melting note.

RECITATIVE.

Yet, e'er the holy rites begin,
The conscious shrine within,
    Bid your magic song impart,

---

[*] The Brethren in their white aprons.

AIR.

How within the wasted heart,
Shook by passion's ruthless power,
Virtue trimm'd her faded flower,
To opening buds of fairest fruit:
   How from majestic nature's glowing face
   She caught each animating grace,
And planted there th' immortal root.

EPODE.

RECITATIVE.—*(accompanied).*

Daughter of gods, fair Virtue, if to thee,
   And thy bright sister, universal Love,
Soul of all good, e'er flowed the soothing harmony
   Of pious gratulation, from above,
To us, thy duteous votaries, impart
   Presence divine.—

AIR.

—The sons of antique art,
  In high, mysterious jubilee,
    With pæan loud, and solemn rite,
    Thy holy step invite,
    And court thy listening ear,
    To drink the cadence clear
  That swells the choral symphony.

CHORUS.

To thee, by foot profane untrod,
Their votive hands have rear'd the high abode.

RECITATIVE.

  Here shall your impulse kind
  Inspire the tranced mind:

AIR.

And lips of truth shall sweetly tell
    What heavenly deeds befit
      The soul by wisdom's lesson smit;
What praise he claims who nobly spurns
      Gay vanities of life, and tinsel joys,
For which unpurged fancy burns.

CHORUS.

What pain he shuns, who dares be wise;
  What glory wins, who dares excel!

XXV.

FAITH, HOPE, AND CHARITY.

(Tune, *Anacreon in Heaven, but recently set to Original Music. Written by Brother* HENRY LEE, *Author of "All's Right,"* &c. &c.

WHEN Faith left her mansions celestial for earth,
    On seraphim plumes she was borne through the sky;
The crown o'er her temples betoken'd her birth,
    The gem on her bosom behests from on high.
Gliding softly thro' clouds by her radiancy clear'd,
Sweet Hope, with a smile, like an angel appear'd;
As friends they approach'd, interchanging the sign,
On earth thus cementing a union divine!

To join this lov'd pair, while discoursing below,
    Mild Charity came, their associate and guide;
All the blessings of life 'twas resolv'd they'd bestow,
    Where honour, with virtue and truth should preside;

This world Faith supported — Hope promised another,
While Charity bound man to man as his brother;
By signs, words, and tokens this system began —
The eye of the Deity sanctioned the plan!

An abode free from guile these fair strangers now
    sought,
    Where Folly with footstep unhallow'd ne'er trod,
Where Wisdom held converse—Morality taught,
    And man paid due homage to virtue and God.
Despairing they droop'd, long in darkness astray,
Till a light, like a star from the east, led the way:
They enter'd the lodge—all their wishes were crown'd!
Here Faith, Hope, and Charity ever are found.

O'er Masons presiding, these virtues combine—
    Faith beckons to join the Grand Master above,
Hope points through heaven's arch to the regions
    divine,
    And Charity teaches peace, friendship, and love!
To all who deserve be these principles shown;
The Craft is most honour'd when most it is known:
May Truth's sacred records to man be unfurl'd,
And Faith, Hope, and Charity govern the world.

XXVI.

Ode for the Dedication of Free-masons' Hall, by the Rev. Brother DANIEL TURNER, *A. M., Woolwich, Kent.*

STROPHE.

RECITATIVE AND CHORUS.

WHAT sacred sounds on Zion's top were heard,
    When rising light t'illume new worlds appear'd!

Seraphic bands all join'd the lay,
And hail'd creation's natal day.

RECITATIVE—*Accompanied.*

'Twas then Old Chaos stood amaz'd
  Before the Almighty's face.
Heaven and earth assumed their place;
  The all-pervading hand
  Divided sea and land,
Then beauty, grace, and order first were rais'd.

CHORUS.

The mighty Architect design'd
An emblem of His spotless mind:
Perfection glow'd throughout the whole,
And harmony was nature's son.

AIR.

Unfinish'd still the great intent,
Once more th' Almighty word was sent
  To fill the wond'rous plan:
The new-form d dust in majesty arose,
And with his Maker's image glows,
  Prince of creation,—Man.

ANTISTROPHE.

RECITATIVE AND CHORUS.

Celestial spirits loudly sounding,
Holy harps through heaven resounding,
Sweep the strings with touch divine,
Masons will the concert join!
While the notes in highest strain,
Wake all nature to a song;

AIR.

Praise to Masons doth belong,
    Masons, sons of art reveal'd.
    Tenets pure, though deep conceal'd,
Craft and Master extol,
    While truth and life remain.

RECITATIVE.

Concord's each peculiar son
Sure will baneful passion shun:
Unity's the strongest power;

AIR.

Unity can blessings shower,
O'er a chosen band and free:
Such as is fam'd Masonry.
    Benevolence each heart expands.
Philanthropy extends the willing arm,
To feed, to shelter, and to warm,
    Each who in need of pity stands.
              Cho.— Philanthropy, &c.

EPODE.

RECITATIVE.—*Accompanied.*

Virtue, all hail! before thy shrine we bow,
    Endue our minds with emulation's fire;
To tread the paths of heroes let us now
    Attempt, and after lasting fame aspire.
To our endeavours aid divine impart,
And grace the works mysterious of our art.

AIR.

Science! gaudiest plume of reason,
   Now to thee, in this their dwelling,
   Masons, all mankind excelling,
   Yield the palm of grateful praise.
   And a joyful chorus raise,
Which shall last through every season.

CHORUS.

Long may the social bond remain,
While arts and virtue grace its reign.

RECITATIVE.

Its influence shall hold,
Till death doth all unfold.

AIR.

Tread gently o'er this sacred ground,
   Here the dome aspiring,
   Breasts Masonic nobly firing,
   Leads to honour, merit, glory,
From deep foundations proudest structures rise,
Thence lofty monuments do strike the skies,
   Such as bear renown in story.

FIRST CHORUS.

May bliss eternal, pleasures fair,
Crown the compass and the square!

GRAND CHORUS.

Happy, happy, happy he,
Who tastes the joys of Masonry.

EULOGIES.

I.

ON CHARITY.

From Prior.

DID sweeter sounds adorn my flowing tongue
    Than ever man pronounc'd, or angel sung;
Had I all knowledge, human and divine,
That thought can reach, or science can define;
And I the power to give that knowledge birth
In all the speeches of the babbling earth;
Did Shadrach's zeal my glowing breast inspire
To weary tortures and rejoice in fire;
Or had I faith like that which Israel saw,
When Moses gave them miracles and law:
Yet, gracious Charity! indulgent guest,
Were not thy power exerted in my breast,
Those speeches would send up unheeded pray'r;
That scorn of life would be but wild despair:
A cymbal's sound were better than my voice:
My faith were form, my eloquence were noise.
    Charity, decent, modest, easy, kind,
Softens the high, and rears the abject mind;
Knows with just reins and gentle hand to guide
Betwixt vile shame and arbitrary pride.
Not soon provoked, she easily forgives;
And much she suffers, as she much believes;

Soft peace she brings wherever she arrives;
She builds our quiet as she forms our lives;
Lays the rough paths of peevish nature even,
And opens in each heart a little heaven.
    Each other gift which God on man bestows,
Its proper bound and due restriction knows;
To one fix'd purpose dedicates its power,
And, finishing its act, exists no more.
Thus, in obedience to what heaven decrees,
Knowledge shall fail, and prophecy shall cease:
But lasting Charity's more ample sway,
Nor bound by time, nor subject to decay,
In happy triumph shall for ever live,
And endless good diffuse, and endless praise receive.
    As thro' the artist's intervening glass
Our eye observes the distant planets pass,
A little we discover, but allow
That more remains unseen than art can show:
So whilst our mind its knowledge would improve,
(Its feeble eye intent on things above),
High as we may lift our reason up,
By faith directed and confirmed by hope:
Yet are we able only to survey
Dawnings of beams, and promises of day:
Heaven's fuller effluence mocks our dazzl'd sight;
Too great its swiftness, and too strong its light.
    But soon the mediate clouds shall be dispell'd:
The sun shall soon be face to face beheld,
In all his robes, with all his glory on,
Seated sublime on his meridian throne.
    Then constant Faith and holy Hope shall die;
One lost in certainty, and one in joy;
Whilst thou, more happy pow'r, fair Charity,
Triumphant sister, greatest of the three,

Thy office and thy nature still the same,
Lasting thy lamp, and unconsumed thy flame,
    Shalt still survive—
Shalt stand before the host of heaven confess'd,
For ever blessing, and for ever blest.

II.

STANZAS ON MASONRY.

Translated from the French.

SHALL envy's tongue, with slander foul,
    My brothers, brand our race august,
Incessant shall thy fury howl,
    Licking black venom from the dust?
No, 'tis too much these ranc'rous taints to bear:
    Rise, generous muse! our spotless fame
    To the wide world aloud proclaim,
And freely what a Mason is declare.

In virtue clear we court the light,
    Rever'd the more the more we're known;
And fain the muse would here incite
    Each worthy man the name to own.
Let the Free-mason, then, to all appear;
    Behold the man each prince admires,
    Behold the friend each man desires,
For ever loyal, zealous, and sincere.

Fair Liberty, with Order bland,
    And radiant Pleasure, lov'd so well,
With Temp'rance sage, in seemly band,
    Within our walls for ever dwell.

From vulgar eyes our pleasures tho' we screen,
    Yet rigorous laws our acts restrain;
    Remorse or anguish ne'er can pain
The Mason's breast, nor cloud his mind serene.

The constant aim of all our plans,
    Is to restore Astrea's reign;
That awful Truth may guard our lands,
    While hateful guile shall prowl in vain.
Each lonely path with structures we adorn,
    And all the buildings which we raise
    Are temples that the virtues grace,
Or prisons close for the foul vices form.

While thus to man our praises sing,
    Let not the softer sex repine,
Nor angry charge against us bring,
    That we their favours dare decline.
If from their steps our sanctuaries we guard,
    When they the reason just shall know,
    Resentment they can never show,
But rather with due praise our caution will reward.

Resplendent sex! in whom combine
    Each brilliant charm, each tender grace,
With awe we bow before your shrine,
    But still we fear you while we praise;
For in our earliest lesson it is said,
    If Adam had but once withstood
    From female charms what seem'd so good,
Nature each man, most sure, a Mason would have
    made.

CATCH.

FOR THREE VOICES.

(Tune, *Hark! the bonny Christ Church Bells.*)

HARK! the Hiram sounds to close,
    And we from work are free;
We'll drink and sing, and toast the King
    And the Craft with a hearty three times three.
Hark! the clock repeats high twelve,
    It can't strike more we all well know,
Then ring, ring, ring, ring, ring the bell,
    For another bowl before we go:
Coming, coming, coming, sir, the waiter cries,
    With a bowl to drown our care;
We're a hearty set, on the level met,
    And we'll part upon the square.

GLEES.

I.

Sung at the Summerset House Lodge.

Written by G. DYER. *Set to Music by* R. SPOFFORTH.

LIGHTLY o'er the village green
   Blue-eyed fairies sport unseen,
Round and round, in circles gay;
Then at cock-crow flit away:
Thus, 'tis said, tho' mortal eye
Ne'er their merry freaks could spy,
Elves for mortals lisp the prayer,—
Elves are guardians of the fair.
    Thus, like elves, in mystic ring,
    Merry Masons drink and sing.

Come, then, brothers, lead along
Social rites and mystic song!
Tho' nor Madam, Miss, nor Bess,
Could our mysteries ever guess,
Nor could ever learn'd divine
Sacred Masonry define,
Round our order close we bind
Laws of love to all mankind!
    Thus, like elves, in mystic ring,
    Merry Masons drink and sing.

Health, then, to each honest man,
Friend to the Masonic plan!
Leaving cynics grave to blunder,
Leaving ladies fair to wonder,
Leaving Thomas still to lie,
Leaving Betty still to spy,
Round and round we push our glass,—
Round and round each toasts his lass.

> Thus, like elves, in mystic ring,
> Merry Masons drink and sing.

II.

Masonic Glee, at Laying the Foundation Stone of a Lodge.

By Stanfield.

MASONS uniting raise the hallow'd pile,
   Sacred to virtue, by science plann'd;
Power celestial o'er the fabric smile,
   And join in kindred tones th' exulting band.

Strength, mighty artist! lay the ample base—
   Wisdom, stretch forth thy potent wand—
Beauty, adorning, give the modest grace—
   And, Science, thou complete with sovereign hand.

III.

Composed by Brother ATTWOOD, *for three voices.*

IN Masons' hearts let joy abound!
  Let the fraternal health go round!
Fill up the bowl, then—fill it high!
Fill all the goblets there!—for why
When Masons meet should they be dry?
Why? sons of candour, tell me why?

Our work is done. We've fed the poor:
We've chased the wolf from sorrow's door.
Fill up the bowl, then—fill it high!
Fill all the goblets there!—for why
Should every mortal drink but I?
Why? sons of mortals, tell me why?

IV.

Composed by Brother KELLY.

THE well known sign we mark, and fly
  The wound to heal—to still the sigh—
And wipe the tear from sorrow's eye.
For ours the aim is, ours the art
To meliorate the human heart;
Of wild desires to stem the flood,
And act as if of kindred blood.

V.

Composed by Brother KELLY.

L O! see from heaven the peaceful dove,
    With olive branch descend!
Augustus shall with Edward join,
    All rivalry to end;
And, taught by their fraternal love,
Our arms our hearts shall intertwine,
    The union to approve.

SONNET.

EXTEMPORE,
BY
DR. PERFECT.

Hail, Mystic Science! Seraph Maid!
    Imperial Beam of Light!
In robes of sacred Truth array'd,
    Morality's delight.
O give me wisdom to design,
    And strength to execute;
In native beauty e'er be mine,
    Benevolence, thy fruit.
Unsullied pearl! of precious worth,
    Most grateful to my soul,
The social virtues owe their birth
    To thy unmatch'd control.
Celestial spark, inspir'd by thee,
We pierce yon starry arch on wings of piety.

AN ORATORIO.

As it was performed at the Philharmonic Room, in Dublin, for the Benefit of Sick and Distressed Free-masons.

The Words by MR. JAMES EYRE WEEKS.

The Music composed by MR. RICHARD BROADWAY, *Organist of St. Patrick's Cathedral.*

DRAMATIS PERSONÆ:

SOLOMON, the Grand Master.
HIGH PRIEST.
HIRAM, the Workman.
URIEL, Angel of the Sun.
SHEBA, Queen of the South.
Chorus of Priests and Nobles.

ACT I.

SOLOMON.

RECITATIVE.

CONVENED, we're met: chief oracle of heav'n,
    To whom the sacred mysteries are given;
We're met to bid a splendid fabric rise
Worthy the mighty Ruler of the Skies.

HIGH PRIEST.

And lo! where Uriel, Angel of the Sun,
Arrives to see the mighty business done.

AIR.

Behold! he comes upon the wings of light,
And with his sunny vestment cheers the sight.

URIEL.

RECITATIVE.

The Lord supreme, Grand Master of the skies,
Who bade creation from a chaos rise,
The rules of architecture first engraved
    On Adam's heart.

CHORUS OF PRIESTS AND NOBLES.

To Heaven's High Architect all praise,
    All gratitude be given,
Who deign'd the human soul to raise,
    By secrets sprung from heaven.

SOLOMON.

RECITATIVE.

Adam, well vers'd in arts,
Gave to his sons the plumb and line:
By Masonry sage Tubal Cain,
To the deep organ tun'd the strain.

AIR.

And while he swell'd the melting note,
On high the silver concords float.

HIGH PRIEST.

RECITATIVE.—*Accompanied.*

Upon the surface of the waves
    (When God a mighty deluge pours)
Noah a chosen remnant saves,
    And lays the Ark's stupendous floors.

URIEL.

AIR.

Hark from on high the Mason-word!
    "David, my servant, shall not build
"A lodge for heaven's all-sovereign Lord,
    "Since blood and war have stain'd his shield;
"That for our deputy, his son
"We have reserv'd—Prince Solomon. *Da Capo.*

CHORUS OF PRIESTS AND NOBLES.

Sound great JEHOVAH'S praise!
Who bade young Solomon the temple raise.

SOLOMON.

RECITATIVE.

So grand a structure shall we raise,
That men shall wonder! angels gaze!
By art divine it shall be rear'd,
Nor shall the hammer's noise be heard.

CHORUS.

Sound great JEHOVAH'S praise!
Who bade King Solomon the temple raise.

URIEL.

RECITATIVE.

To plan the mighty dome,
Hiram, the Master-mason's come.

URIEL.

AIR.

We know thee by thy apron white
    An architect to be:
We know thee by thy trowel bright
    Well skill'd in Masonry.
We know thee by thy jewel's blaze,
    Thy manly walk and air
Instructed, thou the lodge shalt raise;
    Let all for work prepare.

HIRAM.

AIR.

Not like Babel's haughty building,
    Shall our greater lodge be fram'd;
That to hideous jargon yielding,
    Justly was a Babel nam'd:
There confusion all o'erbearing,
    Neither sign nor word they knew!
We our work with order squaring,
    Each proportion shall be true.

SOLOMON.

RECITATIVE.

Cedars, which since creation grew,
    Fall of themselves to grace the dome;
All Lebanon, as if she knew
    The great occasion, lo, is come.

URIEL.

AIR.

Behold, my brethren of the sky,
The work begins, worthy an angel's eye.

CHORUS OF PRIESTS AND NOBLES.

Be present, all ye heavenly host;
The work begins, the Lord defrays the cost.

ACT II.

MESSENGER.

RECITATIVE.

BEHOLD, attended by a numerous train,
   Queen of the south, fair Sheba greets thy reign!
In admiration of thy wisdom, she
Comes to present the bended knee.

SOLOMON TO HIRAM.

RECITATIVE.

Receive her with a fair salute,
Such as with majesty may suit.

HIRAM.

AIR.

When allegiance bids obey,
We with pleasure own its sway.

Enter SHEBA, *attended.*

Obedient to superior greatness, see,
Our sceptre hails thy mightier majesty.

SHEBA.

AIR.

Thus Phœbe, queen of shade of night,
    Owning the sun's superior rays,
With feebler glory, lesser light,
    Attends the triumph of his blaze.
Oh, all-excelling Prince, receive
    The tribute due to such a king!
Not the gift but will believe!
    Take the heart, not what we bring. *Da Capo.*

SOLOMON.

RECITATIVE.

Let measures, softly sweet,
Illustrious Sheba's presence greet.

SOLOMON.

AIR.

Tune the lute and string the lyre,
    Equal to the fair we sing!
Who can see and not admire
    Sheba, consort of the king!
Enliv'ning wit and beauty join,
    Melting sense and graceful air:
Here united powers combine,
    To make her brightest of the fair. *Da Capo.*

SOLOMON.

RECITATIVE.

Hiram, our brother and our friend,
Do thou the queen with me attend.

SCENE II. *A view of the Temple.*

HIGH PRIEST.

RECITATIVE.

Sacred to heaven, behold the dome appears;
Lo! what august solemnity it wears;
Angels themselves have deign'd to deck the frame,
And beauteous Sheba shall report its fame.

AIR.

When the Queen of the South shall return
    To the climes which acknowledge her sway,
Where the sun's warmer beams fiercely burn,
    The princess with transport shall say,
"Well worthy my journey, I've seen
    "A monarch both graceful and wise,
"Deserving the love of a queen;
    "And a temple well worthy the skies." *Da Capo.*

CHORUS.

Open, ye gates, receive a queen who shares,
With equal sense, your happiness and cares.

HIRAM.

RECITATIVE.

Of riches much, but more of wisdom see,
Proportion'd workmanship and Masonry.

HIRAM.

AIR.

O charming Sheba! there behold
What massy stores of burnish'd gold,
    Yet richer is our art:

Not all the orient gems that shine,
Nor treasures of rich Ophir's mine,
   Excel the Mason's heart.

True to the fair, he honours more
Than glitt'ring gems or brightest ore
   The plighted pledge of love;
To ev'ry tie of honour bound,
In love and friendship constant found,
   And favoured from above.

SOLOMON AND SHEBA.

DUET.

SHEBA — One gem beyond the rest I see,
And charming Solomon is he.

SOLOMON — One gem beyond the rest I see,
Fairest of fair ones, thou art she.

SHEBA. Oh thou surpassing all men wise!
SOLOMON. And thine excelling women's eyes.

HIRAM.

RECITATIVE.

Wisdom and beauty both combine
Our art to raise, our hearts to join.

CHORUS.

Give to Masonry the prize,
Where the fairest choose the wise;
Beauty still should Wisdom love;
Beauty and Order reign above.

CHARITY OR LOVE.

A principle necessary to every Free-mason.

BLEST is the man whose soft'ning heart
    Feels all another's pain;
To whom the supplicating eye
    Was never rais'd in vain.

Whose breast expands with generous warmth
    A stranger's woe to feel;
And bleeds in pity o'er the wound
    He wants the power to heal.

He spreads his kind supporting arms
    To every child of grief;
His secret bounty largely flows,
    And brings unask'd relief.

To gentle offices of love
    His feet are never slow;
He views, through mercy's melting eye,
    A brother in a foe.

To him protection shall be shown;
    And mercy from above
Descend on those who thus fulfil
    The perfect law of love.

My passions still my purer breast inflame,
To sing that God from whom existence came;
Till Heaven and nature in the concert join,
And own the author of their birth divine.

                                              BOYCE.

PROLOGUES.

I.

Delivered January 14th, 1774, before a Play performed by desire of the Union Lodge, Exeter.

AS lately, brethren, from the lodge I came,
　　Warm'd with our royal order's purest flame,
Absorbed in thought—before my ravish'd eyes
I saw the Genius Masonry arise:
A curious hieroglyphic robe he wore,
And in his hand the sacred volume bore;
On one side was divine Astræa plac'd;
And soft-eyed Charity the other grac'd;
Humanity, the gen'ral friend, was there,
And Pity, dropping the pathetic tear;
There too was Order,—there with rosy mien
Blithe Temp'rance shone, and white-robed Truth was
　　seen.
There, with a key suspended at his breast,
Silence appear'd—his lips his finger press'd:
With these, soft warbling an instructive song,
Sweet Music, gaily smiling, tripp'd along.
Wild laughter, clam'rous noise, and mirth ill-bred,
The brood of Folly, at his presence fled.
　　The Genius spoke—" My son, observe my train,
"Which of my order different parts explain:
"Look up—behold the bright Astræa there,
"She will direct thee how to use the square;

"Pity will bid thee grieve with those who grieve,
"Whilst Charity will prompt thee to relieve;
"Will prompt thee ev'ry comfort to bestow,
"And draw the arrow from the breast of woe;
"Humanity will lead to honour's goal,
"Give the large thought, and form the gen'rous soul;
"Will bid thee thy fraternal love expand
"To virtue of all faiths, and ev'ry land.
"Order will kindly teach her laws of peace,
"Which discord stop, and social joys increase;
"Temp'rance instruct thee all excess t' avoid,
"By which fair fame is lost, and health destroy'd;
"Truth warn thee ne'er to use perfidious art,
"And bid thy tongue be rooted in thy art;
"Silence direct thee never to disclose
"Whate'er thy brethren in thy breast repose:
"For thee shall Music strike th' harmonious lyre,
"And, whilst she charms thy ear, morality inspire.
"These all observe—and let thy conduct show
"What real blessings I on man bestow."
 He said, and disappeared—and oh! may we,
Who wear this honoured badge, accepted, free,
To ev'ry grace and virtue temples raise,
And by our useful works our order praise.

II.

AS a wild rake who courts a virgin fair,
 And tries in vain her virtue to ensnare,
(Tho' what he calls his heaven he may obtain
By putting on the matrimonial chain),
At length, enraged to find she still is chaste,
Her modest fame maliciously would blast;
So some at our fraternity do rail.

Because our secrets we so well conceal,
And curse the sentry with the flaming sword,
That keeps eavesdroppers from the Mason's word;
Though, rightly introduced, all true men may
Obtain the secret in a lawful way,
They'd have us counter to our honour run;
Do what they would blame us for when done;
And when they find their teasing will not do,
Blinded with anger, height of folly show,
By railing at the thing they do not know.
Not so the assembly of the Scottish kirk,
Their wisdoms went a wiser way to work:
When they were told that Masons practis'd charms,
Invok'd the deil, and rais'd tempestuous storms,
Two of their body prudently they sent,
To learn what could by Masonry be meant.
Admitted to the lodge and treated well,
At their return the assembly hop'd they'd tell:
"We say nae mair than this," they both replied,—
"Do what we've done, and ye'll be satisfied."

III.

As some crack'd chymist of projecting brain,
    Much for discovering, but more for gain,
With toil incessant labours, puffs, and blows,
In search of something nature won't disclose,
At length, his crucibles and measures broke,
His fancy'd gain evaporates in smoke.
So some, presumptuous, still attempt to trace
The guarded symbol of our ancient race;
Enwrapp'd in venerable gloom it lies,
And mocks all sight but of a Mason's eyes;

Like the fam'd stream enriching Egypt's shore,
All feel its use, but few its source explore.

All ages still must owe, and every land,
Their pride and safety to the Mason's hand,
Whether for gorgeous domes renown'd afar,
Or ramparts strong to stem the rage of war;
All we behold in earth or circling air,
Proclaim the power of compasses and square.

The heav'n-taught science, queen of arts, appears,
Eludes the rust of time and waste of years.
Through form and matter are her laws display'd,
Her rule's the same by which the world was made,
Whatever virtues grace the social name,
Those we profess, on those we found our fame;
Wisely the lodge looks down on tinsel state,
Where only to be good is to be great.

Such souls by instinct to each other turn,
Demand alliance, and in friendship burn;
No shallow schemes, no stratagems nor arts,
Can break the cement that unites their hearts.
Then let pale envy rage, alone to shame
The fools mistaking infamy for fame;
Such have all countries and all ages borne,
And such all countries and all ages scorn;
Glorious the temple of the sylvan queen,
Pride of the world, at Ephesus was seen;
A witless wretch, the Pritchard of those days,
Stranger to virtue and unknown to praise,
Crooked of soul and fond of any name,
Consigned the noble monument to flame;
Vain madman! if so thinking to destroy
The art which cannot but with nature die.
Still with the Craft, still shall his name survive,
And in our glory his disgrace shall live;

While his cowans no more admittance gain,
Than Ephraimites at Jordan's passage slain.

IV.

*Delivered January 31st, 1772, before a Play perform-
ed by desire of the Union Lodge, Exeter.*

SPEAKERS. { A FATHER,
            A MOTHER,
            A DAUGHTER, about ten years old.

*The curtain draws up and discovers the Mother sitting
at a table, knotting, upon which lies a play bill; the
Daughter enters and takes it up.*

DAUGHTER.

BY desire of the Union Lodge!—What's this?
This Union Lodge, Mamma?

MOTHER.

Free-masons, miss.

DAUGHTER.

Free-masons, my good Madam! Lack-a-day!
What sort of things (I long to know) are they?

MOTHER.

All women from their order they exclude.

DAUGHTER.

Do they, Mamma?—Indeed that's very rude.
Fond as I am of plays, I'll ne'er be seen
At any play bespoke by such vile men.

MOTHER.

Call them not vile—I Masons much approve;
And there is one whom you with fondness love;
Your father—but, behold, he now appears,
And from the lodge the Mason's badge he wears.

The Father enters, clothed as a Mason, the Daughter runs towards him.

DAUGHTER.

Papa, are you a Mason?—Do tell me,
Now do my good papa, what's Masonry?

FATHER.

I will, my dear. Our order is designed
To expand the human heart, and bless mankind.
Wisdom herself contriv'd the mystic frame;
Strength to support, t' adorn it Beauty came.
We're taught, with ever grateful hearts, t' adore
The God of All, the Universal Power;
To be good subjects, ne'er in plots to join,
Or aught against the nation's peace design.
We're taught to calm destructive anger's storm,
And bring rude matter into proper form;
Always to work by the unerring square,
With zeal to serve our brethren; be sincere,
And by our tongues let our whole hearts appear.
Lowly of mind, and meek, we're bid to be,
And ever clothed with true humility.
All children of one gracious Father are,
To whom no ranks of rich and poor appear;
"He sees with equal eye, as God of All,
"A monarch perish, and a beggar fall."
We're taught our conduct by the plumb to try,

To make it upright to the nicest eye.
The compass is presented to our eyes,
And "circumscribe your actions" loudly cries.
We're strictly order'd never to pass by
Whene'er we see a fellow creature lie
Wounded by sorrow—but with hearts to go,
Which with the milk of kindness overflow,
And make a careful search each wound to find,
To pour in oil and wine, and gently bind;
On our own beasts to place him—to convey
Where all may strive to wipe his tears away.

MOTHER.

Go on, ye good Samaritans, to bless,
And may your generous hearts feel no distress!

FATHER.

Whoe'er believes in an Almighty Cause,
And strict obedience pays to moral laws,
Of whatsoever faith or clime he be,
He shall receive a brother's love from me.
"For modes of faith let graceless zealots fight,
"We know he can't be wrong whose life is right."
What tho' we here such diff'rent roads pursue,
All upright Masons, all good men and true,
Shall meet together in the lodge above,
Where their good names shall certain passwords prove.

MOTHER.

No, God respects not persons, but will bless
Those of all climes who follow righteousness.

FATHER.

Whene'er philosophy, by rigid law,
And brow severe, to virtue strives to draw,
Men are disgusted; we take diff'rent ways,
And make fair Virtue and her lessons please.
We at our work are rationally gay,
And music call to tune the moral lay.
Intemp'rance never at our lodge appears,
Nor noisy riot e'er assails our ears;
But Pleasure always, with her bosom friends,
With Cheerfulness and Temp'rance, there attends.
Our secrets (of importance to mankind)
The upright man who seeks may always find.

MOTHER.

But women, ever seeking, seek in vain;
Be kind enough this mystery to explain.

FATHER.

Tho' women from our order we exclude,
Let not that beauteous sex at once conclude
We love them not — or think they would reveal
What we as secrets wish them to conceal.
We fondly love, and think we might impart
(Sure of their faith) our secrets to their heart.
But we're afraid, if once the lovely fair
Were at our happy lodges to appear,
That love and jealousy would both be there.
Then rivals turn'd, our social bonds destroy'd,
Farewell the pleasures now so much enjoy'd!
We're taught to build 'gainst vice the strongest fence,
And round us raise the wall of innocence:
Happy! thrice happy! could we Masons see
Such perfect workmen as they're taught to be;

Could we behold them everywhere appear
Worthy the honourable badge they wear.
Thus I've explained, my child, our royal art.

DAUGHTER.

I'm much obliged, I thank you from my heart;
All you have said I have not understood,
But Masonry, I'm sure, is very good;
And if to marry 'tis my lot in life,
If you approve, I'll be a Mason's wife.

V.

Delivered at a Provincial Theatre, by a Brother at his Benefit.

DIVESTED of all lightness, fancy's pow'r,
　　The mere amusement of an idle hour,
I now appear, with no alluring wile,
To raise the long-loud laugh, or gen'ral smile.
Cloth'd in this dress, therein accosting you,
Fictitious scenes and satire must adieu.
My present pride's to boast this noble grace,
And own my union to an ancient race.
This grace is noble, virtue makes it so,
And stamps the man who wears it, high or low,
As he his actions to the world doth show.
Our order's age to Time himself's unknown,
And still shall flourish when his scythe's laid down.
When th' æra came for Nature to arise,
Pleas'd with the work she hasted through the skies;
Beauty, and Strength, and Wisdom then arose,
Attendant to fulfil her various laws;

Quick th' immortals hasten'd to descry
Her great designs, and saw with wond'ring eye
Discord and darkness fly before her face,
And sweetest Beauty fill the boundless space.
They saw the planets dance their wond'rous round,
By attraction's secret force in order bound.
They saw the earth in glory rise to view,
Surprized they stood, each different scene was new.
The crowning wonder next arose, and charm'd
Their minds with greater force, for man was form'd;
In whom the various graces all were join'd,
And Beauty, Strength and Wisdom were combin'd.
Their admiration then gave birth to praise,
They sung the Architect in glorious lays;
Their lyres they tun'd with sweetest harmony.
And hail'd the matchless name of Masonry!
Such is the genial power whose laws we own, ⎫
Whose wisdom animates each duteous son, ⎬
Tho' witlings laugh, fools sneer, and bigots frown. ⎭

    When sad corruption tainted human kind,
Aud prejudice shed darkness o'er the mind,
Men fled her presence, dazzled at her light,
And chose to wander in the wilds of night;
Griev'd at the scene, reluctant she retir'd,
And in a seven-fold veil her face attir'd.
No more in public are her truths reveal'd,
From all but a chosen few she keeps conceal'd.
No mix'd gaze, no clam'rous noise she loves,
Wisdom in soberness her mind approves.
But still (so 'tis decreed) she must retain
Some among men her science to maintain.
For them the noblest fabrics she rears,
To crown their virtues, and to ease their cares.
Within those walls no trivial merit's known,
No wild ambition. Envy's jealous frown,

Jaundic'd Suspicion, Satire's vengeful sneer,
Dare not intrude; immortal Truth is there,
Friendship and Love, with all their charming train,
In Masonry's bright temples ever reign,—
No characters are on her altars slain.
What tho' the weak may point, with foolish sneer,
At those who're Masons but by what they wear,
And sagely ask, if Masonry's so good,
Why are the lives of these so very rude?
Yet candid minds (and such do here abound)
Will own the good, tho' bad ones may be found.
Search orders through, e'en sacred are not free
From those who are not what they ought to be.
Still so exact are Masonry's bright rules,
They none offend, but vicious men, or fools.
Brethren, to you, by whom these truths are known,
I now beg leave to turn. For favours shown
My thanks are due; accept them from a heart
That feels the brother's tie in every part.
Long may your lodge remain the honour'd seat
Of each Masonic virtue, good and great!
May every member as a Mason shine,
And round his heart its every grace entwine!
While here below, may heav'n upon him show'r
Its choicest gifts, and, in a distant hour,
Gently from the lodge below his soul remove
To the grand lodge of Masonry above!

VI.

Spoken at Dublin, in the character of TEAGUE, *for the Benefit of an English Free-mason in Distress.*

Written by BRO. LAU. DERMOTT, D. G. M.

GOD save you, gentlefolks, both great and small—
I'm come to tell—*(pause)*—phuh! I forgot it all.
You, Mr. Prompter, there behind the screen,
Why don't you spake, and tell me what I mean?
I have it now, I'm sorry, I confess,
A brother Mason is in great distress;
Nothing to ate, and, what you all will think
Is ten times worse, the divil a sup to drink.
To-day I ax'd him, how did matters go?
He shook his head and cried, "But so and so."
"What want you?" said I, "come now, tell me, honey."
"Nothing" said he "but a small bag of money,
For want of which my bowels all are aching"—
Why do you laugh there? Is it game your making?
                            [*To the galleries.*
Burn me, but he'll be after running crazy,
                                   [*In a heat.*
Except this night you make his stomach easy.
In London born, he's a true patriot, really,
And I'm his brother, born here in Shileally.
Arrah! why not?—I prithee, where's the blunder?
It is but just three hundred miles asunder.
What though our parents never saw each other,
Faith, that's no reason that he's not my brother:
For we are Masons, and our union hence
Hath made us brothers in the strictest sense.

Our union such that it no difference makes
If England, Ireland, or the Land o' Cakes;
Nay, round the globe, if e'er a Mason roam,
He finds a brother, and a kindly home.
Therefore, my jewels, let us all befriend him,
And when in danger, Hannum an Doul defend him.

VII.

Spoken by Mr. Griffith, at the Theatre Royal, Dublin.

IF to delight and humanize the mind,
   The savage world in social ties to bind;
To make the moral virtues all appear
Improv'd and useful, soften'd from severe:
If these demand the tribute of your praise,
The teacher's honour, or the poet's lays;
Thrice honour'd and mysterious Masonry!
By thee erected spacious domes arise,
And spires ascending, glittering in the skies;
The wond'rous whole by heavenly art is crown'd,
And order in diversity is found;
Through such a length of ages still how fair,
How bright, how blooming do thy looks appear;
And still shall bloom. Time, as it glides away,
Fears for its own before thine shall decay:
The use of accents from thy aid is thrown,
Thou form'st a silent language of thy own:
Disdain'st that records should contain thy art,
And only liv'st within the faithful heart.
Behold, where kings and a long shining train
Of garter'd heroes wait upon thy reign,
And boast no honour but a Mason's name.

Still in the dark let the unknowing stray;
No matter what they judge, or what they say;
Still may thy mystic secrets be conceal'd,
And only to a brother be reveal'd.

VIII.

*Spoken before the Union Lodge, Exeter,
January 19th, 1776.*

IN earliest times, as man with man combin'd,
   And science taught them, and the arts refin'd,
The tragic muse arose, and o'er the stage
Wept with feign'd grief, or rav'd with mimic rage;
Nor these alone her talents to convey
Th' instructive moral in a pleasing lay;
To paint fair virtue in her loveliest guise,
Or hold the frightful mirror up to vice:
'Twas her's beside, by strokes of magic art,
To raise the feelings, and expand the heart;
To touch those secret springs within, that move
The tender sympathy of social love;
To melt us to compassion's softest mood,
And rouse the slumb'ring soul to active good.
    Whilst nature thus by art her hand-maid dress'd,
Refines and modulates the human breast;
Here to assist the muses' great design,
With smiles the sons of Masonry may join.
Benignant art! whose heaven-born precepts tend
In larger paths to that same glorious end.
Blest art! in whose harmonious, sweet control,
Soul vibrates perfect unison with soul:
Which prompts the precious drop in Pity's eye,
And lifts the graceful hand of Charity;

Enkindles love and friendship's sacred flame,
And gives a foe distress'd a brother's name.
    Ye who this night (to mild affections prone)
Relieve our feelings, and indulge your own!
Still be your task to feel and to relieve!
Still may you share that comfort which you give!
And whilst the scenes our Shakespear's pencil drew,
Stand thus approv'd, and sanctified by you;
Whilst here his moving tale shall reach your heart,
May your good deeds abroad this truth impart:
The tear which feign'd distress has taught to flow,
Will shed its lenient balm o'er real woe.

IX.

Written and spoken by MR. WOODS, *at the Theatre Royal, Edinburgh, in January, 1783, previous to the Comedy of "Which is the Man?" By desire of the Right Honourable and Most Worshipful* DAVID STEWARD ERSKINE, *Earl of Buchan, Grand Master; and the Worshipful Fraternity of Free and Accepted Masons.*

IN early times, ere science, like the sun,
   Beam'd forth, and worlds from mental darkness won,
What wretched days mankind for ages knew,
Their cares how selfish, and their joys how few!
How tasteless was the cup on mortals press'd,
By social arts untended and unblest!
    If nature now a brighter aspect shows,
Improved by graces science only knows;
In tracing knowledge to its first essays,
How much Free-masonry deserves our praise!

Whose early efforts wit and genius lov'd—
When Hiram plann'd, and David's son approv'd:
Hiram! whose name still leads enquiring youth;*
The chosen star that points the way to truth.
Cities, where commerce keeps her golden store,
Temples, where grateful saints their God adore,
Th' abodes rever'd from whence fair science springs,
And palaces, that mark the power of kings;
These stamp the Mason's fame; yet higher art
He nobly tries—t' amend the human heart.
   Hence, 'midst the ruins of three thousand years,
Unhurt, unchang'd, Free-masonry appears:
Her tow'rs and monuments may fade away,
Her truth and social love shall ne'er decay.
These she with care extends to distant lands,
'Cross frozen seas, o'er wild and barren sands; †
All who can think and feel she makes her friends,
Uniting even foes for moral ends.
The wanderer's drooping heart she loves to cheer,
The wretch's comfort when no aid seems near;
Her actions tending all to one great plan—
To teach mankind what man should be to man;
Each selfish passion boldly to destroy,
That all the world, like us, may meet in joy.
   Do sceptics doubt the Mason's gen'rous aim?
One truth beyond all cavil sets our fame:
Since to the craft a Buchan's care is giv'n,
It must be dear to virtue and to heav'n.

---

  * Candidates for Free-masonry.
  † Alluding to the lodges established in remote parts of the world.

X.

Spoken in the character of an Irish Free-mason, at the Theatre Royal, in the Hay Market.

Written by LAU. DERMOTT, D. G. M.

I, DARBY MULROOMY, from Moat of Grenoge,
Beg leave to be speaking by way of prologue:
And first to begin, sirs, this night is the day
Fix'd for brother L'Estrange's benefit play:
I heard him, just now, about telling an actor
He'd soon be as rich as a Jew or contractor;
His lodge congregated, and ready for certain,
To open in form, just behind this big curtain.
But he admits women, because they are skill'd in
(As well as Free-masons) the new art of building:
O the sweetest of creatures! they're cunning projectors,
They build without rule, square, compass, or sectors;
Their ashlars are curls, their bricks are all wool,
Their mortar's pomatum, foundation a skull;
On which they can build (and I'm sure 'tis no lie,)
As broad as a turf stack, but three times as high.
The men, too, can build, as their fancy best suits,
With curls on each side, like a pair of volutes,;
High toupees in front, something like a key-stone,*
To wedge up the brains in those skulls that have none.
For frieze and festoons they all use Brussels laces,
And, like the fine ladies, can whitewash their faces;
With long tails behind, and with nothing before,
Except down their waistcoats a little tom bore.
        [*Meaning tambour.*

---

* The fashions of 1775.

Thus some have depicted our actors at large,
You, visitors, are not compris'd in this charge.
                [*Bowing to the audience.*
In our ancient craft true friendship abound;
I wish amongst all men the like could be found.
Were all Yankees Free-masons, and Englishmen too,
They'd hearken to reason, old friendship renew;
Would drink, and shake hands, and become mighty
    civil,
And pitch all their guns and their swords to the devil.
But I'll say no more—*(pause)*—for the time's very
    quare,
And poor Darby shall never be caught in a snare:
My business to night is to welcome you here.
Welcome, brethren of the square and compass;
Welcome, bucks, who love to make a rompus;
Welcome, cits, who love to sit in quiet;
Welcome, above, who never love to riot:
Welcome, critics, dread of every poet,
You spare the craft because you do not know it.
Ten thousand welcomes Darby does decree
To all the ladies; welcome, gra ma chree.*

XI.

Spoken at Exeter, February 5th, 1773.

LADIES, perhaps you've heard of Gyges' ring,
    Of which historians write, and poets sing:
Form'd by a Lydian sage, with potent spell
This ring its wearer made invisible.

---

* My heart's love.

After his death it often chang'd its master,
At length fate destin'd it to Zoroaster.
By his successors carefully possess'd,
Long did the magi flourish in the east;
'Till Ammon's son with Thais thither came,
Who fir'd Persepolis to please the dame.
Beneath its ruins long the treasure lay,
'Till by an Arab robber brought to day.
Unconscious of the prize he trudg'd along,
And sold it to a Brahmin for a song.
Thence in Bengal through various hands it pass'd,
And to a kinsman of my own at last;
By which such deeds he saw (the more's the pity)
As ne'er will be explained to the Committee:*
He dying gave it me, its virtues rare
Unfolded, and soon left a joyful heir:
To pass where'er I pleas'd, unseen and free,
O what a feast for curiosity!
No more shall Masonry, I cried, conceal
Its mysteries; all its secrets I'll unveil!
No more the fair shall languish; I'll explain
What they all wish to know, and wish in vain.
I said, and clapp'd my ring upon my finger,
Away I went in haste; I did not linger;
At a fat brother's back, close as his shade
I follow'd, and with him my entry made.
The brethren all were met, a social board;
I saw, unterrified, the guardian sword.
I saw—I saw—and now your ears prepare,
What I then saw I'll publicly declare.
Clear'd was my mental eye—I saw each grace
And each protecting genius of the place:

---

* A Committee of the House of Commons, then sitting to examine into East India affairs.

Friendship on wing ethereal flying round,
Stretch'd out her arm, and blest the hallow'd ground.
Humanity, well pleas'd, there took her stand,
Holding her daughter Pity in her hand;
There Charity, which soothes the widow's sigh,
And wipes the dew-drop from the orphan's eye;
There stood Benevolence, whose large embrace,
Uncircumscribed, took in the human race;
She saw each narrow tie, each private end,
Indignant Virtue's universal friend;
Scorning each frantic zealot, bigot fool,
She stamp'd on every breast her golden rule.
And though the doors are barr'd 'gainst you, ye fair,
Your darling representative was there,
Sweet Modesty amid the moral lay,
To you her tribute did remembrance pay;
I saw each honest heart with transport flow,
I saw each honest cheek with rapture glow;
These little absences, I found, would prove
But added fuel to the torch of love.
Smit with delight—at once reveal'd I stood,
And begged admission of the brotherhood:
They kindly heard, and pardon'd my offence,
I barter'd curiosity for sense.
My magic ring destroy'd, reduc'd to dust,
Taught what was right, and generous, and just;
For Masonry, though hid from prying eyes,
In the broad world admits of no disguise.

XII.

To the Play of "Know your own Mind," spoken by MR. SUTHERLAND, *in Mason's clothing, at Dundee Theatre, in October, 1778. Written by* J. R. LAMY, ESQ., *a Member of St. David's Lodge, Dundee, No. 97 of the Grand Lodge of Scotland.*

MUSIC, be hush!—let catgut cease to trill,
   I come to speak a prologue, if ye will.
To close the day, Sol sinks into the west,
And the pale moon proclaims the hour of rest:
Now silence reigns! and nature from her treasure
Pours forth to mortals ev'ry lib'ral pleasure.
Those badges of an ancient art I wear,
Which grace the prince, and dignify the peer.
The sister lodges bade me kindly say,
They love the drama—and they've chose the play,
"Know your own mind"—It is no common thing;
Some fickle minds are ever on the wing.
When sprightly Fancy once begins to roam,
She little thinks of anything at home;
Such wand'ring minds in ev'ry place are known,
Who know your minds much better than their own.
This is no secret, though we've secrets too,
Secrets as yet unknown to some of you;
Without the aid of devils, spells, or charms,
The coquet fair-one drops into our arms.
Honour and virtue all our actions guide,
We woo the virgin, and we kiss the bride;
But never blab—for blabbing is forbidden,
Under the clothing the grand secret's hidden.
I have a mind one secret to disclose,
(Come forth, sweet secret, from the blushing rose),
The tale unfolded, to the world discovers,
That we Free-masons are no luke-warm lovers;

Sly, leering looks, and soft and tender presses,
Are signs and grips no other man possesses;
And when a brother tries the maid to move,
He whispers Phillis that the word is—Love.

XIII.

OF all the orders founded by the great,
    The wise and good, of old or modern date,
None, like the Craft of Masonry, can claim
The glorious summit of immortal fame.
Upon her principles creation stands,
Form'd by the first Almighty Mason's hands,
Who by the rules of geometry display'd
His power and wisdom through the worlds He made.
The soul of man with knowledge He impress'd,
And taught him Masonry to make him bless'd;
But soon fond man forsook the pointed road,
And lost his knowledge when he left his God.
Long time he wander'd, sore with woe oppress'd,
And dire remorse stung home his conscious breast.
At length he pray'd; and heav'n receiv'd his prayer,
Pleas'd to behold with pity, and to spare;
And taught a way the science to regain,
Through arduous study and laborious pain.
But 'twas forbid the secret to declare,
That all might equally the labour share:
And hence it is the best alone can claim
The noblest character, a Mason's name;
And that the art, from other eyes conceal'd,
Remains a secret, as if ne'er reveal'd.
Let cowans, therefore, and the upstart fry
Of Gormagons, our well earn'd praise deny.

Our secrets let them as they will deride;
For thus the fabled fox the grapes decried;
While we, superior to their malice live,
And freely their conjectures wild forgive.

XIV.

Spoken at Exeter, January 7th, 1771.

THOUGH slander follows wheresoe'er I go,
    To vilify the art she does not know,
Undaunted, (guilt alone has cause to fear),
Cloth'd with this honour'd badge I now appear,
Owning myself a Mason; at the name
No guilty redness dyes my cheek with shame:
Let slander follow, I her darts defy,
And laugh at sneering folly's oft-told lie.
But what our order teaches I will show,
The lessons you must love when once you know:
It always bids us humbly to adore
Th' Almighty Architect, by whose great pow'r
The universe was built; to His decree,
Which wisdom ever guides, resign'd to be.
It makes us zealous in our country's cause,
True to its prince, and faithful to its laws;
For ever bids us, with the strictest care,
To act with all the world upon the square;
Never to publish a frail neighbour's shame,
Or filch away a brother's honest name;
To be sincere; his secrets ne'er reveal,
And him to serve with fervency and zeal.
With true philanthropy it warms our breast,
With useful zeal to succour the distress'd;
Bids us show mercy when we have the pow'r,

And to the houseless stranger ope the door;
The naked with warm vestments to infold,
And guard the shiv'ring wand'rers from the cold:
To feed the hungry, bid them eat and live,
And to the thirsty lip the cup to give;
To visit wretches tortur'd by disease,
Make smooth their bed, and pour the balm of ease;
The widow's tale, the orphan's cry to hear,
And from their eyes wipe off affliction's tear;
"To know each office, each endearing tie,
"Of soft-eyed heav'n-descended Charity."
Upright it bids us walk; to put a rein
On sensual appetites, and pride restrain.
It roots out narrow notions from the mind,
And plants a gen'rous love for all mankind;
Regards not modes of faith, but cries, "Unite
With all who work by the nice rule of right;
All have one Father; all good men and true,
In different roads the same great end pursue."
When to the lodge we go, that happy place,
*There faithful friendship smiles in every face.
What though our joys are hid from public view,
They on reflection please, and must be true.
*The lodge the social virtues fondly love;
*There wisdom's rules we trace, and so improve:
There we (in moral architecture skill'd),
Dungeons for vice—for virtue temples build;
*Whilst scepter'd reason from her steady throne,
*Well pleas'd surveys us all, and makes us one.
There concord and decorum bear the sway,
And moral music tunes th' instructive lay:

---

* The lines marked with this reference are closely imitated from the Free-masons' beautiful and well-known Anthem.

There on a pleasing level all appear,
And merit only is distinguish'd there,
Fraternal love and friendship there increase,
And decent freedom reigns, and lasting peace,
Secrets we have—but those we gladly show
To proper persons, who apply to know.
Be not offended, lovely, beauteous fair,
That you from Mason's rights excluded are;
'Tis not because we think you would disclose
Whate'er within your breasts we might repose;
But we're afraid (and sure our fears are true)
Were you admitted, love would enter too;
That jealousy might then our hearts inflame,
And to a rival's turn a brother's name;
Break all our bonds, annihilate our joy,
And soon our ancient order quite destroy.
Be not offended! we your sex adore,
And pay true homage to your sov'reign pow'r.
Thus I the lessons which we're taught have shown,
Which surely must be lov'd as soon as known;
If e'er with these our actions disagree,
Censure the men—but blame not Masonry;
We do not blame, when Christians go astray,
The light that came from heav'n to show their way.

XV.

Spoken at Exeter, January 27th, 1777.

THE mighty conq'rors who aspire to fame,
  And who by wide-spread ruin raise a name,
Who glory in the battles which they gain,
And ride, exulting, o'er th' ensanguin'd plain;
Such men as these my heart can ne'er approve,
Terror they cause—but cannot win my love;

These, by eternal justice were design'd
For righteous ends, the scourges of mankind.
My heart delights in these,—the truly wise,
Who, men to make most happy, civilize;
The band illustrious,—the benignant few,
Who teach the boist'rous passions to subdue;
Instruct mankind in ev'ry gen'rous art,
And, by example, humanize the heart;
Who, like the sun, their blessings widely spread,
Who comfort give to grief—to hunger, bread;
Whose minds, contracted by no narrow plan,
Own as a brother ev'ry virtuous man;
Who science and morality improve,
And to all climes diffuse fraternal love,
These, only, heroes in my mind appear;
And such I more than honour,—I revere.
To form such heroes Masonry was given,
Most gracious gift of ever bounteous heaven!
And oh! what pleasure now expands my mind,
To see around the friends of human-kind;
My brethren—sons of mercy—who bestow
With lib'ral hand the balm for mortal's woe;
Who unconfin'd benevolence impart,
Dilate the narrow soul, and mend the heart.
Go on, ye wise philanthropists, pursue
The certain path which leads to honour true;
Still live as ye are taught, that men may see
What human nature can, and ought to be;
Then Masonry, the source of truth and peace,
Will spread its influence far, and far increase;
Unfading glory deck the Mason's name,
Whilst built on virtue stands his spotless fame.

XVI.

Spoken at Exeter, January 12th, 1775.

THROUGH many an age, amid the shock of arms,
    Religion's jars, and party's fell alarms;
Mid folly's lies, and slander's forged stains,
Still unsubverted, Masonry remains,
Begot by Wisdom, and upheld by Truth,
Still feels the vigour of unfading youth.
The mystic building stands mid envy's flood,
And evil finds itself o'ercome by good.
Still lock'd in secrecy the hallow'd tie,
Its generous virtues meet the public eye;
And actions now are candidly confess'd,
To show the hidden motives of the breast.
Hypocrisy awhile may cheat the sight,
But time will bring the sneaky pest to light.
Ages have stamp'd a value on our art,
But 'tis our deeds that must convince the heart.
    The Mason views yon glitt'ring orbs on high,
Fix'd in the vast, o'er-arching canopy,
And from the Architect benignant draws
His humbler actions, less extensive laws,
Benevolence is hence his darling theme,
His waking monitor, his midnight dream.
He views the various races of mankind,
And views them always with a brother's mind.
No modes of faith restrain his friendly zeal;
The world is but one larger common-weal.
Yet not alone the fruitless will to bless,
The Mason's heart is open to distress;
His eye sheds pity's dew,—his hand is near
To wipe away affliction's starting tear;
The widow smiles;—compassion weaves her wing;—
The prisoner leaps for joy,—the orphans sing.

O brethren! still pursue the task divine;
For us hath rectitude mark'd out the line.
Behold Humility the level bear,
And Justice, steady-handed, fix the square.
Within our lodge hath Friendship plac'd her throne;
There Unity hath knit her sacred zone;
There Reason, with simplicity of soul;
There modest Mirth and Temp'rance guard the bowl;
There moral Music lifts her tuneful lore,
And Secrecy sits smiling at the door,
Conscious, though not to prying mortals giv'n,
That all our actions are approv'd by heav'n;
Conscious that all who aim at Virtue's goal,
Bear our essential myst'ries in their soul.
    To you, ye fair, adorn'd with every grace,
Though ancient custom hath forbid that place,
We know your worth, your excellence we prize,
We own your charms—the magic of your eyes;
The wretch who loves not you—upon our plan—
Forfeits the name of Mason, and of man.

XVII.

Written by Mr. Woods, *and spoken by him at the New Theatre, Edinburgh, on Monday Evening, February 18th, 1793, when was performed, "I'll Tell you What!" by desire of the Most Worshipful and Most Noble* George, Marquis of Huntly, *Grand Master of Scotland.*

THE glorious temple rais'd by David's son,
    Where Hiram's skill with matchless splendour shone,
In many a verse hath spoke the Mason's fame,
And equall'd with the King's the Master's name.
    The ample base, where sculpture twines the wreath,
And fondly bids departed Virtue breathe,

The beauteous column that ne'er tires the eye,
The lofty spire that seems to pierce the sky,
All these, and more, the Mason's skill display;
Press'd by the hand of Time, they melt away:
More fix'd the fame his moral aims impart;
On the foundation of an upright heart
He rears a structure chance can ne'er annoy,
Malice deface, or Ignorance destroy.

   None but the favour'd band, who boast the will
A brother's generous purpose to fulfil,
May with due rites and formal reverence tread
The sacred paths by mystic science made:
Hence vain conceit hath often aim'd to throw
Contempt on maxims it could never know;
But, though religion does her face enshrine
In awful clouds, we own her voice divine;
Masons with anxious zeal their myst'ries guard,
Yet of the Mason's worth who hath not heard?
Their publc acts by truth to fame consign'd,
Speak them the liberal friends of human kind:
And might the muse their gracious deeds recite,
She'd not forget the kindness shown to-night.

   In Gallia's fields, when English Harry fought,
His drooping soldiers in their tents he sought;
"The man to-day that draws for me his sword,
"Shall be my brother!"—was the hero's word:
The name of brother touched each soldier's breast,
He grasp'd his arms, and shook with pride his crest.
Th' event is known—the boasters forc'd to yield,
Fled, while the band of brothers scour'd the field—
If thus the name of brother, like a charm,
Could frozen valour into action warm,
What solid virtues 'mongst this band must grow,
Who own a brother's name, and all his duties know!

XVIII.

Spoken by Brother JOHN JACKSON, ESQ.,* *afterwards Patentee of the Theatre Royal, Edinburgh, before the Play of "The Recruiting Officer," by desire of the Right Honourable and Most Worshipful* EARL OF ELGIN, *Grand Master of the Most Ancient and Honourable Fraternity of Free and Accepted Masons, April 17th, 1762,* A. L. 5762.

WHEN the Grand Master, and great Lord of All,
Call'd up from chaos this terrestrial ball,
He gave the word, and swift o'er eldest night
Beam'd the first dawning of celestial light.
Confusion heard His voice, and, murm'ring, fled,
Whilst Order rul'd and triumph'd in its stead;
Discordant atoms, rang'd from pole to pole,
Forgot to jar, and peace possess'd the whole;
The fiercest foes in mutual concord strove,
And all—at once—was harmony and love.

By this example taught, Free-masons join,
And full in sight pursue the heavenly sign.
With love's firm bands connected hand in hand,
On Friendship's solid base secure we stand;
While confidence and truth, by turns impress'd,
Beam heavenly influence on each conscious breast.
No party feuds, no fierce intestine jars,
No senseless tumults, no pernicious wars,
Disturb our calm repose, where peace alone,
In decent order, fills the friendly throne.

---

* In the character of a Master Mason.

Can Wisdom's self a nobler method find
To charm the soul and harmonize mankind
Than we adopt, who labour still to prove
Unblemish'd truth, firm faith, and mutual love?
And ye (unconscious of the heavenly ray)
Who smile, perhaps, at what these numbers say,
Confine the rash reproach, and, warn'd, forbear
To spurn our laws because some brothers err.
In nature's fairest products faults arise,
But shall we thence all harmony despise?
Or think creation's beauteous scheme undone,
Because some specks appear upon the sun?

XIX.

WHEN heaven's eternal Architect began
    To frame that noble superstructure, man,
His plan He laid with wisdom all divine,
And Power Almighty fill'd the great design:
An outward form He gave, throughout complete,
Where strength and softness, pow'r and beauty meet
Where native majesty maintain'd her throne:
The fair, though faint, resemblance of His own:
A front erect, the Godhead to adore,
To view His work, and tremble at His pow'r:
And in this frame a godlike soul He placed,
With reason, knowledge, and discernment graced.
Alike His goodness did to all dispense
A due proportion of directing sense.
One only gift there still remain'd behind,
But for the few, the chosen few, design'd;
'Twas sacred Masonry, that crown'd the whole,
And to a nobler height exalts the soul.

Of this great art the secrets to obtain,
Mankind for ages past have strove in vain;
In vain shall strive—till lawfully acquir'd,
The noble truths we teach their breasts have fir'd—
Yet to th' unlearn'd thus far let it be known,
Our darling secret's honesty alone:
Howe'er through depths or mysteries explor'd,
Still Virtue is our grand, our master word;
In that great secret centres all our art,
For each good man's a Mason at his heart.

XX.

WHILE others sing of wars and martial feats,
   Of bloody battles, and of famed retreats,
A nobler subject shall my fancy raise,
And Masonry alone shall claim my praise:
Hail, Masonry! thou royal art divine!
Blameless may I approach thy sacred shrine;
Thy radiant beauties let me there admire,
And warm my heart with thy celestial fire:
Ye wilful blind, seek not your own disgrace,
Be sure you come not near the hallow'd place,
For fear too late your rashness you deplore,
And terrors feel, by you untaught before.
With joy my faithful brethren here I see,
Joining their hearts in love and unity;
Endeav'ring still each other to excel
In social virtues, and in doing well:
No party jars, political debate,
Which often wrath excite, and feuds create;
No impious talk, no wanton jests nor brawls,
Are ever heard within our peaceful walls;

Here, in harmonious concert, friendly join
The prince, the soldier, tradesman, and divine,
And to each other mutual help afford;
The honest farmer and the noble lord.
Freedom and mirth attend the cheerful bowl,
Refresh the spirits and enlarge the soul;
Refreshment we with moderation use,
For temperance admits of no abuse;
Prudence we praise, and Fortitude commend,
To Justice always and her friends a friend:
The scoffing tribe, the shame of Adam's race,
Deride those mysteries which they cannot trace;
Profane solemnities they never saw,
For lying libels are to them a law;
The books of Masonry they in vain explore,
And turn mysterious pages o'er and o'er;
Hoping the great arcanum to attain,
But endless is their toil, and fruitless all their pain;
They may as well for heat to Greenland go,
Or in the torrid regions seek for snow;
The Royal Craft the scoffing tribe despise,
And veil their secrets from untutor'd eyes.

XXI.

Written by RICHARD GARDINER, ESQ., *and spoken by* MRS. DYER, *before the Play of "Love for Love." performed by desire of the Great Lodge at Swaffham, Norfolk, May 6th, 1765.*

WHILE royal splendour and theatric state
    On princely Barry and king Garrick wait,
How little can we hope an humble stage,
Void of all pomp, can your applause engage!
For which among you ladies can discern
A Covent Garden in a Swaffham barn?
Yes, 'tis a barn—yet, fair ones, take me right—
Ours is no play—we hold a lodge to-night!
And should our building want a slight repair,
You see we've friends among the brethren there.
        [*Pointing to the Masons on the stage.*
Reply the Scalds,* with miserable frown,
"Masons repair! they'd sooner pull it down,
A set of ranting, roaring, rumbling fellows,
Who meet to sing 'Old Rose' and 'Burn the Bellows;'
Champagne and claret, dozens in a jerk,
And then, O Lord, how hard they've been at work!
Next for the secret of their own wise making,
Hiram and Boaz, and grand master Jachin,
Poker and tongs! the sign! the word! the stroke!
'Tis all a nothing, and 'tis all a joke.
Nonsense on nonsense! let them storm and rail,
Here's the whole history of their mop and pail;
For 'tis the sense of more than half the town,
Their secret is—a bottle at the Crown."
But not so fast, ye enemies to light,
I, though no Mason, am their friend to night;

---

* The Scald Miserable Society.

And, by your leaves, 'tis something strange, I trow,
To slander that which none of you can know.
We women, though we like good Masons well,
Sometimes are angry that they will not tell;
And then we flaunt away from rout to rout,
And swear, like you, we've found the secret out.
But O vain boast! to all enquiring eyes
Too deep the mine where that bright jewel lies.
That Masons have a secret is most true;
And you, ye beauties, have a secret too;
Now, if the Masons are so rigid grown,
To keep their secret to themselves alone,
Be silent in your turns, 'tis that allures,
Silence! and bid the Masons find out yours.
Thus far conjecture in the comic way,
But let not fancy lead your thoughts astray.
The ties of honour only Masons bind,
Friends to each other and to all mankind;
True to their king, and for their country bold,
They flew to battle like their sires of old;
Banish'd the trowel for the barbed spear,
And where loud cannons thunder'd form'd the square.
Gallant and gay at Minden's glorious plain,
And the proud Moro storm'd, alas! in vain!
In peace with honest hearts they court the fair,
And most they triumph when they triumph there.
Their actions known, their bitt'rest foes approve,
For all that Masons ask is—Love for Love.

XXII.

YOU'VE seen me oft in gold and ermine dress'd,
    And wearing short liv'd honours on my breast;
But now, the honourable badge I wear
Gives an indelible high character:
And thus by our Grand Master am I sent,
To tell you what by Masonry is meant.
If all the social virtues of the mind;
If an extensive love to all mankind;
If hospitable welcome to a guest,
And speedy charity to the distress'd;
If due regard to liberty and laws,
Zeal for our king and for our country's cause;
If these are principles deserving fame,
Let Masons then enjoy the praise they claim;
Nay, more: though war destroys what Masons build,
Ere to a peace inglorious we would yield,
Our squares and trowels into swords we'll turn,
And make our foes the wars they menace mourn;
For their contempt well no vain boaster spare,
Unless by chance we meet a Mason there.

EPILOGUES.

I.

Spoken before the Union Lodge, Exeter, in the character of COLIN MACLEOD, *in the Comedy of "The Fashionable Lover," January 27th, 1777.*

COLIN MACLEOD you see again appears,
 And these white gloves and this white apron wears,
He's a Free-mason—you, brethren, ken it well;
But how you ken it, that I shanna tell.
Frown not, my pretty lasses, though from you
Our secret is conceal'd, we still are true;
None will more constant lovers prove, believe me;
And we're no Masons if we e'er deceive ye.
In Edinburgh I lately was, and there
Of Masons muckle good I chanc'd to hear:
They told me they were helpful to the poor,
Lov'd all mankind, and ope'd their friendly door
To men of mean as well as noble blood,
If they had honest hearts—were true and good.
Aw my poor father left was honesty,
And, by my soul, it is not spent by me;
I offer'd—was receiv'd—and quickly found
What they had told me was not empty sound.
Then I to lodges, overjoy'd, repair'd,
And I will now disclose what there I heard:
They told me in my dealings to be just,
To keep my word, be faithful to my trust;

To love the man whose heart no falsehood knew,
Whether a Turk, a Christian or a Jew;
They told me that the gracious God above
Did guid men of all faiths and climates love.
They said—ne'er let affliction pass thee by,
And not ask what it ails—they bade me try
To ease the troubled mind, to wipe the tearful eye.
Ah! when I see distress my heart receives
Ecod! sic grief, and sic a pull it gives,
I canna for my soul, without great pain,
I canna get it bock t' its place again;
And to my lips it jumps for joy, when I
Can find the means to stop a brother's sigh:
I want to help all those who feel distress,
Cold hearts all hanna who cold climes possess.
Since heav'n has done so much for me, I were
A graceless loon a little not to spare;
A little, my dear brethren in distress!
Muckle I'll spare to make your suff'rings less;
I canna happy be, and you not so,
I take a share in every human woe.
 Oh! Masonry, 'twas you my heart inclin'd
Thus with effectual love to love mankind;
You taught me mercy, and enlarged my mind.
May all your lessons through the world extend,
Then man will be of man the certain friend;
No different faith or party disunite,
And doing gude be every mon's delight.

II.

Spoken on a like occasion, February 5th, 1773.

MRS. H. *(struggling as if to come on the Stage.)*

EXCUSE me, Sir—I'll not be held—go to!
   I fancy I can speak as well as you;
I'm not prepar'd you say—perhaps you'r bit—
Alas, you little know of women's wit.
Prologues, and songs, and all! 'tis rather hard
I should not in deal put in my card.
Encroach on Mason ground! no lodge is here,
I'll speak the Epilogue, that's flat and fair.
                          Coming forward.
Brethren, (for by your smiles I well can see,
You bear our sex no great antipathy)
Forgive this little bustle and intrusion,
For whence did order spring but from confusion?
And sure you'll deem a lady not absurd,
To claim her right in having the last word.
Besides, to be more plain, and tell you true,
We have our mysteries as well as you.
In short (though I'm not apt to be laconic)
Our aprons, though not sheep's-skin, are Masonic.
                   [*Pointing to her head dress.*
Behold this tower suspended in the air,
What Master Mason with his line and square,
E'er form'd a juster plan? 'tis built t' a hair.
   [*Turning half round and pointing to the hinder hair.*
This demi-bastion! is it not complete?
See you not here the beautiful and great?
Am I not qualified to give a lecture,
Who boast such noble piles of architecture?
You fix your scale—or spread your compass wide—
Eccentric fashion is the noblest guide.

Your figures! pshaw! e'en Euclid's self perhaps
'Twould poze to draw the figure of our caps.
And as for squares and hexagons, ye wise,
We beat you quite, for instance—Christmas pies.
Talk you of instruments! our simple feet
Shall dance, and form a labyrinth of Crete:
In circles most exact you deal,—mere rote;
What circle's equal to our petticoat?
You sage philosophers may laugh or stare,
But if we please, we'll make the circle square:
Think you you e'er will see in Bedford Place,
An oval finer than the female face?
But not to matter and its laws confin'd,
Our nicer heart attempts the human mind.
We turn the soil, fix firm foundation there,
And fanes to love and sacred Hymen rear.
As the ground varies, whether vale or hill,
We Masons vary our materials still.
Some use gay airs, yet innocently free,
Join'd with a dash of harmless coquetry;
Some coy reserve, some wit's enlivening fire,
Others, Amphion-like, the melting lyre.
The prude, indeed, could never build at all,
For scandal's sandy pillars quickly fall.
Two radiant eyes have often rais'd a pile,
As the sun quickens insects in the Nile;
Yet time, we own, will shake our firmest mound,
Unless by Virtue's lasting cement bound;
Unless good temper veils each latent flaw,
And decency her polish will bestow:
Thus, brethren, stands our claim to Masonry.
Let a free sister then accepted be:
Know, then, that all true adepts have their sign,
Discover yours, I'll frankly tell you mine.

III.

Addressed to the Friendly Brothers of St. Patrick.

BY MR. BROOKE.

HOW happy once, on heaven's primæval plan,
    Lived the resembling brotherhood of man;
When, ev'n on earth, as in the realms above,
All was goodwill, and unity, and love,
When social hearts, with feelings unconfin'd,
Heav'd for the weal and woe of human kind.
  'Till passion came, attended by debate,
Dissention follow'd, and then enter'd hate;
Contracting bosoms poorly beat for pelf,
And, like dark lanterns, form'd new bounds for self;
Man, lastly, loos'd on man (tremendous trade)
Destroy'd the being he was born to aid.
As, when alarm'd, the blood from ev'ry part
Recedes, to warm and fortify the heart,
Humanity disclaim'd the barb'rous crew,
And to Hibernia's fost'ring clime withdrew.
    Hail, Ireland! highly favour'd from above,
Of learning, once, and still the land of love;
Hail! thou prolific parent of the bless'd,
Old Isle of Saints, old home of the distress'd:
While guardian elements around thee wait,
And chase all poisons from thy sacred seat,
Whose social coasts, with ardour comprehend
The public patriot, and the private friend.
    Hail! I repeat, thou parent of the bless'd!
Old Isle of Saints, old home of the distress'd,
Who tak'st the way-worn stranger to thy breast.
Yes—to this truth the circling world must sign,
The rights of hospitality are thine.
O! may thy sons, who late on nature's plan
Form'd the new league and brotherhood of man,

May they stand forth the joint and worthy heir
Of that heroic Saint whose name they bear;
In them may our reviving voices hail
The patriot pillars of their country's weal;
In them may all the charities conspire,
The widow's husband, and the orphan's sire.
  May their choice union solely comprehend
What merits that supreme of titles—friend;
And, in one hallow'd circle, hold combin'd
The graces, gifts, and worth of human kind.

IV.

Spoken at Exeter, by MRS. HUDSON,
January 12th, 1775.

IN days of yore, 'tis said, the merry Greek,
  Old Æsop—held that birds and beasts could speak;
Owls moraliz'd—jackdaws could reason finely,
Horses neigh'd sense—apes chatter'd most divinely.
Lucky it is for you this gift is lost,
A rat might else have lurk'd beneath a post;
Though you expel us women from your house,
You could not banish each insidious mouse:
A fly might then have whisper'd to the gale,
A tiny cricket might have told the tale.
Happy the woman!—happy were the men!
You could have kept no secrets from us then.
Yet can our days some prodigies afford,
The Cock-lane ghost scratch'd on the vocal board;
Fanny revisited the upper air,
And caught all London by the list'ning ear;
The Stockwell conj'rer his enchantments brew'd,
Saucers and cups with motive powers endu'd;

The active glasses nimbly danc'd the hays;
Th' unwieldy dresser, and the wooden trays,
Jump'd rigadoons—the pudding piping hot
Came tumbling, rolling, bouncing from the pot.
Now, my good sirs, if all these facts have been,
Why may not greater miracles be seen?
Things that can move against the course of nature,
May likewise speak—you grant it—*ergo datur.*
O should I learn the secret from your bowl,
Would it not vex you to the very soul?
What say'st thou, honest bowl?—when met together
What's the chief subject of discourse? the weather?
True Englishmen's discourse—'tis cold to night—
'Tis very cold indeed,—you'r right, sir, right.
Or is it scandal, honest bowl?—Oh me!
I ask your pardon, that's the vice of tea.
Or is it politicks?—the Boston boys?
Tarring and feathering? rioting and noise?
    But, serious now, all raillery apart,
I honour and esteem you from my heart;
Knowing yourselves, you scorn the dead-born jest;
Yours is the feeling mind, the virtuous breast.
Should the laugh echo from the weak and vain,
The laugh of folly cannot fix a stain.
Your souls attend to pity's voice sincere;
Friendship and mild affection harbour there.
Your wives, your children, will approve the lay,
And, conscious, own the truth of what I say.
On you the fair with safety may rely,
Masons exist but by fidelity.
Accept this eulogy upon your art,
The humble tribute of a grateful heart:
I to its worth, its benefits agree;
The time is not far off, then think of me,

V.

Spoken at Exeter, January 31st, 1772.

(Enter A. followed by B. speaking to him.)

NAY, but my dear good brother, why so nice?
　I vow that secrecy is grown a vice!
You say you've given your promise—all a joke,
A promise, like a pie-crust, should be broke;
Tell me your secret, I'll tell you a score.

A. You beaux tell everything you know, and more,
But we, who walk by reason's friendly aid, Neither
betray, nor fear to be betray'd: Nor think it fit that
wisdom's sacred rules, To all divulg'd, become the
sport of fools; With these, thank heav'n, we seldom
are perplex'd.

B. Well preach'd, good brother, and without a text,
Though you wont tell the secret, I could guess If I
knew what to make of that strange dress;
Gloves, square, and apron, to be sure they're
　　spruce,
But rather seem too nice for workmen's use.
Perhaps,—*(pauses)*—ay, that will do—you leave
　　your spouses,
And at the lodge conspire to build card houses.
There, as at White's, your tedious vigils keep,
And 'tis quadrille, or whist that murders sleep:
Subjects perhaps of Pleasure's golden reign,
Mirth is your business, and the word, champagne:
Perhaps of harmony you own the pow'r,
And sprightly glees beguile the fleeting hour;
Or else around the busy scandal flies,
And at each breath a lady's honour dies.

You mark their little foibles there, and rate 'em;
Since you exclude 'em, to be sure you hate 'em.
If this is all you meet for, this you'll see
In more perfection at the Coterie;
But in one thing we differ much—for there
In all our joys the ladies have a share;
At our harmonic meetings they preside,
And love and wine the blissful scene divide;
There dazzling lights each wond'ring scene
    confound,
And there we seem to dance on fairy ground;
And there—*A.* A moment's respite, if you can,
And hear how widely you mistake our plan:
Know, if in splendours any joys you place,
Superior lights our happy lodges grace;
Serenely bright, they lead no sense astray,
But point to wisdom's throne the arduous way;
Yet think not that we pass the churlish night
Without refreshment.—*B.* Then I'm in the right.

A. The moderate glass with caution we dispense, Not to bewilder, but to cheer the sense. We Masons aim not to be more than men, Music we have too.—*B.* Then I'm right again.

A. Yet no loose strains excite unchaste desire, Nor wanton sounds profane Urania's lyre; Chaste as the muse the lessons we are taught, Nor cards nor scandal there deserve a thought.

B. No cards!—no scandal! now you've spoil'd the
    whole—
A very pretty meeting, by my soul!
A modest set, who neither game nor swear!
Egad! I fancy you'll not catch me there.

In search of joys I vanish to Soho.
But stay—I'll leave one secret e'er I go:
  [*Affects to whisper.*
I find your order suits not lads of spirit.

A. For ever welcome to it men of merit. To such, of every clime, of every station, We give, at once, a general invitation.

VI.

Spoken at Exeter, January 19th, 1776.

OH! pray pardon my hurry—indeed I'm so heated!
Well! to see with what insolence women are treated!
I protest what this white-apron'd fellow has said
Has put the whole epilogue out of my head.
Good lack! 'twas the fairest, the prettiest petition,
That you Masons repeal your old stale prohibition,
And grant to us females an equal admission.
"What! shall they (says yon brute) on our lodges intrude,
Whom the church, and the bar, and the senate exclude?"
Struck dumb at this insult, with mortification,
Straight hither I flew to give vent to my passion;
But here each mild brother wears such a kind face,
That I feel more inclined in the epilogue's place,
Thus cooly and fairly to argue the case.
  To these you aver we have no right of common—
Like the crown of the French, fruit forbidden to women:
For the church you object, with (be sure) deep discerning,

That we fail of your meekness, your grace, and your
    learning.—
At the bar it perhaps may be urged that our clack
Would confound right with wrong, or turn white into
    black;
You might question our conscience to either fee pliant,
Or doubt our concern for the wrongs of a client;
In the senate, when women sit there, you will say,
Poor ruin'd old England will rue the sad day:
For a title the sex Magna Charta might barter,
Or the great Bill of Rights for a ribbon or garter;
But whilst man, mighty man, at the bar shall preside,
Guard the fold of the church, or the state-rudder
    guide,
In security (doubtless) religion shall smile,
And law and sweet liberty brighten our isle.

 Yet, O, ye select ones, who boast of your feeling,
Your charity, candour, and fair open dealing;
Ye Masons! come, now for your reasons, and tell us
Why you from your order for ever expel us?
Is it some treas'nous plot that you wickedly dive in?
No—a plot would have called for fine female contriving;
Or is it for fear we should blab all we know?
No—you'll own we can keep some few secrets from
    you;
Or is it—but hold—I've a tale in my head,
('Tis a story mayhap you have formerly read)
How Samson was wheedled and teas'd by his wife,
'Till he gave up his secret, his strength, and his life.

 Alas! if we thus, like Dalilah, should court ye,
'Till our piano at last charm you out of your forte,
Who knows, (and I fairly acknowledge my fears)
But like her we may bring an old house o'er our ears?

Then be warn'd, O ye fair! curiosity cease,
Let us leave them their myst'ries and secrets in peace;
And with candour confess the men most to our mind,
Whom secrecy, truth, and fidelity bind.
The fruits of their union our blessing shall prove,
For the heart that buds friendship must blossom with love.

VII.

Spoken by MRS. HORTON.

WHERE are these hydras? let me vent my spleen,
Are these Freemasons? bless me! these are men!
And young and brisk too; I expected monsters;
Brutes more prodigious than Italian songsters.
Lord, how report will lie! how vain this pother;
These look like sparks who only love each other!
(Ironically.)
Let easy faiths on such gross tales rely,
'Tis false by rules of physiognomy,
I'll ne'er believe it poz, unless I try:
In proper time and place, there's little doubt
But one might find the wondrous secret out;
I shrewdly guess, egad! for all their shyness,
They'd render signs and tokens too of kindness;
If any truth in what I here observe is,
They'll quit ten brother's for one sister's service.
But hold, wild fancy, whither hast thou stray'd?
Where man's concern'd, alas, how frail's a maid!
I'm come to storm, to scold, to rail, to rate,
And see, th' accuser's turned advocate.
Say, to what merits may I not pretend,
Who, though no sister, do yet prove your friend:

Would beauty thus but in your cause appear,
'Twere something, sirs, to be accepted there:
      (Pointing to the boxes.)
Ladies, be gracious to the mystic arts,
And kindly take the gen'rous Masons' parts;
Let no loquacious fop your joys partake,
He sues for telling, not for kissing's sake;
Firm to their trust, the faithful craft conceal;
They cry no roast meat, fare they ne'er so well;
No tell-tale sneer shall raise the conscious blush,
The loyal brother's word is always—hush.
What though they quote old Solomon's decree,
And vainly boast that thro' the world they're free;
With ease you'll humble the presumptuous braves,
One kind regard makes all these freemen slaves.

VIII.

Spoken by MRS. THURMOND, *a Mason's Wife.*

WITH what malicious joy, e'er I knew better,
 Have I been wont the Masons to bespatter;
How greedily have I believed each lie,
Contriv'd against that fam'd society;
With many more complaints. 'Twas very hard
Women should from their secrets be debarr'd,
When kings and statesmen to our sex reveal
Important secrets which they should conceal,
That beauteous ladies, by their sparks ador'd,
Could never wheedle out the Mason's word;
And oft their favours have bestowed in vain,
Nor could one secret for another gain:
I thought, unable to explain the matter,
Each Mason, sure, must be a woman hater;

With sudden fear and dismal horror struck,
I heard my spouse was to subscribe the book.
By all our loves I begg'd he would forbear;
Upon my knees I wept and tore my hair.
But when I found him fix'd, how I behav'd,
I thought him lost, and like a fury rav'd;
Believed he would for ever be undone,
By some strange operation undergone.
When he came back I found a change, 'tis true,
But such a change as did his youth renew;
With rosy cheeks and smiling grace he came,
And sparkling eyes that spoke a bridegroom's flame,
Ye married ladies, 'tis a happy life,
Believe me, that of a Free-mason's wife,
Though they conceal the secrets of their friends,
In love and truth they make us full amends.

IX.

WELL, heaven be prais'd, the mighty secret's out;
    The secret that has made so strange a rout:
This moment I was taught behind the scenes,
What every word, and sign, and token means;
A charming secret, but I must conceal it,
If time at nine months' end does not reveal it,
What monstrous, horrid lies do some folks tell us;
Why, Masons, ladies, are quite clever fellows,
They're lovers of our sex, as I can witness,
And ne'er contrary act to moral fitness; *
If any of ye doubt it, try the Masons,
They'll not deceive your largest expectations;
Let no misguided apprehensions seize ye,

---

  * Alluding to Chubb's Essay, so entitled.

They won't do anything that can displease ye;
They're able workmen, and completely skill'd in
The truest arts and mysteries of building;
They'll build up families, and, as most fit is,
Not only will erect, but people cities;
They'll fill as well as fabricate your houses,
And propagate a race of strong built spouses.
If such their gifts, such, ladies, is their merit,
So great their skill, and strength, and life, and spirit;
What female heart can be so very hard,
As to refuse them their deserved reward?
Once on a time (as heathen stories say)
Two Mason-gods to Troy town took their way;
Arriv'd, and hir'd to work, to work they fell;
Hard was their task, but executed well,
With more than human strength, these heav'nly powers
Raised the impregnable Dardanian towers;
Those towers which long secur'd the Trojan dames
From Grecian ravishers, and Grecian flames;
Gratis they did it, whatsoe'er was done,
Wrong'd of their pay by king Laomedon,
Base, sordid soul, of princes the disgrace,
But heaven his guilt avenged upon his race,
Most justly did his Troy at length expire,
Reduc'd to ashes by vindictive fire.
Ladies, this story's written for your learning,
Let Troy's example fright you all from burning;
Let it this truth in every breast inspire,
That every workman's worthy of his hire;
But sure such virtue in the present age is,
None will defraud the brethren of their wages;
None will transgress the laws of common sense,
Which give both sexes due benevolence:
A Mason's full reward, then, do not grudge,
Since every Mason is your humble drudge.

X.

Spoken by MRS. BELLAMY.

WELL, here I'm come to let you know my thoughts;
Nay ben't alarm'd, I'll not attack your faults;
I'm in good humour, and am come to prattle,
Han't I a head well turn'd, d'ye think, to rattle?
But to clear up the point, and to be free,
What think you is my subject?—Masonry!
Though I'm afraid, as lawyers' cases clear,
My learn'd debate will leave you where you were.
What think you, ladies, ain't it very hard,
That we should from this secret be debarr'd?
How comes it that the softer hours of love,
To wheedle out this secret fruitless prove?
For we can wheedle when we hope to move.
What can it mean? why all this mighty pother?
These mystic signs, and solemn calling brother?
That we are qualified in signs is known;
We can keep secrets too, but they're our own.
When my good man first went to be a Mason,
Though I resolv'd to put the smoother face on,
Yet, to speak truly, I began to fear
He must some dreadful operation bear;
But he return'd, and on his face appear'd
A pleasing smile that every scruple clear'd;
Such added complaisance, so much good nature,
So much, so strangely alter'd for the better,
That, to increase the mutual dear delight,
Would he were made a Mason every night.

XI.

Spoken in the character of VIOLANTE, *after "The Wonder" or "A Woman keeps a Secret," performed by desire of the Union Lodge, at Exeter, January 14th, 1774.*

YE who possess that secret, which to gain
    We oft have sued, as often sued in vain!
Ye, whom th' entreaties of the fair you love,
In some soft moment never yet could move!
Once more with you, the brethren of the Union,
Our injur'd sex claims full and free communion.
Nay, after what you've heard and seen to night,
We ask no favour—we demand our right;
Since neither fear, nor shame, nor love, could wrest
The sacred trust from Violante's breast.
And let me tell you, sirs, the trial's such
I doubt you'd squeak were you press'd half as much.
Well then—out with your secret—What! all dumb!
Will you accept of us?—Deuce take your mum!
    I vow these Masons are mere Turkish fools,
Who dare believe we women have no souls;
And yet, I'm sure, amongst them all who flout us,
Not one can fancy Paradise without us.
But henceforth, if they still deny our merit,
We'll show them, if no soul, we have a spirit.
'Tis plainly all a plot against your wives,
But we may lead your worships blessed lives:
Ye who abroad with aprons gaily roam,
May sadly find the breeches worn at home;
Masters of lodges, not so of their houses,
May read their treas'nous lectures 'gainst their spouses;
Yet say, ye gallant sons of architecture,
Could not we match you with a curtain lecture?

Should this not mend you, we such tricks may show
As did the sex some thousand years ago;
The ladies then—(who dares the fact dispute?)
As now were curious, and the men as mute;
At length, beyond all female patience grown,
They constituted lodges of their own;
Had their own signs, and words, and (doubtless) jewels,
Aprons, and squares, and compasses, and trowels;
Nay, arm'd with sword and buckler to defy 'em,
And murder'd every male who ventur'd nigh 'em.
How 'twould affright you mute masonic dons,
Should we revive the lodge of Amazons!
Heav'ns!—neither promise, threat, nor love prevails;
Indeed!—and will you Masons ne'er tell tales?
'Faith then I will—and own, as 'tis but just t'ye,
Since you're so close, why we may safely trust ye;
For sure, my lovely sisters, they alone
Can keep our secrets who can keep their own.

APPENDIX
TO
MASONIC SONGS.

APPENDIX.

I.

By Bro. W. T. Harding, *Batley*.

A MASON'S heart is prone to love,
    To love and loyalty;
To cherish his time-honour'd Craft—
    Of ancient Masonry:

To cheer the languid hopes of life
    With feeling sympathy,
And greet, with friendship's warmest smiles,
    The sons of Masonry.

To guide us through the shoals of life,
    Thy beacon light appears,
To steer our bark with safety through
    This world of hopes and fears.

Within the bonds of brotherhood,
    In love and unity,
We still adhere to virtue's cause,
    To love and Masonry.

Within the halo of thy light
    O may we ever be
Like stars, resplendent, shining bright,
    Blest sons of Masonry.

And may the compass points direct
    Our hearts to heaven and Thee,
Our Ruler and great Architect,
    The hope of Masonry.

II.
THE FINAL TOAST.

By Bro. D. L. Richardson.

Music by Bro. J. R. Fletcher, *Bury.*

"Are your glasses charged in the West and the South?" the Worshipful Master cries;
"They're charged in the West, they're charged in the South," each Warden prompt replies;
Then to our final toast to-night, your glasses fairly drain,
"Happy to meet,—sorry to part,—Happy to meet again."

Cho.—Happy to meet, &c.

The Mason's social brotherhood around the festive board,
Reveals a wealth more precious far than selfish miser's hoard;
They freely share the priceless store that generous hearts contain,
"Happy to meet,—sorry to part,—Happy to meet again."

Cho.—Happy to meet, &c.

We work like Masons free and true, and when our task is done,
A merry song and a cheering glass are not unduly won;
And only at our farewell pledge is pleasure touched with pain,
"Happy to meet,—sorry to part,—Happy to meet again."

Cho.—Happy to meet, &c.

Amidst our mirth we drink, "To all poor Masons o'er the world,"
On every shore our flag of love is gloriously unfurled;
We prize each brother, fair or dark, who bears no moral stain:
"Happy to meet,—sorry to part,—Happy to meet again."

Cho.—Happy to meet, &c.

The Mason feels the noble truth the Scottish peasant told,
That "rank is but the guinea stamp, the man himself the gold."
With us the rich and poor unite, and equal rights maintain,
"Happy to meet,—sorry to part,—Happy to meet again."

Cho.—Happy to meet, &c.

"Dear Brethren of the 'Mystic tie'" the night is waning fast;
Our duty's done, our feast is o'er, this song must be our last;
Good night,—good night,—once more, once more repeat the farewell strain—
"Happy to meet,—sorry to part,—Happy to meet again."

Cho.—Happy to meet, &c.

III.

IN THE HEART OF A MASON'S LODGE.

By BRO. JOHN FAWCETT SKELTON, *Lodge No. 146.*
(*Written specially for the present work*).

(Tune, *"On board of a Man-of-War."*—1710.)

AROUND the festive board, we sit all at our ease,
And, keeping all Masonic, we do whate'er we please;
  The Graces all are there,
  With Love upon the square,
In the heart of a Mason's Lodge.

  Cho.—In the heart of a Mason's Lodge,
  In the heart of a Mason's Lodge,
  The Graces all are there,
  With Love upon the square,
  In the heart of a Mason's Lodge.

The symbols of the Craft, in beauty hang around;
There's food for deep reflection on the tesselated ground;
  The faces on the wall
  Only happy days recall,
In the heart of a Mason's Lodge.
  Cho.—In the heart, &c.

We sing a merry song, smoke the "calumet of peace,"
And gaily chat together in our cabinet of bliss;
  Each brother does his best
  To entertain the rest,
In the heart of a Mason's Lodge.
  Cho.—In the heart, &c.

No angry look is seen, each face is bright and gay,
And ev'ry risky topic of debate is put away;
  We keep the jubilee
  Of the jolly "Fourth Degree,"
In the heart of a Mason's Lodge.
   Cho.—In the heart, &c.

Our troubles in the world stop at the mystic door,
And nothing inharmonious may pass the threshold o'er,
  For Sorrow, Grief, and Care
  Never sit upon the square,
In the heart of a Mason's Lodge.
   Cho.—In the heart, &c.

May the canker-worm of strife ne'er enter to destroy
The glowing fruits of Masonry, its beauty and its joy;
  But Love and Honour dwell,
  With Charity, as well,
In the heart of a Mason's Lodge.
   Cho.—In the heart, &c.

IV.

By Bro. S. N. Evans, *Wolverhampton.*

(Tune, *"The brave old Oak."*)

A SONG for the Craft—the proud old Craft—
    Which has weather'd the storm so long;
Which has won renown from the cowl and the crown,
    And a lay from the child of song.
Its emblems stand on ev'ry land
    Where the foot of man hath been,
And every clime in the march of time
    Hath its signs and symbols seen.
        Then sing to the Craft—the proud old Craft—
           Which has weather'd the storm so long;
        And still may it be the boast of the free,
        And the theme of the deathless song.

In the days of old, when the wise and bold
    Had honour and power alone,
'Twas a greater pride o'er a lodge to preside,
    Than to sit on a monarch's throne:
The sceptre proud to the gavil bow'd,
    And the courtier bent his knee,
And humbly sought to be placed and taught,
    At the foot of the Mason free.
        Then sing to the Craft, &c.

It attained its prime in the olden time,
    When Solomon's temple rose,
But it shows to-day no sign of decay,
    And no lack of its vigour knows.
In the future's days shall its beacon blaze
    Thro' the gloom of surrounding night,
And serve to guide, o'er the troubled tide,
    The brother who knows its light.
        Then sing to the Craft, &c.

V.

THE BRAVE OLD CRAFT.

BY BRO. T. R. HOFLAND, *Lodge 130, Preston.*

(Tune, *"The brave old Oak."*)

A SONG to the Craft—the brave old Craft—
    That hath rul'd in the world so long;
Here's success to the Art—the time honoured Art—
    And its pillars so fair and strong.
On its fame and renown the sun ne'er goes down,
    But shines ever clear and bright;
The East and the West have its glory confess'd,
    And the North and the South own its might.
        Then sing to the Craft—the brave old Craft,—
            That hath rul'd in the world so long;
        And still may its worth illumine the earth,
            When ten thousand years are gone.

It dawned in the time when the grand eastern clime
    Was thrill'd with a voice divine;
When the heart and the soul first own'd the control
    Of the arts that exalt and refine.
Then a structure was reared—thus early revered—
    Devoted to friendship and love:
Sweet Charity smiled,—heaven's best belov'd child—
    From her mansions of beauty above.
        Then pledge to the Craft—the brave old Craft, &c.

Though states have decayed, and the laws they have made
    Are lost in the shadowy past;
Unfaded by time, in its grandeur sublime,
    Still our order stands firm and fast:
And still to man's heart it the truth doth impart,

He should be to his brother kind;
That honour and worth—brightest gems of the earth—
 In his bosom should ever be shrin'd!
  Then fill to the Craft—the brave old Craft, &c.

With feelings sincere he should wipe the sad tear,
 From the sorrowing mourner's cheek;
His mission is bless'd, to protect the oppress'd,
 And to comfort the lone and the weak.
The Great Architect's Eye, from his throne in the sky,
 Looks down and approves of our plan;
For Faith shall be pure, and Religion secure,
 While Masonry teacheth Man.
  So fill high to the Craft—the brave old Craft, &c.

VI.

MASONS' RULES.

(Tune, "Derry Down.")

ATTEND, brother Masons, while I faintly describe,
 The rules from our Tools we all may imbibe,
How from simple things greatest wisdom is drawn,
From whom of our Craft the advantage is known.
  Derry down, down, down, derry down.

You first must endeavour to form a good plan,
For at random who acts is not a wise man;
Who minds not proportion we count a great fool,
And what is he better who walks without rule?
  Derry down, &c.

Right to temper the Mortar true Masons should see,
Without proper Temper no mortals agree:
And to build by your line you'll find a great beauty,
For none keep direct without Line of Duty.
       Derry down, &c.

To keep within bounds from your Square you may learn,
To keep all things even your Plumb it will warn.
From your Cement, well wrought, be taught, too, you may,
In what due proportion to moisten your clay.
       Derry down, &c.

Your Trowel will teach you to be truly polite,
And how different bodies in one to unite:
And if still most smoothly through life you would steer,
Attend to your Compass, lest Danger be near.
       Derry down, &c.

From each of your tools you may knowledge extract:
The Mell teaches driving when men will not act;
Learn polish from Chizel, by Hammer ends meet;
Thus all from their tools may be Masons compleat.
       Derry down, &c.

From the various materials your Building is made,
Know Strength must arise from Union in Trade;
And from different parts supporting each other,
Each Mason should learn to take care of a brother.
       Derry down, &c.

Hence success we may drink to the Craft of a Mason,
For never a monarch could think it a base one:
But how can you amongst us find any disorders,
Since we're noted for minding all the Five Orders?
       Derry down, &c.

VII.
BEAUTIFUL SPIRIT.

BY BRO. J. ROGERS, P.M. 1219.

(Tune, "*Beautiful Venice.*")

BEAUTIFUL Spirit! Fountain of Love!
    Whose spring hath its source in the regions
        above;
How rich are the treasures thy symbols unfold,
To the heart that is versed in thy legends of old.
Sweet Charity's smile sheds a beam o'er thy path,
To chase ev'ry shadow of envy and wrath.
I have sung many themes, but the sweetest to me,
Is the beautiful Spirit of Masonry free.
        Cho.—Beautiful Spirit, &c.

Beautiful Spirit! Pride of the World!
O'er each region of earth are thy banners unfurled,
From the zone where the sun sheds her tropical beam,
To the pole where the Ice King makes captive the
        stream.
Of the mighty of old— of the noble to-day,
The brightest and proudest have bow'd to thy sway.
'Mid poesy's themes not a sweeter can be
Than the beautiful Spirit of Masonry free.
        Cho.—Beautiful Spirit, &c.

VIII.

(Tune, *"The Prince and Old England for ever."*)

BROTHER Masons, assembled as Masons should be,
  In worth, truth, and harmony's cause:
My song is a theme truly noble and free,
  And founded on Masonry's laws,
Like the sun-star of day is its lustre supreme,
  A lustre no foe can destroy;
And this we'll insist on, whatever folks dream,
  Our laws are the fountain of joy:
O! yes, and this fountain, so crystalline bright,
  To preserve is each Mason's endeavour:
And now for a toast, and a toast of delight,
  Here's Masons, Freemasons, for ever—huzza!
    The lodge of Freemasons for ever—huzza!
    And now for a toast, and a toast of delight,
    Here's Masons, Freemasons, for ever!

From the north to the south, the east to the west,
  Our Order is known to appear;
And the plume that so gracefully blazons its crest,
  To justice and mercy is dear!
Like the air that we breath in, it bears no control,
  So potent it waves for our good:
While *Faith, Hope,* and *Charity's* proud to enrol
  A cause that we'll seal with our blood;
Oh! yes, and this Order, so brilliant and bright,
  No malice nor demon can sever;
And now for a toast, and a toast of delight,
  Here's Masons, Freemasons, for ever—huzza!
    The lodge of Freemasons, &c.

Like man bound to man in true brotherly love,
    Our lodge rears its eagle-wing'd head;
And, under an *All-seeing Eye* from above,
    By white-rob d Benevolence led!
Blest Charity! where doth thy stream purer flow
    Than that which our *schools* has endowed?
Like the hymn-charm of angels, it vanquishes woe,
    And Freemasons sing it aloud:
Oh! yes, and this stream, too, so noble and bright,
    No envy nor hatred can sever:
And now for a toast, and a toast of delight,
    Here's Masons, Freemasons, for ever—huzza!
        The lodge of Freemasons, &c.

IX.
(Tune, *"Bachelor's Hall."*)

COME, come, brother Masons, assemble with joy,
    Let friendship and mirth still our labours employ,
Let vigour possess us in this glorious cause,
That gains from the heart most certain applause;
Still our work shall repel every envious shaft,
And honour ourselves, our country, and Craft.
    Come away, come away, to the lodge-room repair,
    For union and truth are the badges we wear.

The compass our guide, doth this lesson impart,
Content in our station and upright in heart;
The paths we pursue are with virtue combined,
And conscious in truth, we are level in mind.
Here unite all opinions, what's here understood,
Is the light we receive, "be just and be good."

The world may endeavour our secrets to gain,—
Industry and worth can the mystery obtain;
Here all are alike, no distinctions are known;
When Friendship invites us her dictates we own;
No politics ever we mix in our cause,
Though we honour our king, our religion, and laws.
Our hearts are expanded at Charity's call;
No ambition or pride our enjoyments appal;
The secrets that bind us are pure and refined,
And diffuse in our bosoms goodwill to mankind.
'Tis thus we unite, and with firmness endeavour,
For the king and the Craft, and Old England for ever.

X
By Brother Oborne. (1765).

COME, come, my dear brethren, and list to my song,
It is of the praise which to Masons belong,
The happiest of folks are the Masons that's free,
Who in love and true friendship do ever agree.

Each one that comes here must be true and sincere,
And the strictest enquiry his character bear;
For whoever's unworthy we never admit,
'Mongst Masons that's free and accepted to sit.

Here reason and judgment together combine,
And religion's great truths for to aid our design,
Mankind to instruct, and virtuous to be
Are the doctrines we teach unto Masons that's free.

Let disputes and confusion 'mongst us ne'er be heard,
Be decorum and decency ever observed;
And let us rejoice, and be merry, and sing,
And drink a full glass to the Craft and the King.

XI.

OURS IS THE LIFE TO PURSUE.

By Bro. John Fawcett Skelton, *Lodge No. 146.*

(Tune, *"Come, let us be happy together"*)

COME, let us be happy together,
    Affectionate Masons all round;
Assisting and cheering each other,
    Where in lodge or in life we are found.
Let us look to our glorious symbols,
    And practise what they but suggest;
Our jewels keep bright on our bosoms till death,
    For the life of a Mason's the best;
        His life is the best,
        His life is the best.
Then here's to the Craft, and God bless it!
    May ev'ry Freemason be true;
The world, then, were forc'd to confess it,
    That ours is the life to pursue.
        Cho.—Then here's to the Craft, &c.

How ancient the Craft that we treasure!
    Our service, how beautiful through!
Our music, how grand in its measure!
    Our precepts, how noble and true!
Then let us be proud of our Order,
    The oldest, the fairest, the best;
The grandest of all ever founded on earth;
    By heaven supported and blest;
        Supported and blest,
        Supported and blest.

Then here's to the Craft, and God bless it!
   May ev'ry Freemason be true;
The world, then, were forc'd to confess it,
   That ours is the life to pursue.
      Cho.—Then here's to the Craft, &c.

May "the Architect Great" that's above us
   Guard us, and "Freemasonry," too;
Enlighten, encourage, and love us,
   And strengthen our Order anew.
It bids us adore Him—our Maker—
   The Light of the Lodge-Room above!
And, here, to our brethren, and neighbours, and all,
   To act with Truth, Friendship, and Love!"
      "Truth, Friendship, and Love,
      Truth, Friendship, and Love!"
Then here's to the Craft, and God bless it!
   May ev'ry Freemason be true;
The world, then, were forc'd to confess it,
   That ours is the life to pursue.
      Cho.—Then here's to the Craft, &c.

XII.

By Brother Oborne. (1765).

(Tune, *"Hearts of Oak"*)

COME, ye Masons so free, who do ever agree,
   In harmony, friendship, and justice, and love;
And thereby to all show an emblem below,
   Of the harmony reigning in heaven above.

CHORUS.

   We are Masons that's free,
   And we always agree;
      We always are ready,
      Steady, brothers, steady,
   To assist the distrest, and be honest and free

Let each join his aid the lodge to support,
And constantly make it his place of resort;
And when he comes there let him chearfully join
And assist in the rites of our science divine.
    Cho.—We are Masons, &c.

And when business is o'er, if the master 'll permit,
Let some worthy brother, as together they sit,
In praise of our Art give a Freemason's song,
For to Masons all honour and praise do belong.
    Cho.—We are Masons, &c.

Then fill up a bumper to great BEAUFORT'S name,
Oh! long may it stand on the records of fame;
Be his name the toast, and let it thrice go round,
And may Masonry flourish and ever abound!
    Cho.—We are Masons, &c.

XIII.

INITIATION.

COURAGE, brother, do not stumble,
　　Though thy path be dark as night,
There's a star to guide the humble,
　　"Trust in God and do the right."
　　　　Cho.—Do the right! do the right!
　　　　　　Trust in God, and do the right.

Trust no party, sect, or faction;
　　Trust no leaders in the fight;
But in every word and action,
　　"Trust in God, and do the right."
　　　　Cho.—Do the right, &c.

Simple rule and safest guiding,
　　Inward peace and inward might,
Star upon our path abiding,
　　"Trust in God, and do the right."
　　　　Cho.—Do the right, &c.

XIV.

THE GRIP OF MASONRY.

By Bro. W. T. Harding, *W. M. Nelson of the Nile Lodge, Batley.*

FILL high the cup of rosy wine,
　　And let all a goblet drain;
And quaff its nectar'd sweetness,
　　To warm each manly vein;

Bid morbid cares adieu for once,
    And let us merry be,
And grasp each hand with friendship's grip,
    The grip of Masonry.

For what is there like Masonry,
    What can such joys impart?
As to inculcate fraternal love,
    The precepts of our Art;
In social bonds of union,
    Congenial and free,
        We grasp each hand, &c

Our hearts vibrate with gladness,
    The Muses gently move,
In joyous strains of melody,
    To tune the soul to love,
Our spirits blend at reason's shrine,
    To calm life's troubled sea,
        And grasp each hand, &c.

Fair Science beams in golden rays,
    On Wisdom dwells a smile;
While Strength and Beauty both unite,
    To grace our noble pile;
Then "All the Craft," dear brethren,
    And may the impulse be,
        To grasp each hand, &c.

Thrice welcome, then, confederates true,
    Ye sons of moral worth;
May Charity's congenial rays
    Shine o'er the boundless earth;
And, e'er we part, let's drink a toast
To Mexbro' and to Lee;
        And grasp each hand, &c.

XV.

By Bro. W. T. Harding, *W. M. Nelson of the Nile Lodge, Batley.*

(Tune, *"Bruce's Address."*)

FREEMASONS all, where'er ye be,
    Sons of Light, ye Masons free,
May virtue and may honour be,
    The Ornaments of Masonry.
With fervent zeal, with heart and hand,
May love cement our mystic band;
And for our cause let's make a stand;
    For glorious Masonry.

Freemasons all, from pole to pole,
May love unite and truth control;
If sorrows come, what can condole
    Our griefs like Masonry?
With kindly smiles we all have met,
To welcome each, and not forget
The absent whom we now regret,
    On grounds of Masonry.

Ye Craftsmen all, may love impart
A warmth unto each honest heart;
And oft consult that faithful chart,
    The guide of Masonry.
And when the spirit hence has fled,
May angels o'er their pinions spread,
And crown with bliss each Mason's head,
    With heavenly Masonry.

XVI.

HAIL, FREEMASONRY!

By BRO. JOHN FAWCETT SKELTON, *Lodge No. 146.*
(Written specially for the present work).

(Tune, *"Hey, John Barleycorn!"—By Bro.*
Geoghegan, Lodge 221.)

FREEMASONRY, of all the Arts, is fairest, first,
    and best;
  Old as the hills, its glory fills North, South, and
    East and West.
Whoe'er obtain its honours, with its privileges find
Its sterling worth o'er all the earth, for men of ev'ry kind.
    Hail, Freemasonry!
    Grand old Masonry!
   In thy "charge" is the world at large,
      Freemasonry!

All scientific is its base—all learning it invites—
All beautiful its ritual—all solemn are its rites.
Truth lies within its crystal well; its charity all bless'd,
In streams o'erflows to succour those whom Fortune
    hath distress'd.
      Cho.—Hail, Freemasonry! &c.

For mortal man, whose vessel frail is toss'd on life's
    rough main,
Our glorious Craft will aid to waft it safe in port again;

  N.B.—The foregoing Song may also be sung to the Tune of *"The fine old English Gentleman,"* with the following words for the Chorus:—
    All glorious Freemasonry!
    Best Art of the olden time.

She leads the brethren safely on through life to death's
   dark door,
Nor turns her head until they tread the Mason's golden
   shore.
      Cho.—Hail, Freemasonry! &c.

The Craft, all hail! in glowing strains as ever poet
   sung;
Honour and fame to Masons came while yet the world
   was young.
Ye rising brethren, full of zeal, bestir yourselves to
   raise
Our standard high, 'neath ev'ry sky, as in the ancient
   days.
      Cho.—Hail, Freemasonry! &c.

XVII.

HERE'S TO OUR BROTHERS ABROAD.

By BRO. JOHN FAWCETT SKELTON, *Lodge No. 146.*
   (Written specially for the present work.)

(Tune, *"The Red, White, and Blue."*)

FREEMASONRY! the pride of the Nations!
   The joy of the cream of mankind!
The world rings with constant ovations
   Re-echoed on every wind.
The Craft hath its sons on ev'ry ocean—
   Its followers—to death—on ev'ry strand,
Yet all *one* in the deepest devotion,
   Around our *one* altar we stand.

CHORUS.

Then here's to our brothers abroad!
Soon to see them again from abroad!
Though afar, they are faithful Freemasons,
Then here's to our brothers abroad!

Where the cannons of war loudest rattle,
    Ashore or afloat may be seen
Our brethren in arms, doing battle
    For God! Home! Old England! and Queen!
And roaming, for commerce or pleasure,
    Are hosts of our brethren to day;
But they join us in ev'ry mystic measure,
    And each for the other will pray.
        Cho.—Then here's to our brothers, &c.

The cup! worthy stewards, then bring hither,
    And fill it, good brothers, to the brim;
Freemasonry never shall wither,
    Nor the star of its glory grow dim.
No fate can our unity sever,
    Which age after age shall applaud!
It is destined to flourish for ever!
    Then here's to our brothers abroad!
        Cho.—Then here's to our brothers, &c.

XVIII.

By Brother WILLOUGHBY FLOWER, *of the Friendly Lodge, No. 521, Barnsley.*

(Tune, "*Hearts of Oak.*")

FROM time immemorial Freemasonry's stood,
Its tenets so noble, its precepts so good,
It is built on a rock both abroad and at home,
And Masons are called to polish the stone.

CHORUS.

Then to work brothers all,
And attend to the call,
Be cautious and steady,
And always be ready
Your Master's commands to obey, one and all.

May Faith, like the bright eastern star, lend its ray,
To illumine the path and direct us the way;
When Hope finds relief, and in every land
May Charity stretch forth her bountiful hand.
Cho.—Then to work, brothers all, &c.

These virtues united, the Craft need not fear
On pillars like these their temples to rear;
The fruits of their labour the future may reap,
The arts they are taught with fidelity keep.
Cho.—Then to work, brothers all, &c.

All brothers, their morals to polish with care,
Should work on the level, by plumb, line, and square,
And keep within compass, be true to the gauge,
To honour the Craft as the pride of their age.
Cho.—Then to work, brothers all, &c.

May the Friendly Lodge brothers, with caution and care,
Their labour pursue when assembled they are,
Ne'er suffer intrusion their work to retard,
But hope sweeten labour to meet their reward.
    Cho.—Then to work, brothers all, &c.

XIX.

FREEMASONRY.

By BRO. JOHN FAWCETT SKELTON, *Lodge No. 146.*

(Tune, *"The Hardy Norseman."*)

HAIL, Masonry! thou glorious Art!
    In beauty may'st thou shine,
While life glows in the human heart,
    Or love in the Divine!
May Friendship, boundless as the sea,
    And Love, pure as the snow,
With Truth, in heavenly harmony,
    Delight our Lodge below.

Alas! we do not—dare not say
    Our Mason-brethren all
Are perfect as the light of day,
    And never know a fall.
Our rules are good, our laws are grand,
    Our precepts are divine,
And we, indeed, might spotless stand,
    Could we but toe the line.
    Cho.—Our rules, &c.

But this we boldly do declare,
    In face of earthly hosts,—
Who nearest works up to the "square"
    Our "constitution" boasts:
He is a Mason and a Man
    As noble as the best,—
One, who, when busy life is done,
    May claim eternal rest.
        Cho.—He is a Mason, &c.

Then, Brothers, pledge we in a draught.
    With pride the most profound,—
Success and honour to the Craft
    The spacious earth around!
May e'en the world outside its gates
    Confess, as ages roll,
Freemasonry high elevates
    And purifies the soul.
        Cho—May e'en the world, &c.

XX.

HAIL to the great Masonic powers!
Yes, cheerfully I'd pass my hours
In darkness, prisons, without shame,
That ne'er can shade a Mason's name.

All his delight is doing good:
Long, long his ancient craft has stood,
And never, never yet met blame—
It cannot touch a Mason's name.

Then raise the glass,—may Love and Truth
Guide us in age or fervid youth;
And forward on the page of Fame,
First may appear the Mason's name.

XXI.

HAIL to the Order first endowed on earth!
Blest in creation from its earliest birth:
Yes, the great badge in humble pride we wear,
Type of our mystic arts and character.

We prize the social virtues of the mind,
Shown in a brother's love to all mankind;
With hospitality we cheer each guest,
And pity—comfort yield to the distrest.

Zeal for our king and for our country's cause,
To check the evil, and spread Virtue's laws:
If these are principles deserving fame,
Let honour then bedeck the Mason's name.

XXII.

THE WIFE OF AN ACCEPTED MASON.

(*Written specially for the present work*).

(*Sung to the melody of "The Lancashire Witches."*)

Written and Composed by BRO. J. B. GEOGHEGAN,
Lodge No. 221.

HOW happy the woman must be
   Who a Mason and brother espouses,
No trouble she ever will see,
   But her home be the brightest of houses.
No austere commands to obey,
   'Tis love keeps the marital race on,
For reason and right hold the sway,
   With a free and an accepted Mason.

CHORUS.

Then hurrah for the wife of a Mason!
No trouble will e'er leave its trace on
The brow of the fair
Who her home has to share
With a free and an accepted Mason.

Her days will be cheerful and long,
   Her slumbers be peaceful and mellow;
And the love of her husband be strong,
   For a Mason's a true-hearted fellow:
She'll be honour'd as mother and wife,
   And good fortune will sit with a grace on
The woman who travels thro' life,
   With a free and an accepted Mason.
      Cho.—Then hurrah for the wife, &c.

She will live in, and learn from, a school
 Whose precepts are honest and fair;
For a Mason is governed by rule,
 And his actions are all on the square.
Discretion she'll take for her guide,
 And "Truth" be the motto she'll place on
Her heart, when she's hail'd as the bride
 Of a free and an accepted Mason.
   Cho.—Then hurrah for the wife, &c

Then a health to the ladies all round,
 Whether matron, maid, widow, or wife,
But a double health when they are found
 Tightly tied to a Mason for life;
May fortune heap joys on their heads,
 And favour prepare the best place on
This earth, for the woman who weds
 With a brother, a friend, and a Mason.
   Cho.—Then hurrah for the wife, &c.

XXIII.

THE FELLOW CRAFT'S SONG.

By Bro. S. N. Evans.

(Tune, *"I'm afloat."*)

I AM pass'd, I am pass'd, I'm a Craftsman become
Each Mason's my brother, the Lodge is my home!
Up! up! fill my glass, and I'll quaff it with glee,
To the health of each Mason Accepted and Free!

I'm the brother of Monarchs, the Prince and the Peer,
I am sure of a friend wheresoe'er I appear;
And however dejected or helpless I lie,
I shall never lack aid while a brother is nigh.
Quick! quick! raise your glass, let its brim kiss your lip,
And I warrant your heart will expand while you sip;
Let the toast be "The Craft," over land, over sea,
May it flourish, unclouded, the Star of the Free!

Whilst thousands around us lie buried in night,
We bask in the beams of the Fountain of Light!
What to us are the sneers of the prejudiced mind?
To our principles strange, to their influence blind.

The voice of the syren may tempt us in vain,
Our signs are our secrets, and still shall remain,
With motives the purest that mortals can sway,
Our duties we'll do and our laws we'll obey.

Hurrah! my brave brethren, while earth shall revolve,
Our ties of affection shall never dissolve!
East, west, north, and south, over land, over sea,
Our Craft still shall flourish the Star of the Free!

XXIV.
THE GRAND MASTER

I CALL on each Mason a bumper to fill
    Of the liquor which pleases him best;
Be it water or wine, let him take what he will,
    'Tis the toast that shall give it the zest.
When the lodge and its labours awhile are postponed,
    And each brother is called to refresh him,
With our hearts and our voices to harmony toned,
    We'll drink, "Our Grand Master, God bless him!"

The jewels and gold of an Emperor's crown
    On a tyrant's stern brow may repose,
And the face of diplomacy smooth out its frown,
    More surely to harass its foes.
But the heart of a Mason would scorn such deceit,
    Nor may tyranny's fetters oppress him;
And his sway so benign that whenever we meet,
    We'll drink, "Our Grand Master, God bless him!"

XXV.
THE FINE OLD MASON.

BY BRO. J. H. MERRIDEW, *Lodge No. 88.*

(Tune, *"The Old English Gentleman."*)

I'LL sing you a Masonic song,
    Made by a Mason's pate,
Of a fine Masonic brother,
    (Though he had no fine estate),
Who, always at his post in time,
    Ne'er made a brother wait;

Or, when he came, disturbed the Lodge
    With too much learned prate.
        Like a fine Masonic Brother,
        One of the olden time.

His head was stored with symbols,
    With token, sign and word,—
Their deep and solemn meanings.
    Within his heart were stored;
He worked a section or degree,
    As now is seldom heard,
No sentence was e'er missed by him,
    No portion of it slurr'd.
        Like a fine, &c.

When his lodge met, whate'er his post,
    He came at duty's call,
And prouder was he in that room,
    Than in a Baron's hall;
Or at a banquet table,—
    Or at Masonic ball,—
This fine Masonic brother
    Found time and smiles for all.
        Like a fine, &c.

But life, if sweet, is passing fleet,
    Though the Masonic eye
That's kept the faith in constant view,
    Fears not the hour to die;
His Art has told of better worlds,
    Where comes not tear or sigh,
And he trusts he leaves his lodge on earth
    For a Grand Lodge in the sky.
        Like a fine, &c.

Now is not this much better far
    Than any vain parade
Of fine, hard words, and grand harangues,
    We sometimes now hear made;
Oh! let our Constitutions
    Be rigidly obeyed,
And let us copy his good deeds,
    To whom this tribute's paid.
        The fine Masonic Brother, &c.

XXVI.

A ROYAL ARCH SONG.

BY COMP. W. S. BARLOW, P.Z. CHAP. 128.

(Tune, *"A Warrior Bold."*)

IN eastern clime,—in olden time,—
    When Cyrus held the sway,
A Mason band through Syria's land
    Pursued their toilsome way:
      The sandal shoon they wore,
      Were stain'd and wet with gore,
Yet still they cried, as on they hied,—
    "We'll keep the vow we swore,
And, live or die, we'll raise on high
    Our Temple-walls once more!"

And when at last, the desert pass'd,
    On Salem's hill they stand;
Tell how they wrought,—tell how they fought,
    With foes on ev'ry hand!
      Yet, as they battled sore,
      Or fell, to rise no more,

This war-cry rung from ev'ry tongue,—
   "We've kept the vow we swore,
And, though we die, have raised on high
   Our Temple-walls once more!"

Whoe'er shall claim a Mason's name,
   May act a Royal part;
And raise secure a Temple pure
   In each Companion's heart:
      Who does the good he can,—
      Who loves his fellow-man,—
May greet the blow which lays him low,
   And, smiling, yield his breath;
Yea, undismayed, may walk the Shade,
   For Love alone shall conquer Death!

XXVII.

SONG—ST. CECILIA.

Glasgow, 1779.

Communicated by BRO. G. P. BROCKBANK, *Bolton.*

(Tune, *"An old woman clothed in grey."*)

IN spite of the prejudiced hate
   The vulgar against us maintain,
Let us new attachments create,
   And strengthen each link to our chain.
Without ceasing they slander us still,
   And fling at us many a joke;
But those who of Masons speak ill,
   Are not worthy their wrath to provoke.

We challenge the witty or sage,
    Our merits or deeds to gainsay,
Since those of the primitive age
    We are bound to esteem and obey.
A friendship that's warm and sincere
    Does always her favours dispense;
And our hearts to be swayed will appear
    By the dictates of nature or sense.

Perhaps some may deem it a fault
    That we so mysterious are,
But Virtue alone we are taught,
    Is the object that's worthy our care.
Assured of being honest, we taste
    This cheerful amusement at leisure,
With the presence of decency graced,
    Which regulates every pleasure.

Hence it is that we see ev'ry brother
    An affable air entertain,
And excusing the faults of each other,
    A sociable spirit maintain:
Without hatred or jealousy thus,
    United we Masons do live,
And he only is envied by us,
    Who his friends the most pleasure can give.

XXVIII.

THE GRAND OLD GAME.

Words and Music by BRO J. B. GEOGHEGAN,
Lodge No. 221.
(*Written specially for the present work*).
(*To the melody of "The same old game."*)

IN the days of long ago,
    When great Jupiter and Co.
Assembled on the fam'd Olympian mount,
    They would grasp each other's hand,
    As they sat in council grand,
All their glorious conceptions to recount:
    And as their converse warm'd
    They a band of brothers form'd,
It was mighty, and Masonic was its name,
    And thus the gods combined
    For the good of all mankind,
And we'll carry on the grand old game.
    The grand old game,
    The grand old game,
The whole wide world our actions will acclaim,
    As in our lodge we raise
    Our songs of joy and praise,
And carry on the grand old game.

    Straightway the sons of earth,
    In their majesty and worth,
Embraced the good the gods to them had giv'n,
    For Friendship, Truth, and Love,
    Are descended from above,
And give to men a sweet foretaste of heaven.
    Our own beloved Prince
    Doth his loyalty evince,
To Masonry and all its ancient fame;

> And may He who rules the spheres,
> Grant him health and length of years,
> To carry on the grand old game.
> The grand old game,
> The grand old game,
> Adding lustre to his station and name,
> Stately manhood, age, and youth,
> Honour, Charity and Truth,
> So we'll carry on the grand old game.
>
> Then, while we have the powers,
> Let us seize the happy hours
> That friendship and fraternity provide,
> And when we've sang and quaff'd,
> Doing honour to the Craft,
> May prudence and discretion be our guide;
> And, as Old Time rolls on,
> Calling brothers, one by one,
> Unto the earth from whence each brother came,
> May those we leave behind
> Have the will, the means and mind,
> To carry on the grand old game.
> The grand old game,
> The grand old game,
> Let deeds of love our good intents proclaim,
> And till we turn to dust,
> As at last each brother must,
> Let us carry on the grand old game.

A NOTE OF APOLOGY.

> I AM but a 'prentice hand,
> So the knowledge I command
> Of Masonry, is limited and short;
> But in the course of time,
> When I up the ladder climb,
> I may send you rhymes (perhaps) of a better sort.

XXIX.

SONG FROM "ST. CECILIA"

Published at Glasgow, 1779.

(Tune, *"In the garb of old Gaul."*)

In the dress of Freemasons, fit garments for Jove,
  With the strongest attachment, true brotherly love,
We now are assembled, all jovial and free,
For who are so wise, so social as we!

CHORUS.

And since we're bound by secrecy to unity and
    love,
Let us, like brethren, faithful still to ev'ry brother
    prove:
  Thus hand in hand let's firmly stand,
    All Masons in a ring,
  Protectors of our native land,
    The Craft and the King.

Though some with ambition for glory contend,
And when they've obtained it despise a poor friend;
Yet a Mason, tho' noble, his fame to ensure,
Counts a Mason his brother tho' ever so poor.
                    Cho.—And since, &c.

But not to our brethren alone we confine
That brotherly love, that affection divine!
For our kind-hearted sisters in that bear a share,
And as we admire, we're belov'd by the fair.
                    Cho.—And since, &c.

With Justice, with Candour, our bosoms are warm'd,
Our tongues are with Truth and Sincerity armed;
We're loyal, we're trusty, we're faithful to those
Who treat us as friends, and we laugh at our foes.
      Cho.—And since. &c.
We bend to the King, to our Master we bend,
For these are the rulers we're bound to defend;
And whenever such Kings or such Masters arise.
As Britons, as Masons, we've cause to rejoice.
      Cho.—And since, &c.

XXX.
MASTER MASON'S SONG.

I SING the Mason's glory,
 Whose prying mind doth burn,
Unto complete perfection,
 Our mysteries to learn;
Not those who visit Lodges
 To eat and drink their fill;
Not those who, at our meetings,
 Hear lectures 'gainst their will:
Cho.—But only those whose pleasure
 At every Lodge can be,
T' improve themselves by lectures,
 In glorious Masonry.
   Hail, glorious Masonry!

The faithful, worthy brother
 Whose heart can feel for grief,
Whose bosom with compassion
 Steps forth to its relief:
Whose soul is ever ready
 Around him to diffuse

The principles of Masons,
   And guard them from abuse:
Cho.—These are thy sons, whose pleasure
   At every Lodge will be
   T' improve themselves by lectures
   In glorious Masonry.
         Hail, glorious Masonry!

King Solomon, our patron,
   Transmitted this command,—
"The faithful and praiseworthy
   True light must understand;
And my descendents, also,
   Who're seated in the East,
Have not fulfilled their duty
   Till light has reached the West."
Cho.—Therefore, our highest pleasure
   At every Lodge should be,
   T' improve ourselves by lectures
   In glorious Masonry.
         Hail, glorious Masonry!

The duty and the station,
   Our Master in the chair,
Obliges him to summon
   Each brother to prepare;
That all may be enabled,
   By slow, though sure, degrees
To answer in rotation,
   With honour and with ease.
Cho.—Such are thy sons, whose pleasure
   At every Lodge will be,
   T' improve themselves by lectures
   In glorious Masonry.
         Hail, glorious Masonry!

XXXI.

By Mrs. Alsop.

(Tune, *"The Old English Gentleman."*)

I WILL sing you a new song,
   That was made by a young pate,
Of a Free Accepted Mason,
   Who had a small estate;
     He kept a conscience clear,
   And avoided all debate,
And submissively he bowed
   To the laws of Craft and State,
      Like a Free Accepted Mason,
      One of the olden times.

His house so neat was not bedeck'd
   With pikes, or guns, or bows,
But precepts good, that had been proved
   To stand against all foes;
And such was his domestic peace,
   Nought could him discompose,
For Faith and Hope joined hand in hand
   To strengthen the repose
      Of this Free Accepted Mason,
      One of the olden time.

Nor wind, nor rain, nor frost nor cold,
   E'er chill'd his glowing breast,
For Charity, fair maid of old,
   He made a welcome guest;
'Twas there the orphan, widowed fair,
   Soon found a balmy rest,

For soothing all their real griefs
    Gave to the labour zest,
        Of this Free Accepted Mason,
        One of the olden time.

He oft had wished, with scanty means,
    But oft he wished in vain,
To found a Mason's Institute,
    The orphan to maintain;
That wish was wafted to the poles,
    And echoed back again;
And soon the fabric rose complete,
    And stood amid the plain,
        By Free Accepted Masons,
        All of the olden time.

Like Phœbus with his golden train,
    In eastern splendour drest,
He rose majestic in the morn,
    With virtue for his crest;
Meridian glory he attained,—
    Then sinking in the west,
Th' horizon beamed with rosy hue,
    And told the brighter rest
        Of this Free Accepted Mason,
        One of the olden time.

Though times and seasons circling change,
    And customs pass away,
Yet Masons' hands and Masons' heads
    Are still the same to day;
The lovely fair unite with us,
    And, smiling, seem to say,—
Go on and prosper in the work,
    And act in the same way
        As this Free Accepted Mason,
        One of the olden time.

XXXII.

By Bro. Robert Hodgson, *St. John's Lodge,*

No. 95, Sunderland.

(Tune, *"My own beloved Italy."*)

LET faction's tools their systems weave,
    And deep in strife mankind embroil;
Let plotting knaves their dupes deceive,
    Till vengeance on themselves recoil.
But Masons free, the world shall see,
    Can meet in love upon the square;
And brothers be in unity,
    For such all true Freemasons are!
Chorus—Then fill a bumper to the brim,
    And round the board the toast shall be,
May the oil of kindness ever trim
    The lamp that lights Freemasonry!

Its fame has waked the poet's lyre,
    And swelled the tone of minstrelsy;
True hearts have warmed with nobler fire,
    When kindled by Freemasonry:
'Tis written on historic page,
    Its power the demon Strife could charm,
For in the battle's hottest rage
    The *sign* has stay'd the warrior's arm
Chorus—Then fill a bumper to the brim,
    And round the board the toast shall be,
May Time's oblivious hand ne'er dim
    The record of Freemasonry.

In Charity it has its source,
    In Secrecy it has its power;
Its temple is the universe,
    Its light is shed on every shore:
Though we may stroll through foreign lands,
    Where Moor and Turk their turbans wear;
Or roam o'er Afric's burning sands,
    We're sure to find a brother there.

Chorus.—Then fill a bumper—fill again—
      And round the board the toast shall be,
    May Love, and Truth, and Peace remain
    For ever with Freemasonry!

XXXIII.
MY MOTHER LODGE.

By BRO. JOHN FAWCETT SKELTON, *Lodge No. 146.*
(*Written specially for the present work*).

(Tune, "*Ye banks and braes o' bonnie Doon.*")

MY Mother Lodge! a hymn of praise
    And gratitude I sing to thee;
For in thine arms I first was rais'd
    To life Masonic, full and free.
The cowan-crowd outside thy doors—
    Thy doors so closely prov'd and tyl'd,
Know not the varied charms and joys
    Thou hast for ev'ry faithful child.
Cho—My Mother Lodge! My Mother Lodge!

May all within thy walls be blest—
    Thy labours all in love abound;
May ev'ry son thou dost invest,
    One true Freemason more be found.
My Mother Lodge inspires my muse
    To sing with filial love unfeign'd;
Nor would I her sweet favour lose
    For all that monarchs ever gain'd.
Cho.—My Mother Lodge! My Mother Lodge!

There first I learn'd our sacred signs,
    And how to act upon the square;
And saw throughout our grand designs,
    The hidden truths of Nature fair.
Can happiness on earth be found,
    Or blissful harmony like thine?
Thou art a bit of holy ground,
    And thy good spirit shall be mine.
Cho.—My Mother Lodge! My Mother Lodge!

XXXIV.

By Bro. Young.

(Tune, *"Fly not yet"*)

Now, brothers, let's with one accord,
    While seated round this jovial board,
In mirth and glee and song unite,
To spend the happy festive night
    In tuneful harmony.

The labours of the lodge are o'er,
Refreshment spreads its cheerful store;
The smiling glasses sparkle round,
And true hilarity is found.
    O stay! O stay!
Friendship here to-night shall reign,
And bind us in the golden chain
    Of glorious Masonry!

Our worthy Master's Hiram sounds,
And in the west and south rebounds;
He gives "The Queen," with honours due,
And "Our Royal Grand Master" too:
    Each in full bumpers round.

Thus loyalty and duty's join'd,
And pleasure is with both combin'd;
'Tis so our social hours are spent,
Free from all care and discontent,
    O stay! O stay!
Where can we sweeter moments spring,
Or what more true delight can bring,
    Than here this night is found.

XXXV.

By Bro. J. H. Merridew, *Lodge No. 88.*

(Tune, *"Kate Kearney."*)

OH! did you e'er meet with a Mason,
A fraternal smile his kind face on:
From the glance of his eye, you may easily spy,
He's a Free and an Accepted Mason!

He may seem most uncommonly simple,
Yet there's meaning in every dimple;
And who may him hail, will but seldom fail,
A Brother to find in a Mason!

Now should you e'er meet with a Mason,
And to greet him may have an occasion;
Just give him a smile, let the place be in tile,
And a welcome you'll get from a Mason!

His eyes may be carelessly beaming,
The world knows not what he is dreaming;
But show him a sign that he can divine,
And you'll find that you've met a true Mason!

Now, however some feelings we smother,
'Tis pleasant to meet with a brother:
So let all combine our hearts to entwine,
And each be to each a true Mason!

XXXVI.

BY BRO. J. H. MERRIDEW, *Lodge No. 88.*

(Tune, *"The Maids of Merry England."*)

OH! the free accepted Masons,
    The good, the firm and true,
That their allotted path in life
    Right steadfastly pursue.
Their hearts are warm with friendship,
    For they their vows obey,
The Free Accepted Masons,
    What right good friends are they!

They are like a noble army,
    No foes can ever part,
'Tis no mere clinging of the hand,
    Their union's of the heart;
Each other's thoughts delighting,
    With their gallant proud array,
The Free Accepted Masons,
    What right good friends are they!

They've smiles when we are happy,
    They've sympathy when sad,
And happy is each true brother,
    When all around are glad:
And happy is our lodge to-night,
    Under our Master's sway,
The Free Accepted Masons,
    What right good friends are they!

Then ever like true brethren,
    May we join both heart and hand,
With signs and tokens that the world
    Shall never understand;
And that heaven may ever bless us,
    We'll all devoutly pray,—
The Free Accepted Masons,
    What right good friends are they!

XXXVII.

AULD LANG SYNE.

Words by BRO. J. ROGERS, P.M. 1219.

ONE hour with you, one hour with you,
    No doubt, nor care, nor strife,
Is worth a year of weary woe
    To all that lightens life.
One hour with you, and you, and you,
    Bright links of mystic chain;
Oh! may we oft these joys renew,
    And often meet again.

CHORUS.

One hour with you, and you, and you,
    Bright links of mystic chain;
Oh! may we oft these joys renew,
    And often meet again.

Your eyes with love's own language free,—
    Your hands grip strong and true,—
Your heart,—your voice doth welcome me
    To spend an hour with you.
        Cho.—One hour with you, &c.

I go when morning skies are bright,
    To work my Mason's due;
To labour is my chief delight,
    And spend an hour with you.
        Cho.—One hour with you, &c.

I come when evening gilds the west,
    To breathe a fond adieu,
And hope again, by fortune blest,
    To spend an hour with you.
        Cho.—One hour with you, &c.

XXXVIII.

BY BROTHER BRICE. (1760).

(Tune, *"So blithe as the Linnet."*)

OUR grave work is o'er:—high twelve beats the clock,
    High time, high time in chear to regale:
So, whilst we obey the regulating knock,
    Let social, social glee prevail.

By how much soe'er abounds our joy,
    Decorum, decorum wait on each side;
And though requisite the glasses to imploy,
    The graces, graces still preside.

Each kind brother tune, the best as he may,
    In turn, in turn some brotherly song,
And chorusing all, in full harmony,
    The chearful, chearful note prolong.

Be our odes all humane, all generous, and free
    From railing, railing, envy, rage;
Incentive to love, inchanting to agree,
    Nor rude, nor rude contention wage.

Be pride well supprest, ill passions subdued,
    And candour, candour still bear sway;
The pleasant path of peace be e'er pursued,
    Nor self-will, self-will lead astray.

As link'd are our hands, link'd too be our hearts,
    No force nor fraud should break the chain;
To prompt mutual good all do our proper parts,
    And Mason, Mason-faith maintain.

Hark! a sov'reign decree issues from the east
    To charge.—Let's charge; but charge at our will;
No compulsion's allow'd where reason rules the feast;
    We'll comfort, comfort (boys!)—not kill.

Our glasses are crown'd with moderation due:
    Attend, attend the benevolent vote:
Bib at once, bear in mind the triple-thrice cue;
    The table, table, hands and throat.

XXXIX.

"SHOULD AULD ACQUAINTANCE BE FORGOT?"

(*Written specially for the present work*).

BY BRO. JOHN BAMBER, P. M. Lodge No. 962.

(Tune, *"Auld Lang Syne"*)

SHOULD auld acquaintance be forgot,
    And days of auld lang syne?
Should friendship and fraternal love
    Be other than they've been?
May faith be long, and trust be strong,
    As in the days gone by,
When gather'd round on hallowed ground,
    We toast the "mystic tie."

The "sun" should be our brightest guide,
    On life's uneven way;
And, whate'er betide, we'll ne'er divide,
    In doing what we may.
We'll kindly open hand and heart
    To those who succour need;
And ne'er forget the grand old truth,
    That friends are friends indeed.

Act always right and on the "square,"
    Whate'er the case or cause,
Be not dismay'd—be not afraid—
    Through want of vain applause.
The longest lane will have an end,
    Dark night give place to dawn;
Then sing, 'tis ne'er too late to mend,
    Hope cometh with the morn.

Let the "compass" keep us all within
    The path of rectitude;
And when the world seems dark and dim,
    Be sure 'tis for some good:
The lesson oft is hard to bear,
    Life's troubles keenly smart,
But remember still that come they will,
    To strengthen hope and heart.

May "Alpha's" loyal lodge resound
    With true Masonic "fire;"
Our Royal Prince—Our Noble Grand—
    Have all his heart's desire!
Then drown all wrong in cheerful song,
    In sect or party's spite;
And toast "The Craft the world around,"
    And "god protect the right!"

XL.
TRUE AND TRUSTY MASONS.

BY BRO. W. S. BARLOW, *in honour of Prince Edwin Lodge, No. 128.*

(Tune, *"Mistress Prue."*)

SONS of Light! come, tune your lays,
 Lest your pipes grow rusty;
Whilst we cheer in songs of praise
 Masons true and trusty!
In the Lodge which gave us Light
 Skilled Past Masters plenty;
Some whose locks are frosted white—
 Brethren four times twenty!
  Tried and prov'd—of faith unmov'd—
  True and trusty Masons!
   (Repeat last two lines in Chorus).

When pale Cynthia's full-orb'd beams
 Fill the night with beauty,
Well we know her silv'ry streams
 Warn us of our duty:
Wrinkled Care awhile may wait,
 Lodgeward all are turning,
Where, in triple order placed,
 Mystic lights are burning!
  Symbols clear, your hearts to cheer,
  True and trusty Masons!

As the sun, with rosy hands,
 Opes the gates of morning,
In the east the Master stands,
 All his Lodge adorning:

Work begun in Order fair,
   Is in Peace cemented,
Then we part upon the Square,
    In Harmony contented!
      Till we meet again to greet
      True and trusty Masons!

Ere the Hiram sound to close,
   Or our labours ended,
Plead, Fair Charity, for those
   Homeless, unbefriended!
Oh! regard the Orphan claim
   Of brothers dear departed;
Shield the aged, blind, and lame,
   Heal the broken-hearted!
      Till ye hear those words of cheer—
      "Well done, trusty Masons!"

XLI.
FAITH, HOPE, AND LOVE.

SORROW and pain and night are one;
    Darkness comes with all;
    Shadows rise and fall;
The moon's cold light is not her own,
Only the silver stars appear,
Given, as 'twere, by Hope to cheer
    The faint and weary
    When sad and dreary—
      Here!

Faith and Hope and Love are one;
    Sunlight comes to stay;
    Shadows flee away:
The Master sits upon his throne,
A shining light in heaven above,
Ruling men by Faith and Love:
    Turning their mourning
    Into bright morning
      There!

XLII.
FRIENDSHIP AND LOVE.

THE loud trump of Fame willing ushers the day,
    When Cam's social sons first in friendship entwin'd,
When honour and truth lent a kindred ray,
    T'enlighten the heart which to virtue inclin'd.
All bless the great hour, and hailed the blest power,
And prayed smiling Providence ever to shower
Those blessings which only descend from above—
Truth, Charity, Friendship, and Brotherly Love.

Though time makes the dull, sordid mortal repine,
    And each fleeting moment his pleasures annoy,
Such vot'ries of folly ne'er met at my shrine,
    Where mirth, love, and friendship those moments enjoy.
Be wise while ye may, to our lodge come away,
Where Friendship with smiles as celestial as day,
Will give you her hand, and a blessing impart,
Which ev'ry true brother will lock in his heart.

Though envy in brotherly form should assail,
    And malice attempt our true hearts to divide,
Yet friendship defies all their arts to prevail,
    Not formed to enjoy, they will ever deride.
Still Friendship divine refulgent shall shine,
Since Charity's laurels her brow do entwine,
And hail her triumphant on earth to arise,
Till time shall return her again to the skies.

Since life's rosy hour's so fleet on the wing,
    And Friendship and Love can felicity give,
In innocent mirth let us joke, drink, and sing,
    And the summer of youth cannot fade while we live.
This toast be most dear, "the virtuous fair!"
To them we will ever be true and sincere;
May they, when this lodge re-assembled above,
For ever unite us in Friendship and Love.

XLIII.

THE NOBLE ORDER.

By BRO. JOHN FAWCETT SKELTON, *Lodge No. 146.*

(Tunes, *"The sea is England's glory."*—*"Jerusalem the golden."*—*"From Greenland's icy mountains,"* &c.)

THERE is a Noble Order
    Selected from all men,
From earth's remotest border,
    To Britain back again:
From ev'ry northern nation—
    From ev'ry circling zone—
From ev'y southern station
    This Order hath its own.

From widely distant regions,—
    From hills beyond the wind,
It draws its loyal legions
    To benefit mankind.
Brave chiefs with bronzen faces—
    Fair sons of ev'ry tongue—
All tribes, and clans, and races,
    This Order proudly throng.

This noblest of all Orders,
    Most ancient and most free,
Is known to earth's bright borders
    As fair "Freemasonry."

Then wave her flags all prouder,
    On ev'ry hill and shore;
And sing her praises louder
    Than we have done before!

"The Noble Order," brothers,
    Let lips of yours reply;
The star of all the others
    Beneath the starry sky.
Earth's princes bear its banners,
    And to its mandates bow;
Then drink, with all our honours,
    "The Noble Order" now.

XLIV.

I'LL MEET THEM WHEN THE SUN GOES DOWN.

Tune:—
("*I'll meet her when the sun goes down.*"—*American.*)

By BRO. JOHN FAWCETT SKELTON, *Lodge No. 146.*

(*Written specially for the present work.*)

THERE'S a nice little lodge of Masons all,
    As any in the town;
Number [One-Four-Six] on England's roll,
    And I seek it when the sun goes down.
All is there that the brethren can desire,
    Love and Freedom, without a frown,
With a pipe and a glass, and a tuneful choir,
    And I seek it when the sun goes down.

CHORUS.

    And it's oh! how I love my Masonic brothers,
        For they're better than all others;
        Oh! how I love!
    And I'll meet them when the sun goes down.

When the cares of the world-life worry me,
    And I get me a crack on the crown!
Ah! then I think of the lodge with glee,
    And I seek it when the sun goes down.
Oh! the fun and the wisdom there combin'd,
    Hath an old world-wide renown,
So soothing and sweet to my heart and mind,
    So I seek it when the sun goes down.
        Cho.—And it's oh! how I love, &c.

XLV.

HERE'S TO HIS HEALTH.

Music by COMP. J. R. FLETCHER, *Bury.*

THIS world is so hard and so stony,
    That if a man is to get through,
He need have the courage of Nelson,
    And plenty of Job's patience too.
But a man who is kind to another,
    And cheerfully helps him along,
God bless such a man and a brother,
    And here's to his health in a song.

This life is as cheerless as winter
    To those who are cold in the heart;
But the man who is warm in his nature
    Bids winter for ever depart.
The ground that he treads on will blossom
    Till beauties around him shall throng;
God bless such a man and a brother,
    And here's to his health in a song.

As clouds that in sunshine are open,
    And silver'd by light passing through;
So men who are generous in spirit,
    Are blessed by the good things they do.
There's nothing like helping another,
    For getting one's own self along;
Who does this is truly a brother,
    And here's to his health in a song.

XLVI.

By. Bro. J. H. Merridew, *Lodge No. 88.*

(Tune, *"Jeannette and Jeannot."*)

WE have come from far and near, far and near we've come to-night.
To meet around our honour'd shrine, where Faith burns ever bright;
And we've come with warm, true heart,—it should be ever so,—
To cling unto our brethren, alike in weal or woe!

We care not for the ills that our daily life may bring,
Remembering this refuge, its praises we will sing;
And though our breasts may heave with worldly hate or love,
We'll prize and treasure well our lodge, all other things above!

When the Lodge is duly opened, when each office is well fill'd,
What meeting of the worldlings can show so fair a guild?
With our Worthy and our Worshipful, the Master, in the east,
Who would not be partaker of so glorious a feast?
Or at this social banquet, where mirth and muse combine,
Our hearts pledg'd to each other, the closer to entwine:
Oh! pray with me, my brethren, what ever else we do,
That to our Constitutions and to our Lodge we're TRUE!

XLVII.
THE LEVEL AND THE SQUARE.

By Bro. Rob. Morris, P.M.

"We meet upon the level and we part upon the square;"
What words of precious meaning those words masonic are!
Come, let us contemplate them, they are worthy of a thought,
In the very soul of Masonry those precious words are wrought.

We part upon the square, for the world must have its due;
We mingle with the multitude, a faithful band and true;
But the influence of our gatherings in memory is green,
And we long upon the level to renew the happy scene.

There's a world where all are equal—we are journeying to it fast;
We shall meet upon the level there, when the gates of death are passed;
We shall stand before the Orient and our Master will be there,
To try the *blocks* we offer with His own unerring square.

Let us meet upon the level, then, while labouring patient here;
Let us meet and let us labour, tho' the labour be severe;
Already in the western sky, the signs bid us prepare
To gather up our working tools, and part upon the square.

Hands round, ye faithful Masons, in the bright
    fraternal chain;
We part upon the square below to meet in Heaven
    again.
O! what words of precious meaning those words
    masonic are,
"We meet upon the level, and we part upon the
    square."

XLVIII.

THE MASON'S VACANT CHAIR.

(*Written specially for the present work*).

(Tune, *"The vacant chair."*)

WE shall meet around our altar,
    In the Lodge, upon the square;
But our bravest words will falter,
    As we see his vacant chair.
'Twas as yesterday we met him,
    Hand in hand, and heart to heart;
Oh! not soon shall we forget him!
    Oh! 'twas hard for us to part.
    Cho.—We shall meet around our altar,
        In the Lodge, upon the square,
    But our bravest words will falter,
        As we see his vacant chair.

A belov'd and cheerful brother
    Was he who now has gone;
Hard to find we such another
    'Neath our fix'd meridian sun.

Bright for him the same will glisten,
    Where o'er earth soe'er he roam,
In his dreams oft may he listen.
    To the voices dear of home.
        Cho.—We shall meet, &c.

May he prosper 'mong the living—
    May he never lack a friend—
May he have no dread misgiving
    When his life draws to an end:
Like a good and faithful Mason,
    May he join his lodge above,
When his raptur'd soul shall hasten
    From this world to worlds of love!
        Cho.—We shall meet, &c.

XLIX.

DEAD!

By BRO. JOHN FAWCETT SKELTON, *Lodge No. 146.*

(*Written specially for the present work*).

(Tune, *"The vacant chair."*)

WE shall meet around our altar,
　　In the Lodge, upon the square;
But our bravest words will falter,
　　As we see his vacant chair.
Clad in gloom are all our spirits,
　　For our brother dear is dead;
But his mem'ry richly merits
　　All our praises, sung or said.
　　　　Cho.—We shall meet, &c.

He hath done a Mason's duty,
　　He hath kept his jewels bright;
In yon lodge of heavenly beauty
　　May his spirit see the Light!
In the grave we all bewail him,—
　　Here his Lodge is left in woe;
May the Great Grand Master hail him,
　　Where all good Freemasons go.
　　　　Cho.—We shall meet, &c.

L.
WHAT BETTER THEME.

By BRO. JAMES STEVENS, P.M. *25, 720, 1216, &c.*

Music by COMP. J. R. FLETCHER, *Bury.*

WHAT better theme can claim our lays,
  And lend its aid to harmony?
What noble art sheds brighter rays
  Than glorious Freemasonry?
What other virtues can compare
With those 'tween "compasses and square?"
  For Faith and Hope and Charity,
  Brotherly Love and Unity,
  With Order, Peace, and Harmony,
  Are found in true Freemasonry.
    Cho.—For Faith and Hope and Charity, &c.

When first to us the light is shown
  That governs true morality,
Others' distress we make our own,
  In natural equality.
Our steps are then taught to ascend
The ladder staves that upward tend—
  Faith, first upon the muster roll,
  Hope, the sheet-anchor of the soul,
  And *Charity,* that crown the whole
  Foundation of Freemasonry.
    Cho.—For Faith and Hope and Charity, &c.

When Craftsmen's labours we attend
  We're taught the hidden mystery,
By science led to comprehend
  The scope of nature's history;
From nature up to nature's God
Our minds are rais'd above the sod,

And *Wisdom* comes to shield from harm,
Strength hurtful passions to disarm,
Whilst *Beauty* lends a crowning charm
To all our works in Masonry.
  Cho.—For Faith and Hope and Charity, &c.

And next, as Master Masons, we
 Share the sublimest mystery,
And prove how potent then can be
 Fortitude and *Fidelity;*
The terrors of the darkest hour
Are lessened by the Mystic Power,
 And *Virtue's* portals open wide
 Our steps to *Honour's* fane to guide,
 Whilst *Mercy* pleads upon our side
 To Him who rules Freemasonry.
  Cho.—For Faith and Hope and Charity, &c.

And when, our glorious labours o'er,
 We meet for brief hilarity,
Amidst our joys our brethren poor
 Remembered are in Charity:
Each thankful heart expands to bless;
Each willing hand relief will press;
 With *Temperance* God's gifts we share;
 Prudence extends her watchful care,
 And *Justice,* symbolled by the *Square,*
 Perfects our works in Masonry.
  Cho.—For Faith and Hope and Charity, &c.

LI.

WHEN I WAS MADE A MASON.

By BRO. JOHN FAWCETT SKELTON, *Lodge No. 146.*

(*Written specially for the present work.*)

(Tune, "'*Twas in the good ship 'Rover'*"—*Dibdin.*)

WHEN I was made a Mason,
 Now many years ago;
I put my boldest face on,
 All fear to overthrow.
I put my boldest face on,
 All fear to overthrow,
But still it did not answer,
 I quak'd in ev'ry bone;
And though a plucky man, sir,
 I stifled many a groan.
  Cho.—And though a plucky man, sir,
   I stifled many a groan.

I wonder'd what the dickens
 They'd do to me the first!
My heart was not a chicken's,
 But oh! I fear'd the worst.
My heart was not a chicken's,
 But oh! I fear'd the worst.
Low murmurs all around me,
 And solemn music too,
In the darkness did confound me,
 And I was in a stew.
  Cho.—In the darkness, &c.

If I live to be a hundred
    I'll ne'er forget that night,
Nor how I felt and wonder'd
    When first I saw the light.
Nor how I felt and wonder'd
    When first I saw the light.
Some secrets, then, and myst'ries,
    Word, symbol, grip and sign,
With our all ancient hist'ries
    Of brotherhood were mine.
      Cho.—With our all ancient, &c.

Since then I've been a rover,
    And many a goblet quaff'd,
But nothing could discover
    So glorious as the Craft.
But nothing could discover
    So glorious as the Craft.
I'll sing her praises ever,
    With honest pride and glee,
And life throughout endeavour
    A Mason true to be.
      Cho.—And life thoughout, &c

LII.
BY BROTHER OBORNE. (1765).
(Tune, *"Black Jake."*)

WHEN Masons in a lodge do meet,
    Then they each other kindly greet
With friendship true, and hearts sincere,
What mortals, then, so happy are?
Or who with Masons can compare?
    Who chearfully join
    And together combine   } *repeated twice.*
To promote this Royal Mystic Art.

True friendship, like ours, is hard to be found;
With mirth and good humour the glass goes round,
    And each takes his brother and friend by the hand.
Our evening thus we merrily spend;
To our work (which is solemn) we ever attend,
        And the lodge we support
          As our place of resort,
With the utmost fervency, freedom, and zeal.

When thus met together we're jovial and jolly,
We drive away Care and his friend Melancholy,
    And substitute Humour and Mirth in their place;
Then the Master commands, "let each fill his glass,
"And see that the toast in due form round does pass;"
        We his orders receive,
        And attention do give,
Nor e'er from the rules of Masonry swerve.

Thus pleasant and calmly our time slides away,
Respect to our Masters and Wardens we pay,
    And put them to worship as Masons are taught.
May our undertakings, both public and private,
Succeed, and in time may we all arrive at
        The utmost perfection of joy, ⎫
        Bliss, and love,   ⎬ *once only.*
        In the regions of light, in
        The lodge that's above, ⎭
Whose structure shall last till time's no more.

LIII.

By BROTHER ROBERT HALL.

(Tune, *"Rule, Britannia."*)

WHEN Masonry, by heav'n's decree,
    Arose from father Adam's brain;
This was the charter of the fraternity,
    And secrecy shall guard the same.

CHORUS.

Hail, Masonry! for ever may'st thou be
To all but us a mystery.

The brethren all, upright and just,
    Shall ever act upon the square;
Until the world dissolve to dust,
    The needy shall their bounty share.
        Cho.—Hail, Masonry, &c.

True moral men, sincere and free,
    Shall wisdom's dictates still impart,
And mirth and joy, and social unity,
    Shall bless those peaceful sons of art.
        Cho.—Hail, Masonry, &c.

The cowan and the craft knave
    Shall never tread the sacred ground;
The miser, traitor, abject slave,
    In Masons' lodge shall ne'er be found.
        Cho.—Hail, Masonry, &c.

But if he's honest, just and true,
    His life and actions clear and bright;
Report, prepare, invest him too,
    For he's the man shall see the Light.
        Cho.—Hail, Masonry, &c.

LIV.

(Tune, *"Greedy Midas"*)

WITH harmony and flowing wine
　　My brethren all, come with me join,
To celebrate this happy day,
And to our Master homage pay.

Hail! happy, happy, sacred place,
Where Friendship smiles in ev'ry face;
And Royal Art doth fill the chair,
Adorned with his noble Square.

Next sing, my muse, our Warden's praise,
With chorus loud in tuneful lays;
Oh! may these columns ne'er decay
Until the world dissolves away!

My brethren all, come, join with me,
And sing the praise of Masonry:
The noble, faithful, and the brave,
Whose arts shall live beyond the grave.

Let Envy hide her shameful face,
Before us Ancient Sons of Peace;
Whose golden precepts still remain
Free from Envy, Pride, or Stain!

LV.
A MASON'S TRUE JEWELS.

YOU know all the jewels that work each degree,
    As we rise in the lodge, the accepted and free,
The blue and the silver, the purple and gold,
Familiar to Masons—the young and the old;
Yet still the true Mason has jewels more rare,
Which time cannot tarnish, though always in wear.
I'll name them, and if in the naming I'm true,
Let these priceless treasures be chorused by you:
    Sweet Hope, that gives comfort wherever we go,
    The shield of true Faith, that protects from the foe;
    And Charity, seeking to comfort and bless,
    Child, widow, and brother, bow'd down by distress.

A sound heart's the shrine where these relics repose,
Giving grace to our mirth, shedding balm o'er our
    woe,
Shining out through our life with a lustre more bright
Than the diamonds that Ind sends to dazzle our sight.
The Power that spans heaven, and measures the wave,
Gave these to be worn by the good and the brave,
And in closing my song, let me name them again,
And then in full chorus re-echo the strain:
                        Sweet Hope, &c.

CANTATA.

Composed by Mozart, for the Consecration of his Lodge, at Salzburg. Arranged by Bro. J. R. Fletcher, Bury.

CHORUS.

LET the sound of joyous music send a thrill to every heart,
In our song of festive gladness, let each Brother take a part.
    Here, in this our happy meeting,
    Everyone his Brothers greeting;
    Here we seek to weld again
    Brotherhood's all golden chain.

SONG.

Friendship, Goddess, showers her blessings down upon humanity,
Not with pomp, parade, and boasting, but unseen, and silently.
Silent Goddess, in thine honour shall true manhood bend the knee,
For thou warm'st, as with the sunlight, every heart that shelters thee.

DUET.

Let our consecrated Temple be a welcome memory,
Filling us with strong endeavour towards a perfect unity.
Let us bear each other's burdens, full inspired with sympathy;
Holy light from heaven to guide us we shall share right worthily.

Heaven will guide us if we're earnest workers in the
   holy cause;
Much is done, but much needs doing to all-hallow
   Friendship's laws.
  Virtue has our whole allegiance,
  Virtue claims our best obedience,
  Evil thoughts are laid to rest;
  Envy dies, and every discord
  Fades into a perfect concord,
  Filling ev'ry brother's breast.
CHORUS—Let the sound of joyous music, &c.
(*The words of the above Cantata are copyright.*)

DUETS.

I.
(Music by Dr. Boyce.)

HERE let soft charity repair,
 And break the bonds of grief;
Down the harrowed couch of care
Man to man must bring relief.

II.
*Written Extempore, and sung by two Brothers,
both labouring under "colds."*

SOLO.

LET us croak together,
 Sirs! I am not joking,
In this frosty weather
 Singing is but croaking.
And the tune we mean to sing
Is that musty Latin thing,
 Gaudeamus igitur.

DUETTO.

Gaudeamus igitur,
    Juvenes dum sumus:
Post peractam juventutem
Et molestam senectutem
    Nos habebit humus.

SOLO.

Masonry's our subject;
    Old, but yet not rotten;
Tho' abus'd, degraded;
    Half its laws forgotten!
Guiltless joy, and mirth, and glee,
Harmony, and Charity,
    Prop our Institution.

Tho' a set of jolly souls
    All the world may call us,
Drowning reason in our bowls;
    Let them, let them maul us.
They may laugh who win, I think:
Fill your glasses, then, and drink—
    Mirth to every Mason.

Merry let us Masons be,
    Glad on this occasion:
Who should sing, if not the Free
    And Accepted Mason?
May our union never cease:
While we live, let's live in peace,
    Free, Accepted Masons!

GLEES.

I.

(Music, "Here's a health to all good lasses.")

HALL! mysterious, glorious Science
    Which to discord bids defiance;
Harmony alone reigns here:
Come, let's sing to him that raised us
From the rugged path that maz'd us,
    To the Light that we revere!

Glorious Science! glorious Science!
Hail, mysterious, glorious Science!
Which to discord bids defiance;
    Harmony alone reigns here.

II.
HAIL TO THE CRAFT!

Written and Composed by BRO. J. PARRY.

CHORUS.

HAIL to the Craft! which hath for ages stood
    The taunts of Envy, and the threats of power

SOLO AND DUET.

In Friendship firm, obedient to the laws,
The Mason stands the Patriot and the Man!
    Cho.—Hail to the Craft! &c.
    (Ad lib.) Hail to the Craft! to the Craft, all hail!

VERSE,—FULL.

When meek-eyed Pity doth for aid implore,
His heart expands, she never pleads in vain:
The needy's call he freely will obey,
And share the gifts that heaven on him bestows.
   Cho.—Hail to the Craft! &c.

III.
BY A BROTHER *of the Lodge of Three Graces, No. 591.*

(Music, "Life's a Bumper.")

HAIL, triumphant Masonry!
 May thy sons united be;
Nor, like vulgar mortals, spend
Life as 'twere for no great end:
Let this Lodge with truth be crowned,
May its fame be spread around;
Every generous heart combine,
Secresy and Friendship join.

IV.
BY BRO. S. N. EVANS.

(Music, "Faintly as tolls the evening chime.")

JOYFULLY in the Lodge we meet,
 Fondly each other as brethren greet;
Soon as the door is closely tiled,
Masonry issues her precepts mild.
List, brothers, list! the solemn prayer
Fervently floats upon the air.

Why should we to the world unfold
Secrets as precious as beaten gold?
Yet the Accepted, True, and Free,
Who are so ready to teach as we?
Hail we, and claim we, heart and hand,
Brethren, the noblest in the land.

With solemn prayer the Lodge we close,
Who may not safely then repose?
Nature's Great Architect's name invoke;
Terror shall fly like scattering smoke.
Sing, brothers, sing, no danger fear,
Masonry reigns all powerful here.

V.
PROSPER THE ART.

Music by Bro. Hargreaves.

WHEN the Temple's first stone was slowly descending,
    A stillness like death the scene reigned around,
There thousands of gazers in silence were bending,
    Till rested the pond'rous mass on the ground;
Then shouts filled the air, and joy was like madness,
    The founder alone weeping meekly apart,
Until from his lips burst, flowing with gladness,
    The wish that for ever might "Prosper the Art."

When the Temple had reared its magnificent crest,
    And the wealth of the world embellished its walls,
The nations drew near from the east and the west,
    Their homage to pay in its beautiful halls.

Then they paused at the porch with feelings delighted,
    Bestowing fond looks ere they turned to depart;
As homewards they trod with voices united,
    They joined in full chorus—"Prosper the Art."

VI.

WITH A JOLLY, FULL BOTTLE.

Glee for Three Voices, as sung at the Prov. Grand Meeting, Chester, 1857.

WITH a jolly, full bottle be each brother armed,
    We must be good Masons when our hearts are thus warmed.
Here's a health to Old England, the Queen, and the Craft,
Let all present pledge in a hearty good draught.
May England's Grand Master defend our just cause,
Protect our old landmarks, constitutions and laws.

STANZAS.

By a P. Z. of the Chapter of Reason, 406, Stalybridge.

HOW pleasant and how good it is,
    And beautiful to see,
For brethren (as Freemasons are)
    To live in unity.

'Tis heaven-like! and good for all
    Who Masonry do love;
'Tis the command from Him who reigns
    Omnipotent above.

May Masons long united be,
    Their thoughts to God direct;
Who was,—and is,—and will remain
    The World's Great Architect.

"Brotherly love, Relief, and Truth,"
    Freemasons do combine;
Masons agree in "Faith and Hope,"
    And "Charity" divine.

Oh! what a boon to Masons' hearts
    'Tis to relieve distress;
And own from whom their good proceeds,
    Their health, their happiness.

Then, Masons, join to praise the Lord,
    For blessings freely given;
And when we leave this earthly Lodge,
    May we ascend to heaven.

HYMNS.

I.
OPENING HYMN.

BRIEF life is here our portion;
    Brief sorrow, short-lived care:
The life that knows no ending,
    The tearless life is there.

O happy retribution!
    Short toil, eternal rest;
For mortals and for sinners
    A mansion with the blest.

II.
AN OPENING HYMN.

By BRO. JOHN FAWCETT SKELTON, *Lodge No. 146.*

(Tunes, *"St. George" "Easter Hymn,"* &c.)

COME, ye brethren, stand and sing
    Opening welcome, let it ring,
Till this honour'd place resound
From the dormer to the ground.
Here our sorrows we forget—
Here the sun doth never set—
Here all vexing cares we fly,
Where the mystic brethren hie.

Now for duty at the shrine,
With Masonic rule and line;
Now for worship, wrapt in awe,
Round the Book of Sacred Law;
Now for prayer and solemn rite —
Now for glorious work this night—
Then may we expect reward
At the well-earn'd festive board.

Guide us, O thou Mighty Power,
From this solemn opening hour;
Give us grace that we may see
All we owe the Craft and Thee.
All our ritual be Thine,
Great Masonic Source Divine!
Let us love our lodges here,
Till in Thine we all appear.

III.
AN OPENING HYMN.

By BRO. JOHN FAWCETT SKELTON, *Lodge No. 146.*
(*Written specially for the present work*).

OH! the joy when brethren meet,
In the lodge's calm retreat,
To perform Masonic rites
'Neath the great and lesser lights.
May our labours thus begun
All in order, one by one,
In sweet peace be now dispos'd.
And in harmony be clos'd.
(Ad lib.) So mote it be!

No ill feeling enters where
Lodges open "on the square;"
Nought but Love with Friendship vies
Truth within her beaming eyes.
 May our labours, &c.

Come, my brethren of the Craft,
Work our vessel, fore and aft;
Masonry's the ship to brave
Life's wild wind and stormy wave.
 May our labours, &c.

Sing, my brethren, and may we
For this meeting better be:
Masonry shall teach us how
All may happy be below.
 May our labours, &c.

IV.
AN OPENING HYMN.

By BRO. JOHN FAWCETT SKELTON, *Lodge No. 146.*

(Tunes, *"Mariners,'" "Vesper Hymn," "Haydn's," &c.*)

ONCE again, in mystic manner,
 Known but by the favour'd few,
Under our Masonic banner,
 Meet we, brethren, tried and true.
Once again our jewels wearing,
 On the breast, and in the heart,
Working gleefully, and sharing
 Each the honours of our art.

Signs and symbols fondly using,
　　Actions solemn—words profound;
Nothing slighting—naught abusing,
　　While the "loving cup" goes round.
May this meeting, than all former,
　　(If 'twere possible, indeed)
Be completer, sweeter, warmer,
　　Truer to our Craft and creed.

Thus will Masonry for ever
　　Brighter shine, and grander grow,
Till the mighty human river
　　Off the face of earth shall flow.
Architect Divine, look o'er us,
　　While in love we labour here,
And whatever lies before us,
　　Be Thou ever near and dear.

A CLOSING HYMN.

HAIL, Eternal! by whose aid
　　All created things were made:
Heaven and earth Thy vast design;
Hear us, Architect Divine!

May our work, begun in Thee,
Ever blest with Order be;
And may we, when labours cease,
Part in Harmony and Peace.

By Thy glorious Majesty—
By the trust we place in Thee!
By the badge and mystic sign,
Hear us, Architect Divine!

A CLOSING HYMN.

By BRO. JOHN FAWCETT SKELTON, *Lodge No. 146.*
(*Written specially for the present work*).
(Tune, "*Abide with me.*")

NOW all in harmony prepare to close,
　　Like the sweet leaves within the evening rose;
Safely lock up our working-tools again,
With all our secrets from the world profane.

Let ev'ry brother join with voice and heart,
These closing strains before in love we part;
And in the treach'rous world as on we move,
Keep well within the safe Masonic groove.

Meeting and parting! such is life all through,
Till lov'd ones catch our whisper'd last adieu:
Till then, O Thou Great Architect Divine,
Keep us "close tyled" in that dear heart of Thine.

A CLOSING HYMN.

NOW the evening shadows closing,
　　Warn from toil to peaceful rest;
Mystic arts and rites reposing
　　Sacred in each faithful breast.

Fount of Light! whose love increasing
　　Doth to all Thy works extend,
Crown our Order with Thy blessing;
　　Build, sustain us to the end.

Humbly now we bow before Thee,
   Grateful for Thy aid divine;
Everlasting power and glory,
   Mighty Architect be Thine!
               So mote it be.

A CLOSING HYMN.

By BRO. JOHN FAWCETT SKELTON, *Lodge No. 146.*

(*Written specially for the present work*).

OUR mystic labours now are o'er;
   Fill'd is the "loving cup;"
We close the sacred book once more,
   And lock our secrets up.

'Fidelity,' thrice told, we cry!
   Our vows again we swear;
And praise the Architect Most High,
   For his Masonic care.

Secure against the cowan's art,
   We mingle with mankind,
Each brave to play his worldly part
   With true Masonic mind.

In order did our work begin;
   In peace it onward flows;
And now with love our lodge within,
   In harmony we close.

ODES.

I.

On the Installation of H. R. H. THE PRINCE OF WALES, *as Most Worshipful Grand Master, at the Albert Hall, 28th April, 1875, by Brother* WALTER SPENCER, *P.M. and Treasurer of the Bank of England Lodge, &c. &c.*

REMOTEST Past hath left its prints sublime;
    Its ruined Temples everywhere remain,
Admonishing through change of place and time
    By monuments not thus bequeathed in vain,
That all things here must suffer change—save TRUTH.
    Like sand by sand, Earth's crust is worn away,
For Continent and ocean change, as youth
    Changes to age, as night suceeds to-day.

Review the vanished Empires of our earth
    Which budded, ripened—and then faded out
Until, down-trodden in a wintry dearth,
    Their very names became the sport of doubt!
Reckon the leaders who have toiled and wrought
    To leave their mark on Hist'ry's page—in vain;
Whose cherished visions have been brought to nought;
    Whose praises never can be sung again!

Think of the great thoughts that have flashed to light,*
    Thoughts to inspire the coming time and mind,
Whose authors rest neglected, in the night
    Which gave a brighter dawn unto mankind!
Even Religion—see how changed at last
The Creeds that millions clung to in the past!

Is there an Ideal whose perennial youth
Enshrines a living everlasting Truth?
Is there a ray beaming through Hist'ry's night
Which emanated from the primal Light,
Revealing antient symbols, that reflect
The fiat of the world's Great Architect?

Yes! Nature's Truths extending through the Past
    As through the Present, shame man's changeful tale;
And antient Landmarks, founded hard and fast,
    Those primal Truths in graven smybols veil.
Our allegory claims them for its own,
    Echoing a voice which, laden with their lore
Through ages gone, repeats in earnest tone
    Their Solemn formulæ for evermore;
And teaches Masons, an immortal lot
    In "Universal Charity" to found,
Whose centre may be struck at every spot
    And whose circumference no space can bound.

Those Truths, to us in allegory told,
    With Light in the beginning had their birth;
The banded wisdom of the Wise of old
    Memorial altars reared upon the earth.
And ever with the Sun, that *from the East*
    Will *to'ards the West* its living radiance shed,

---

    * For this apostrophe the Author is indebted to "Bailey's Festus."

The sacred flame to glow has never ceased
    Which for our use departed Brethren fed
That we might tend it in our turn: the while
    They numbered years in stone on Carnac's bed,
Recorded Seasons on Stonehenge's pile,
    Or named the stars from off the Pyramid.

We work by the inexorable Laws
    Which the great Cosmos owns for rule of right,
Nor waste our strength upon the quips and flaws
    Over which some dispute and bigots fight!
We gaze up at the canopies of stone
    That from the ground aspire to reach the skies,
And (claiming antient Mason's Art our own
    By which our spiritual temples rise)
Acknowledging a great Ideal divine
    Embodied thus by Mason's toil and sighs
Feel, that the altars which those fanes enshrine
    Are hallowed by the Truths we symbolise!

FREEMASONS work for love unto the Art,
    Not for the hire alone to serve the Lord:
Infusing fervour into every part
    Which grows an earnest of our rich reward.
For at the last, our earthly labours done—
    If worthy, the Great Architect's commands
Will raise up each, a proved and perfect stone,
    Into a Temple builded not with hands.

And here—the heirs unto the men of old
    Will emulate their fervency and zeal:
Joining in courses of symmetric mould
    To strengthen and adorn the commonweal.
Though Roman Pontiffs ban the Mason's Light,
    Nor brook the level laid upon the priest,
Here may the FREE of every creed unite
    Where one rule tries the greatest and the least!

The SONS OF TOLERANCE assemble here,
  Christians or Jews, Parsees or Mussulmen.
The same great Architect we all revere
  With those of yore, bonded by Truth as then.
Under our PRINCE a living dome we build,
  The polished keystone of whose crown is he;
And each, for ever in the Temple filled,
  The Masons'-word seals thrice:—
    FIDELITY!!!

II.
TO THE ROSE-CROIX OF H. R. D. M.

BY BRO. WALTER SPENCER, 30°

AVE Rosa Crucis! When through the dark valley
  The shadows of death mock the pilgrims of woe,
When error and fraud their grim satellites rally,
  Unfaltering under thy banner we go.

Thy vision of Truth, to the soldier believing,
  Gleams bright on the altar, fulfils the desire,
And sheds through the veil of mortality's weaving
  A radiant glory of spiritual fire.

There thrills through our ranks, from thy sweet inspiration,
  A mystic spell like to the sound of the sea.
The charmëd hymn wakes to eternal vibration
  The echoes of Nature in full melody;

It whispers the roll of the infinite muster
    Of worlds that revolve in their orbital race;
Illum'd by thy keen inconceivable lustre
    And held by immutable laws in the space;
Upspreading, it kisses the seal of Creation
    And worships in awe at the signet of God,
Till melting in glow of divine exhalation
    It pours down the path which Emmanuel trod;
Returning it unlocks the mazes of Seven,
    The spheres through which we to perfection press on,
Ere, cheered by the wine-cup and changed with the leaven,
    We gaze on the light which the perfect have won;
It ends in announcing the message of Heaven
    Over which radiates the face of the One,
Proclaiming the crown of the sacrifice given,
    The anguish endured and the triumph begun.

We hear it, the mystical ladder ascending,
    Which yields, at each step, the initial of flame
Whose accents caught up by Archangel, come blending,
    And breathe out, in awe, the Ineffable Name.
The Eagle, exultant, ascends to the morning,
    With Wing golden tipp'd by the Lord of the East.
From ashes the Phœnix, the fire-circle scorning,
    Soars in renewed youth and with beauty increased;
Its innocent brood see the Pelican nourish,
    In shedding its life-blood with pinion unfurled;
And long in our midst may their attributes flourish,
    For these are the types we disclose to the world!
The bold gaze of hate and the sad sigh of sorrow,
    We quell with a Charity stronger than they,

The Faith of the present, the Hope of the morrow,
    Transmit through the ages thy roseate ray.

The past may mistake or the future contemn us,
    Our love is linked firm in the Ancient of Days;
Opponents may harass and ambushes hem us,
    But none from our ranks our great Captain betrays.
With Him, when the eyelash grown wet at His story
    Is dried with the solace 'tis His to bestow,
Our Princes and Sages shall muster in glory,
    Who fought the good fight in the valley below.

A COLLECTION OF MASONIC TOASTS & SENTIMENTS.

A health to the widow's sons, wherever they are dispersed.
    A health to those brethren whose principles are
    Well guided and govern'd by the Compass and Square.
All true friends of the Craft.
A proper application of the 24-in. gauge, so as that we may measure out and husband our time to the best of purposes.
Every brother who keeps the key of knowledge from all intruders, but will cheerfully open the cabinet to a worthy brother.
Every brother who maintains a constancy in love, and sincerity in friendship.
Every brother who stands Plumb to his principles, yet is Level to his brethren.
Genuine Masonry universal.
    Guided by that bright starred letter G,
    May every Freemason his duty see.
Let the diligent apprentice have an eye to his Gauge, Gavel, and Chisel.
May all Freemasons be enabled to act in strict conformity to the rules of their order.
May all Freemasons go hand in hand in the road of virtue.
May all Freemasons live in love and die in peace.
May all Freemasons please and be pleased.
May brotherly love, relief, and truth ever be found amongst Masons.
May concord, peace, and harmony subsist in all regular lodges, and always distinguish the fraternity of Freemasons.
May every brother have a heart to feel, and a hand to give.
May every brother learn to live within the Compasses, and act upon the Square.
May every brother who has merit always find encouragement.
May every brother who is lawfully and regularly entered in our society, which is both ancient and honourable, be as duly instructed in the true morals thereof.

May every Freemason find constancy in love and sincerity in friendship.
May every Freemason have health, peace, and plenty.
May every Freemason have so much genuine philosophy, as that he may neither be too much exalted with the smiles of prosperity, nor too much dejected with the frowns of adversity.
May every Freemason participate in the happiness of a brother.
May every Mason be able to act so as to have an approving monitor.
May every society instituted for the promotion of virtue flourish.
May every worthy brother have a head to earn and a heart to spend.
May every worthy brother who is willing to work and labour through the day, as his condition requires, be happy at night with his friend, his love, and a cheerful glass.
May Freemasons ever be the patterns of virtue.
May Freemasons ever taste and relish the sweets of domestic contentment.
May honour and honesty distinguish the brethren.
May Hypocrisy, Faction, and Strife, be for ever rooted from every Lodge.
May Masonry flourish until Nature expire,
And its glories ne'er fade till the world is on fire.
May Masonry prove as universal as it is honourable and useful.
May mirth in our lodge continually reign,
And Masons their friendship for ever maintain.
May no Freemason desire plenty but with the benevolent view to relieve the indigent.
May no Freemason ever step awry,
But walk upright, and live as he should die.
May no Freemason wish for more liberty than constitutes happiness, nor more freedom than tends to the public good.
May our actions as Masons be properly Squared.
May our conversation be such as that youth may therein find instruction, women modesty, the aged respect, and all men civility.
May peace, harmony, and concord subsist among Freemasons, and may every idle dispute and frivolous distinction be buried in oblivion.
May Sincerity, Charity, and Peace be established in this lodge.

May temperance, fortitude, prudence, and justice (four excellent virtues) ever adhere to the heart, and be found in the actions of a Mason.
May temptation never conquer a Freemason's virtue.
May the brethren in this place be united to one another by the bond of love.
May the brethren of our glorious Craft be ever distinguished in the world by their regular lives, more than by their gloves and aprons.
May the cares which haunt the heart of the covetous be unknown to a Freemason.
May the circle of love, which has no end, ever encompass the heart of a Freemason.
May the deformity of vice in other men teach a Mason to abhor his own.
May the emblems of a Mason ever remind him of his duty.
May the erect posture of man teach him the uprightness of Masonry.
May the foundation of every regular Lodge be solid, its building sure, and its members numerous and happy.
May the Freemason's conscience be sound, though his fortune be rotten.
May the frowns of resentment never be known among us.
May the gentle spirit of love animate the heart of every Mason.
   May the Goddess Fidelity never depart,
   But continue her reign in each Freemason's heart.
May the hearts of Freemasons agree although their ideas should differ.
May the lives of all Freemasons be spent in acts of true piety, and in the enjoyment of tranquillity.
May the lodges in this place be distinguished for love, peace, and harmony.
May the Mason's conduct be so uniform, that he may not be ashamed to take a retrospective view of it.
May the prospect of riches never have such an effect upon a Mason, as to induce him to do that which is repugnant to virtue.
May the Square, Level, and Plumb-rule ever be a Craftsman's guide.
May the Square, Plumb-line, and Level, regulate the conduct of every brother.
May unity, friendship, and brotherly love ever distinguish the brethren of the ancient Craft.

MASONIC TOASTS AND SENTIMENTS.

May Virtue ever direct our actions with respect to ourselves; justice to those with whom we deal; mercy, love, and charity to all mankind.

May we be more ready to correct our own faults than to publish the errors of the brethren.

May we never condemn that in a brother which we would pardon in ourselves.

May we never rashly believe the report we hear, which is prejudicial to a brother.

Peace and plenty to every brother.

Prosperity to Masons and Masonry.

Prosperity to the ancient and honourable Craft.

Relief to all indigent brethren.

The absent brethren of this lodge.

The Grand Lodge of England.

The heart that conceals,
And the tongue that never improperly reveals.

The Memory of the Distinguished Three.

The Right Worshipful Deputy Provincial Grand Master.

The Right Worshipful Provincial Grand Master.

To all genuine Freemasons, wherever oppressed or dispersed.

To all pure and upright Masons.

To all social Freemasons.

To all that live within compass and square.

To all those who steer their course by the Three Great Lights of Masonry.

To all true and faithful Brothers.

To all true Masons and upright,
Who saw the East where rose the light.

To each charming, fair, and faithful she
Who loves the Craft of Masonry.

To each true and faithful heart,
That still preserves the sacred art.

To each faithful brother, both ancient and young,
Who governs his passions and bridles his tongue.

To him that did the Temple rear,
Who liv'd and died upon the Square;
And buried is, and none knows where,
But such as Master Masons are.

To him that first the work began.

To him who all things understood,
To him who found the stone and wood,
To him who luckless spilt his blood,
In doing of his duty.

>   To him who did the wood provide,
>   To him who plann'd the Temple's pride,
>   To him—the Widow's Son—who died
>   So nobly at his duty!

To him who uses the mallet in knocking off those superfluous passions that in any manner degrade the man or the Mason.

>   To Masons and to Masons' bairns,
>   And women with both wit and charms,
>   That love to lie in Masons' arms.

To our Most Worshipful Grand Master.
To our next happy meeting.
To our Visiting Brothers.
To the ancient sons of peace.
To the Fraternity around the globe.
To the increase of perpetual friendship and peace among the ancient Craft.
To the lovers of Masonry.
To the Masters and Wardens of all regular lodges.
To the memory of the Tyrian artist.
To the Mother of all Masons.
To the perpetual honour of Freemasons.
To the Queen and the Craft.

>   To the Queen, good health;
>   The Nation, wealth;
>   The Prince, God bless;
>   The Fleet, success;
>   The Lodge no less.

To the Right Worshipful Acting Grand Master.
To the Right Worshipful Deputy Grand Master.
To the secret and silent.
To the Worshipful Grand Wardens.

REMARKABLE OCCURRENCES IN MASONRY.

	A.D.
ST. ALBAN formed the first Grand Lodge in Britain	287
King Athelstan granted a Charter to Freemasons.	926
Prince Edwin formed a Grand Lodge at York	926
Edward III. revised the Constitutions	1358
Masons' Assemblies prohibited by Parliament	1425
Henry VI. initiated	1450
Grand Masters of the Knights of Malta, Patrons of Masonry	1500
Inigo Jones constituted several Lodges	1607
Earl of St. Alban's regulated the Lodges	1637
St. Paul's begun by Freemasons	1657
William III. initiated	1690
St. Paul's completed by Freemasons	1710
Grand Lodge revived, Anthony Sayer, Esq, G.M.	1717
Valuable MSS. burnt by scrupulous brethren	1720
Office of Deputy Grand Master revived	1720
Book of Constitutions published	1723
Grand Secretary first appointed	1723
Grand Treasurer first appointed	1724
Committee of Charity established	1725
Provincial Grand Masters first appointed	1726
Twelve Grand Stewards first appointed	1728
Lord Kingston gave valuable presents to Grand Lodge	1729
Duke of Norfolk ditto	1731
Emperor of Germany initiated	1735
Frederick, Prince of Wales initiated	1737
The Crown Prince of Prussia (Frederick the Great) initiated	1738
Public Processions on Feast-Days discontinued	1747
Their R. H. the Dukes of York and Gloucester initiated	1766
Registering Regulations commenced, 28th October	1768

Hall Committee appointed..	1773
The King of Prussia sanctioned the Grand Lodge at Berlin..	1774
Two freehold houses, Nos 60 and 61, Great Queen Street (on the site of which Freemasons' Hall and Tavern were afterwards erected) purchased	1774
First stone of Freemasons' Hall laid................................	1775
Five Thousand Pounds raised by a Tontine towards building ditto...	1775
Office of Grand Chaplain revived..................................	1775
Freemasons' Hall dedicated.. (Enlarged 1815 and 1848).	1776
Freemasons' Calendar published by authority of the Grand Lodge..	1777
Several Masons imprisoned at Naples..........................	1777
H.R.H. Henry Fred. Duke of Cumberland elected G.M.	1781
H.R.H. the Prince of Wales (King George IV) initiated	1787
H.R.H. Duke of York initiated.......................................	1787
H.R.H. Duke of Clarence (King William IV.) initiated	1787
Freemasons' Tavern rebuilt	1788
Female School instituted	1788
H.R.H. Duke of Kent initiated.......................................	1790
The Prince of Wales elected G.M. on the death of the Duke of Cumberland	1790
H.R.H. Prince William of Gloucester initiated	1795
H.R.H. Duke of Cumberland King of Hanover)initiated	1796
H.R.H Duke of Sussex initiated	1798
Boys' Institution established..	1798
Liquidation Fund established	1798
Act of Parliament passed containing Enactments respecting the Society...	1799
Foundation Stone of Covent Garden Theatre laid by the Prince of Wales as G. M................................	1808
H.R.H. Duke of Sussex elected G. M. on resignation of H.R.H. the Prince Regent, who took the title of G. Patron	1813
Re-union of all the Freemasons in England under H.R.H. the Duke of Sussex as Grand Master, 27th December..	1813
Constitutions of the United Grand Lodge published	1815

Brother William Preston, of Lodge of Antiquity, gave, by Will, Five Hundred Pounds Consols, to Fund of Benevolence; Five Hundred Pounds Consols to Girls' School; Three Hundred

Pounds Consols for Prestonian Lecture 1819
George IV., after his Accession, signified his pleasure to continue Patron 1820
H.R.H. the Duke of Sussex, G. M. gave five superb carved and gilt Chairs, with velvet cushions, to Grand Lodge 1820
H.R.H. the Duke of York, as P. D. G. M. laid the Foundation Stone of Eton and Windsor Bridge . 1822
Foundation Stone of London University laid by the Duke of Sussex, M.W.G.M. 1827
Charity Medal instituted as an Honorary Distinction to Brethren who have served the offices of Steward for the Girls' School and the Institution for Boys 1829
His Majesty King William IV. on his Accession declared himself Patron of the Order 1830
Sir John Soane gave Five Hundred Pounds to the Fund of General Purposes 1832
H.R.H. the Duke of Sussex gave a Marble Bust of His Majesty King William IV., also the three Gilt Trowels with which H. R. H. laid the Foundation Stones of the London University, the Licensed Victuallers' Asylum, and the Charing Cross Hospital 1833
A piece of Plate weighing 1800 ounces, purchased by the voluntary Subscriptions of Lodges and Brethren, was presented to H.R.H. the Duke of Sussex, on completing 25 years as Grand Master 1838
Resolution of the Grand Lodge to grant Hundred and Fifty Pounds per annum each to the Female School and the Institution for Boys, having previously made grants amounting in the aggregate to Three Thousand Five Hundred and Eighty Pounds to the Girls' School, to Three Thousand Five Hundred and Thirty-three Pounds to the Institution for Boys 1839
Royal Masonic Benevolent Annuity Fund established by the Grand Lodge, with a Grant of Four Hundred Pounds per annum 1842
Five Hundred Pounds given by Grand Lodge to be invested towards establishing a permanent Fund for keeping in repair the Edifice for the Freemasons Female School 1842

450 REMARKABLE OCCURRENCES IN MASONRY.

The Earl of Zetland, Provincial Grand Master, installed as Grand Master	1844
Her Majesty Queen Victoria gave Fifty Pounds to the Royal Masonic Benevolent Annuity Fund	1845
A Marble Statue of the Duke of Sussex, executed by Bro. E. H. Baily, R.A. by vote of the Grand Lodge, was placed in Freemasons' Hall, and opened 29th April	1846
Widows' Fund established by the Grand Lodge, with a Grant of Hundred Pounds per annum	1849
The Grand Chapter granted One Hundred Pounds per annum to the Benevolent Annuity Fund	1847
And Thirty-five Pounds per annum to the Widows' Fund	1849
Amalgamation of the Masonic Asylum at Croyden Common, with the Benevolent Annuity Fund, when the Grand Lodge gave Five Hundred Pounds to be invested towards a Permanent Fund for keeping in repair the Building of the Masonic Asylum	1850
The Foundation Stone of St. George's Hall, at Bradford, Yorkshire, laid by the Earl of Zetland, M.W.G.M	1851
Installation of H.R.H. the Prince of Wales as Most Worshipful Grand Master, at the Albert Hall, London, 28th April	1875
The East Lancashire Systematic Masonic Educational and Benevolent Institution established	1876
H.R.H. Prince Albert Victor initiated by H.R.H. the Prince of Wales	1885

CONTENTS.

¶ THE SONGS ARE ARRANGED ALPHABETICALLY THROUGHOUT BOTH THE BOOK AND APPENDIX.

SONGS FOR SPECIAL OCCASIONS, OFFICERS' SONGS, &c.

PAGE.

Grand Master's Songs	141, 156, 378
Deputy Grand Master's Song	120
Grand Warden's Song	98
Past Master's Song	50
Junior Warden's Songs	104, 150
Master Mason's Song	386
Fellow-Craft's Songs	37, 69, 136, 377
Entered Apprentice's Songs	34, 92
The Treasurer's Song	64
The Secretary's Song	197
The Candidate's Song	108
Initiation	365
The Final Toast : or Tyler's Song	350
Song for St. John's Day	90
Royal Arch Songs	45, 53, 63, 114, 176, 380
Knights Templar Songs	19, 62

CONTENTS.

Laying Foundation Stone	427
To a Departed Brother	413
To a distant Brother or Brethren	369, 411
Funeral Hymn	222
Cantatas	207—210, 422
Duets	211—216, 423, 424
Anthems	217—224
Odes	225—272, 436—441
Eulogies	273—276
Catch	277
Glees	278—281, 425—428
Sonnet	282
Oratorio	283
Prologues	293—327
Epilogues	328—345
Stanzas	429
Opening and Closing Hymns	430—435
A Collection of Masonic Toasts and Sentiments	442
Remarkable Occurrences in Masonry	447

Look for these and other great titles at:
http://www.stoneguildpublishing.com

Book of Ancient and Accepted Scottish Rite by Charles T. McClenachan
The Book of the Holy Graal by A. E. Waite
The Book of the Lodge by George Oliver
The Builders by Joseph Fort Newton
Chymical Marriage of Christian Rosencreutz translated by A. E. Waite
The Doctrine and Literature of the Kabalah by A. E. Waite
Fama Fraternitatis and Confession of the Rosicrucians by A. E. Waite
Freemasonry in the Holy Land by Robert Morris
The Freemason's Manual by Jeremiah How
The Freemason's Monitor by Daniel Sickels
The History of Freemasonry and Concordant Orders
The History of Initiation by George Oliver
Illustrations of the Symbols of Freemasonry by Jacob Ernst
The Kybalion by The Three Initiates
Low Twelve by Edward S. Ellis
The New Masonic Trestleboard by Charles W. Moore
Opinions on Speculative Masonry by James C. Odiorne
The Perfect Ceremonies of Craft Masonry
The Poetry of Freemasonry by Rob Morris
Real History of the Rosicrucians by A. E. Waite
The Symbolism of Freemasonry by Albert G. Mackey
Symbolism of the Three Degrees by Oliver Day Street
Taylor's Monitor by William M. Taylor
Taylor-Hamilton Monitor of Symbolic Masonry by Sam R. Hamilton
Three Hundred Masonic Odes and Poems by Rob Morris
True Masonic Chart or Hieroglyphic Monitor by Jeremy Cross

www.ingramcontent.com/pod-product-compliance
Lightning Source LLC
Chambersburg PA
CBHW070539230426
43665CB00014B/1747